FINDING YOUR VOICE

Barbara Houseman is a well-known and highly respected voice, text and acting coach and a director. She has thirty years' experience in theatre. She initially trained as a teacher at the Central School of Speech and Drama and then as a director at the Bristol Old Vic Theatre School. She won an Arts Council Director's Bursary, after which she directed in repertory theatres and drama schools as well as teaching voice, text and acting.

In 1991 she joined the voice department at the Royal Shakespeare Company. During her six years there she worked with over two hundred and fifty actors and thirty directors on more than sixty classical and modern plays. On leaving the Royal Shakespeare Company she became Associate Director at the Young Vic, where she worked on *The Comedy of Errors* and *More Grimm Tales*.

Freelance, she has conducted voice and text work on productions as diverse as *Doctor Dolittle* by Leslie Bricusse, *Cleansed* by Sarah Kane, *Art* by Yasmina Reza, Complicite's *Mnemonic*, *Further Than the Furthest Thing* by Zinnie Harris, *The Play What I Wrote* by Sean Foley and Hamish McColl, *Treats* by Christopher Hampton and *Equus* by Peter Shaffer. She has also worked in film and television and held workshops in Australia, China, Columbia, New Zealand, Sri Lanka and the United States.

Finding Your Voice is the first of a trilogy of books. The second is *Tackling Text [and Subtext]*, and the third – *Enabling Actors* – will look at ways in which directors and others who work with actors can help them to produce their best work.

Other Titles in this Series

ACTING AND REACTING
Tools for the Modern Actor
Nick Moseley

ACTIONS
The Actors' Thesaurus
Marina Caldarone and Maggie Lloyd-Williams

THE ACTOR AND THE TARGET
Declan Donnellan

THE ARTICULATE BODY
The Physical Training of the Actor
Anne Dennis

BEYOND STANISLAVSKY
The Psycho-Physical Approach to Actor Training
Bella Merlin

THE COMPLETE STANISLAVSKY TOOLKIT
Bella Merlin

DIFFERENT EVERY NIGHT
Freeing the Actor
Mike Alfreds

HOUSE OF GAMES
Making Theatre from Everyday Life
Chris Johnston

THE IMPROVISATION BOOK
How to Conduct Successful Improvisation Sessions
John Abbott

THE IMPROVISATION GAME
Discovering the Secrets of Spontaneous Performance
Chris Johnston

IMPROVISATION IN REHEARSAL
John Abbott

LABAN FOR ACTORS AND DANCERS
Putting Laban's Movement Theory into Practice
Jean Newlove

LABAN FOR ALL
Jean Newlove and John Dalby

OTHER PEOPLE'S SHOES
Thoughts on Acting
Harriet Walter

PERFORMING SHAKESPEARE
Oliver Ford Davies

SINGING WITH YOUR OWN VOICE
Orlanda Cook

TACKLING TEXT [AND SUBTEXT]
A Step-by-Step Guide for Actors
Barbara Houseman

THROUGH THE BODY
A Practical Guide to Physical Theatre
Dymphna Callery

NICK HERN BOOKS

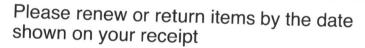

London

A Nick Hern Book

Finding Your Voice
first published in Great Britain in 2002
as a paperback original by Nick Hern Books Limited,
14 Larden Road, London W3 7ST

Reprinted 2004, 2005. 2006, 2007, 2008 (twice), 2009

British Library Cataloguing data for this book
is available from the British Library

ISBN 978 1 85459 659 8

Cover design: Ned Hoste, 2H

Typeset by Country Setting, Kingsdown, Kent CT14 8ES

Printed in Great Britain by the MPG Books Group,
Bodmin and King's Lynn

To Mark Bauwens

without whose inspiration, patience, and support
this book would never have been written

Contents

Foreword *by Kenneth Branagh* ix

Acknowledgements xi

Introduction xiii

1 Before You Start 3

2 Body Work 15

3 Breath and Support 59

4 Breath into Sound: Supporting the Voice 97

5 Releasing the Sound: Freeing the Voice 118

6 Filling out the Sound: Finding Your Resonance 162

7 Extending the Sound: Finding Your Range 182

8 Shaping the Sound: Firming Up Your Articulation 193

Drawing the Work Together 232

Quick Reference Section

Warm-Up 235

Working with Text 242

Vocal Health 244

Troubleshooting 250

Useful Contacts 267

Index 268

Foreword

I first became aware of Barbara Houseman's work some years ago when I was performing with the Royal Shakespeare Company. She was part of the great tradition of voice teaching, which the company encouraged, pioneered by the brilliant Cis Berry.

More recently I have worked with Barbara as a director and as an actor. In both cases she was an enormous inspiration.

This excellent book distils the experience of many years into a tremendously useful manual. Not just for the actor, but for anyone who wishes to work on releasing the full potential of their voice and reap the benefits in their life and work.

The book's advice is practical and flexible. Application is certainly required to see results, but enjoyment of the process is also remembered throughout. The work really is fun. It can be read sequentially or dipped into according to need or specific interest.

My experience is that these techniques and this philosophy result in clearer, more truthful communication, in individuals expressing themselves with greater meaning and truth, and help people, through the joyful release of their vocal potential, to become more fully themselves.

For that gift I thank Barbara, and I wish you joy on the journey.

KENNETH BRANAGH

Acknowledgements

Over the years I have been fortunate to have worked with many gifted and inspirational people. I am grateful to them all; especially to Katya Benjamin, Meribeth Bunch, Mark Meylan, Veronica Smithers, Andrew Wade, Sue Weston and Tessa Van Sertima and the directors and actors at the Royal Shakespeare Company, but four people need a special mention.

Firstly, Rita Melene, whom my mother found when I was five years old. Rita taught me for many years, before I went to the Central School of Speech and Drama at nineteen. She had trained at Central in the 1920s, when Elsie Fogerty, the founder, was still Principal. She taught me to love words; she introduced me to Shakespeare before anyone had suggested it might be difficult, so I was never frightened of it.

When I auditioned for the teaching course at Central, she gave me a list of about seventy-five books – a mixture of plays, poetry and theatre theory – to wade through. She told me I needed to read them all or I would not stand a chance of getting in. So, I dutifully made my way through the entire list. Of course, they never asked me about a single book, but I did not regret having read them.

The next person, to whom I owe so much, is Sonia Moriceau, with whom I studied Shiatsu and Meditation. Her work has influenced mine profoundly. Through her I have discovered much about the link between mental and physical energy and this has proven invaluable both in my own work and in that with actors. I continue to work with her and shall do so as long as she continues to teach.

The third person is Janice Chapman, a superb singing teacher, whom I first met just over ten years ago, when I attended one of her workshops. Right from the start I realised how valuable and exceptionally clear her work on support was. For a time I was able to work with her privately and the majority of the support work I now do is based on her excellent work and research.

The last, but certainly not least, person is Cicely Berry, whom I was very fortunate to be able to work with in my six years at the Royal Shakespeare Company. Cicely has revolutionised the way we work on voice and text, not just in this country but also world wide, and most voice teachers working today have been influenced by her work; whether they know it or not! Watching her at work and working with her was invaluable and she has had a huge influence on my work, especially in terms of text.

Of course, there is one last group of people that I need to thank and that is everyone that I have taught, for indeed it has been their questions, needs and difficulties that have taught me so much.

THANKS TO

Mark Bauwens, Lyle Jobling and Mark Meylan for painstakingly reading various drafts and giving such excellent feedback. Thanks also to Mark Meylan and John Rubin for their contributions to the Vocal Health section and to Meribeth Bunch for checking many of the anatomical details. Thanks to Nicola Endicott for watching me draw endless stick men and patiently trying to teach me about perspective! Finally, thanks to Caroline Downing for such detailed and understanding editing. I could not have wished for a better editor.

Introduction

The potential of voice work

Voice work can release an actor. The voice is the bridge between the inner and outer worlds and, if the voice is free, it can reflect the inner world with great accuracy, revealing each actor's unique response to character, situation and text.

That is the purpose of this book: to support each actor to find their own released voice; to find their own power and expression so they can fully communicate their thoughts and feelings subtly, flexibly and excitingly.

So how does this book work?

This book is about choices, not about correctness. Depending on your experience of voice work you can use it in different ways to build up your own personal tool kit to serve your individual needs as an actor.

If you have done little or no voice work, read through each chapter once quite lightly, so that you get an overview. Then, go back and work through the exercises in that chapter. Once you are comfortable move onto the next chapter and work in the same way. At the end of each chapter I suggest how you can put the exercises together to create a brief workout, so that you are not stuck with an ever-increasing session. Once you have gone through the whole book you will have a much greater understanding of your voice and of which exercises help you most. Then, you can put together your own workout and warm-up or you can use the ones I suggest.

If you have done more voice work, but feel there are gaps you would like to fill in, then, read lightly through the introduction to each chapter to get an overview of the work and then pick and choose the exercises you think will be most helpful.

If you have a particular issue that you want to work on, then, look in the trouble-shooter section. This will give you a brief explanation and direct you to relevant exercises.

Respecting the complexity of the voice

We need to work on the voice with respect. The voice is an expression of self. It expresses our ease or lack of ease both with ourselves and the world. It cannot be bullied into shape.

To work on your voice you need to start by getting to know it: approaching it with curiosity and respect rather than judgement and demand. Then you will start to understand your voice and any necessary change will be much easier and more pleasurable to achieve.

Where not to look for your voice!

Our voices naturally have the potential to express our inner thoughts and feelings so powerfully and accurately yet often this potential becomes obscured. This can lead us to believe that we never had the potential in the first place. As a result we may try to copy someone else, whom we feel does have a powerful and expressive voice. This never works. Such a voice can never reveal our inner responses. If you wish to find a voice that truly touches an audience, you have to find your *own* voice.

Understanding why we lose connection with our voice

Before you can find your own voice it is necessary to understand how its potential to express and reveal so powerfully and accurately is obscured.

When we are very young our voices are strong, free and connected. The reason for this is that we trust ourselves. We have a clear connection with how we feel and we have the freedom and confidence to express this – without doubt, judgement or effort.

Over the years we often lose this trust in ourselves. Doubt and judgement start to erode our sureness and we either draw back, afraid to commit, or we overcompensate.

This happens to a greater or lesser extent to us all. It seems to be part of the maturing process. We start off very sure of our world and confident that how we see and respond to that world is how everybody else sees and responds to it. Then, we come to realise that other people experience the world differently from us. This is a blow. Are we right or are they? Do we abandon our view and take on theirs or fight tooth and nail to protect our beliefs and to persuade them that they are wrong? It can take a lifetime to rediscover an easy sureness in ourselves, which allows us to honour our own world-view and that of others.

Where we have drawn back, the voice will often be quieter and less expressive. Articulation will often be less firm and clear. The voice may lack support and resonance. There may be a sense of the voice being swallowed or trapped in the throat.

Where we have overcompensated, the voice may be strident, and perhaps shrill or tight when emotional. It may be over emphatic, over expressive and over articulated. Although it may seem a strong voice it may still lack support and resonance and instead be pushed from the throat causing, in time, vocal strain.

Finding your voice

Obviously, the whole book deals with the process of finding your voice, but there are some key tools that I would like to introduce now. Using these tools can revolutionise your voice work and make it far more enjoyable and successful.

Quiet sureness and commitment Working with an *attitude* of quiet sureness and commitment helps to remove both tentativeness and over effort from your work. This sureness and commitment is not a *false external* confidence but a *true internal* certainty, the kind of certainty we have about activities we have always found easy. For example, if you have always been good at sports or mathematics or cooking or driving a car you won't be tentative about doing these activities, nor will you feel you have anything to prove, you'll just get on with them. That is quiet sureness.

Quiet sureness allows you to commit completely, without force, to what you are doing and it releases great energy. Also, by simply committing, many so-called problems are immediately solved. So when in doubt, recall a feeling of quiet sureness and instead of pulling back or pushing forward, gently, but firmly commit.

Light but Full Awareness Many problems occur with the voice because we have no idea what we are actually doing. One of the fastest ways to bring about change is, paradoxically, to stop trying to change anything and simply be *aware* of what you are doing. This gives you a chance to *notice* tensions and unhelpful habits and this *awareness* alone will set in motion a change. You can then easily build on this change by doing the relevant exercises.

So, instead of striving to achieve or reeling exercises off mindlessly while you think about something else; just lightly pay attention to what you are doing, without any judgement.

Ease Being aware will help you to notice when you work with ease and when you work with strain. Strain is always the result of excessive or inappropriate effort.

Certainly effort is required when using your voice in performance, otherwise there will be no energy. But it is vital that this is *appropriate* effort. How do you know whether it is appropriate? If you feel physically and mentally at ease, then you are on the right lines.

So make *ease* a high priority when you are working. Anything achieved through strain will be of no use to you on stage.

Interest Ease ensures that you do not *over*-work the muscles, but what assures that you do not *under*-work them?

Well, sureness and commitment go a long way to getting the muscles to work appropriately. The more quietly sure and gently but firmly committed you are, the more energy you will have.

Another great energy-giver is interest. Think of a time when you were working on something which really interested you: remember how alive you felt. Then, think of a time when you were working on something that didn't interest you: remember how lethargic or tensed up you felt.

Interest gives you easy, flexible energy. So, work with interest and curiosity not with judgement and doubt and you'll find you have far more energy and, hopefully, far more fun.

Generosity This may seem a very strange tool to work with. Yet so often, we approach work on ourselves with huge judgement and criticism. We beat ourselves up mentally when we can't do exercises, we put ourselves under huge pressure to achieve. It is no wonder that, as a result, we often give up if we are finding particular work difficult. It is just too painful to continue.

So, you need to work with generosity towards yourself: with the kind of generosity you would show towards someone you care for very much. Think of someone for whom you would have endless tolerance and acceptance and, then, apply that tolerance and acceptance to yourself!

This is not a soft option or a 'wet' way of working. If you work with generosity and acceptance towards yourself, you will find that you can stay with work that is difficult for far longer and, as a result you will achieve far more, far more quickly.

FINDING YOUR VOICE

I

Before You Start

Having given you five key tools to work with in the introduction, I would like to add a few reassurances and some advice on how to approach the work.

A FEW REASSURANCES

There is no need to spend ages practising

It is the *regularity* of practice that is important. It is much better to practice for a short time every day than a long time once a week.

Also, you don't have to do all the exercises at one time. You can separate them into smaller, more manageable chunks that can be done at various points during the day.

Some exercises can be practised as you go about your daily life. This is an excellent way of practising, since the aim is for the work to become natural.

It is better to practise each exercise for only a brief time – two or three minutes at most. After this the quality of attention falls off and you will find you revert to old habits, which is discouraging.

There is no need to think about your voice or any of the exercises whilst you're on stage

It is neither helpful nor necessary to think about the voice, or voice exercises, whilst you are on stage.

If you practise with focus and attention, and warm up as suggested, then, on stage, you can forget about your voice and fully engage with the text and the other actors.

If you do find that you still have problems in performance, look in the trouble-shooter index and work as it suggests. If the problem persists, then you need to find a voice teacher to work with to discover the root of the problem.

Whatever route you take, once on stage forget about your voice!

You won't end up sounding false

All the exercises are designed to develop your *own* voice to its full potential. To make it more responsive to and expressive of your feelings and thoughts.

It is a good idea to think of developing your voice for general use, rather than just having a 'stage' or 'performance' voice. This way it will have greater flexibility and feel more owned. Also, you are less likely to tire or damage it. A great deal of vocal tiredness and damage is the result of demanding social use rather than demanding performance use!

You don't need to get rid of your own accent

It is a nonsense to feel you have to shift from your own accent to 'so-called' Standard English or RP to work as an actor.[1] You *do* need to work on your voice to find its full clarity, richness and expression. If you can't be understood or your voice has a limited expression, the richness of your thoughts and feelings will never be communicated.

You may choose to learn Standard English as an accent, for that is what it is, it is not a neutral. There is no such thing. It simply happens to be the accent spoken by those in power so it is called Standard English. If the seat of government and power had historically been in Liverpool rather than London, then Liverpudlian would be Standard English.

Nor is it necessary that classical plays be done in Standard English. What classical plays do need is an owning of the language, by which I mean looking not only at *what* is said but also at *how* it is said: the words used and the images behind the words (see pages 188-90).

Certain plays, such as those of Coward, Wilde and Rattigan may need a certain way of speaking, but this is as much about character, attitude and

1 RP stands for received pronunciation and comes from the notion that the accent spoken by those 'received' at court was the best and, therefore, should be considered as the standard to aspire to.

class as it is about accent. The accent is an *expression* of who the characters are and how they interact with the world and so developing the appropriate accent is part of building the character.

So, please, work in your own accent on the voice exercises in this book. By all means, if you are working on a play, where you have to speak with a different accent, then go through your voice exercises in that accent. That is a good way of really owning the accent and ensuring you can use it freely and healthily.

Technique is not the actor's enemy

Technique does not need to lead to work that is artificial and studied. Technique does not need to be an enemy of truth. Technique can help you fly.

When you have a role you are happy with, in a play you believe in, working with a director and fellow actors you feel at ease with and stimulated by, your voice and body, imagination and creativity work wonderfully well. However, when all these elements are not in place and you feel less secure, that is when technique comes into its own. It is your rescue remedy. It helps you to *re-find* your best work, to re-enter your creative space, and your technique for doing this will be as personal as your acting itself.

What I have noticed about very experienced actors, who turn out consistently good work, by which I mean fresh, exciting non-predictable work, is that they are able to build a creative space around themselves in which they can flourish, however unhelpful the circumstances. This is the technique I am interested in: exercises that enable you to do your best work, to feel free and creative wherever and with whoever you are working.

Anyway you already know how to use your voice and body well. It is just a question of relearning it!

Unless there is a physiological or psychological problem, all babies can scream the house down, for hours on end, without damaging their voices. All healthy toddlers have great posture and an expressive voice, full of range and colour, which they can use incessantly without getting a sore throat.

So you do already know how to do it. It is all simply buried under a collection of less helpful habits you've acquired along the way.

This work is really a way of returning to your best self, your most expressive self. Once you have done that, then, the more you use the muscles the stronger they will get.

HOW TO WORK

I have already talked about sureness, commitment, awareness, ease and interest and how these can help your work. Below are some more ways of working that can take the pain out of voice work and make it much easier.

Check your approach

How you approach the work is as important as the work itself. So often it is approached tentatively, which de-energises, or with excess effort, which strains. Think about how you have approached voice work in the past.

Have you always drawn back from it a little? If you have you may have found that none of the exercises ever seemed to work fully, that it all felt a little flat and mechanical.

Or have you always tried too hard? If you have, you may have found that you could never do the work without tension creeping in somewhere; that it left you feeling all knotted up.

Try to approach the work with a quiet sureness. Assume that you will be able to do the exercises, even if you have found voice work difficult in the past. Check every so often: *'Am I drawing back or trying too hard?'*

Vocal energy and expression come from vocal muscles that are committed and alive, rather than holding back or grabbing and pushing.

Keep the mind light

Our thoughts have a powerful effect on our body and, therefore, on our voice. A tight mind will lead to a tight body and so to a tight voice. Thoughts of pushing and striving to achieve lead to physical and vocal over-effort whilst thoughts of fear and doubt lead to physical and vocal holding back.

The good news is that if you work with a more relaxed and open mind you can influence the body and voice in a positive way. I talked in the introduction about working with sureness, commitment and interest to bring energy. I also spoke about the importance of working with ease. To achieve physical and vocal ease you need to find ease in the mind. Working with an attitude of patience, of tolerance, of kindness and generosity towards yourself, as I have already suggested, all help to bring about mental and, therefore, physical and vocal ease.

Use mental focus and direction to avoid excess physical effort

Successful voice work relies as much on *mental* focus and attention as it does on *physical* effort.

If you try to achieve any activity through physical effort alone you will end up using more muscle power than you need and there is a very good chance that you won't necessarily use the best muscles for the job.

Using mental focus or direction to stimulate activity leads to much more accurate and efficient use of the muscles, which means that activities are achieved with greater ease and flexibility.

Sports people work in this way. If a tennis player is trying to improve his or her forehand stroke, as well as spending time practising the *mechanics* of the stroke, they may watch examples of a good forehand on video and then try to *visualise* the *whole* stroke. Then, the brain is left to turn this visualisation into action.

In this way, the brain is given the *whole pattern* and left to work out the best way for the body to achieve the activity, which means it can engage the best muscles for the job.

There are three vital components to this process – imagery, touch and mental bounce

Imagery The use of imagery is often hotly debated, with many seeing it as 'airy fairy' and imprecise.

My view is that the problem lies in the *way* imagery is used, not in the use of imagery itself.

An image works because it is simple and yet it carries a complex set of instructions from the brain to the body. *You* only need to focus on one thing – the image – but, as a result, a complex set of processes is set in action.

In order for imagery to work, the image needs to be *precise* and *meaningful* to the person using it. I always explain to people that my image is a starting point and they should feel free to adapt it or change it altogether until it works for them.

It is also important the person focuses on the image *one hundred percent*. Often imagery doesn't work because the person is not paying complete attention to the image. Instead, they may be checking to see if the old, unwanted behaviour is still occurring or they may be consciously 'doing' because they don't trust the image to work by itself.

So, it is important to find the *right image* and, then, put *full attention* on that image and *trust* that the desired activity will occur.

Touch Obviously, you need to focus quite precisely on the area that you wish the image to activate. Otherwise the brain may send a general message, which will activate more muscles than necessary or even activate the wrong muscles altogether.

This is where touch plays such a vital part. If you place your hands on the area you wish to move, that helps the mind to focus on that area.

Imagine the brain's problem. There are millions of motor nerve cells in the brain, which transmit instructions for movement all over the body. If you are trying to build a new behaviour, the brain will be unsure as to which nerve, or nerves, to send the message down. So it may not send the message at all, or else it may send it down the nerves it always has done, so causing the old behaviour, or it may send the message to the general area causing more muscles to work than is necessary or desirable.

By placing your hands very specifically and firmly on the area you wish to be activated, the brain gets sensory feedback, via the sensory nerves, and has a much more accurate idea of which motor nerves to send the message down.

Imagine, for example, you are trying to teach yourself to raise one eyebrow. You may well hold the eyebrow you don't want to move still with one hand and move the other eyebrow up and down with the other hand until the brain works out which nerves will activate the required muscles.

Working with imagery and touch will enable your mind to focus more quickly and help you achieve results without extraneous effort.

Mental Bounce Imagery and touch allow you to give *precise instructions* to the muscles. Mental bounce provides the *energy* for the muscles, enabling them to commit appropriately rather than holding back or forcing.

Mental bounce is an energetic state of mind that comes from sureness, commitment and interest. A good way to access these is to think of flirting or teasing or being a little cocky as you do the voice work. This releases a great deal of easy energy, galvanises the muscles that support the voice and shape our speech, and makes voice work more fun to do.

Work slowly and calmly

Understandably, actors will often exclaim *'But I can't do it that slowly on stage!'* Of course not and no one expects you to. The point of working slowly is to give your brain some time to absorb the new pattern. If you practise slowly the brain will pick up the new habit accurately. Once it has this new pattern clearly imprinted it will naturally be able to speed it up. However, if you work fast, the new habit or pattern is likely to be jumbled and will not be accurately reproduced. So, actually, working slowly leads to quicker results.

Working calmly is important for a similar reason. It gives your brain space. Also, if you work with anxiety or effort or impatience the brain will assume that these are part of the new, desired habit or pattern.

Work on one thing at a time

It is best to focus on the task set in each exercise and not to try and carry over tasks from other exercises unless specifically asked to do so. I call this 'layering' – working on one aspect or layer at a time. This keeps everything simple and makes life much easier. It also achieves much better results. It is a question of working on each piece of the jigsaw and trusting that the pieces will fit themselves together, which indeed they will!

Always focus on the behaviour you want and keep going!

There is a great tendency to keep checking and moving the focus back to the behaviour you don't want. Not only is this disheartening it is also counter-productive because you end up giving more attention to the old habit, that you want to drop, than you give to the new habit, that you want to build. So keep your focus on the desired behaviour and trust that, eventually, the message will get through.

Don't be disheartened when it is difficult

When an exercise is hard it is time to celebrate. It means that you have an opportunity to learn, to extend your skill. If you only do exercises that you find easy you may end up feeling good but you won't necessarily learn a great deal. So when an exercise is difficult – enjoy it!

Of course, this doesn't mean you have to worry if you don't find an exercise difficult! Whatever the exercise, however easy or difficult it may be, don't be impressed or discouraged – just get on with it.

Feel your voice rather than listen to it

It is very tempting to listen to your voice and monitor it that way.

This is unhelpful for two reasons. Firstly, it puts you *outside* yourself in what is potentially the *self-conscious, judging* position, which is never helpful, but especially not for creative work. Secondly, you may strive to recreate the sound you heard and liked and there is no guarantee you'll achieve it through the same means, so there's a danger you'll produce the same sound but in a less efficient or relaxed way.

However, if you focus on the physical feeling of your voice in each exercise, you stay inside yourself, with yourself, in the aware position, which is much more helpful to the creative process and vital when performing. Also, your physical experience of your voice is far more accurate. Once you have located the physical sensation associated with a particular vocal behaviour you will know when you feel that sensation again you are accurately recreating the behaviour you want.

Getting rid of the tyranny of the throat

We all know sound is made in the throat. We may not know exactly how, but this knowledge often leads us to put our attention there, which achieves little or nothing of any use and often leads to inappropriate and unhelpful effort.

It is important to know a couple of facts about the throat before we go any further.

The production of sound is not the only function of the larynx. It also protects the lungs by preventing food and drink entering the windpipe.[2]

In addition, the larynx enables us to engage in physically strenuous tasks by closing the throat and so turning the chest into a non-collapsible cavity. Try the following to understand for yourself what I am talking about:

- ❍ *Push against a wall as if you are trying to move it and feel what happens in your throat. Can you feel a closing or pushing together there?*
- ❍ *If you're not sure about that, try pretending that you're straining to go to the toilet and see if you feel it then.*

'So what?' you may say. *'How is this relevant?'* Its relevance is that the brain associates effort with a need to close or constrict in the throat. Therefore, if your brain perceives speaking in general, or a particular role as effortful it is going to constrict the throat and this is the last thing you want to happen.

How do you avoid this? There are two ways, which might at first seem contradictory.

Firstly, you pay attention to the throat, but in a completely different way from usual. You work on being able to keep the throat open, to 'deconstrict' it.[3] This work is much less technical and much more accessible than it may sound. I'll go through the exercises later in the book.[4]

Secondly, unless 'deconstricting' your throat, you should never put your attention there. Many actors damage their throats through being over-protective of them. They mentally 'hold' the throat and this leads to actual muscular holding. This often occurs if an actor has had trouble with their voice. If it has let them down, they find it hard to just let the throat get on by itself.

2 This is achieved by the epiglottis, a tongue-like flap, closing over the larynx and so blocking the windpipe.

3 'Deconstrict' is the term used by an American singer and speech therapist, Jo Estill, who has done some fascinating research into the workings of the larynx and has devised a whole set of 'figures' or exercises for positively directing the movement of the larynx and vocal folds. To find out more about her work and about workshops in this country see her web site: www.evts.com.

4 See page 138–142.

Similarly, if an actor has a cold, there is a tendency to protect the voice, which again can lead to a type of holding, and which takes the attention *off* the breath support muscles, which would help the voice out.

Note

A word of caution: if you're working with weights at a gym, ensure that you can always breathe in and out freely and fairly quietly as you work and that you are not closing your throat. If you find this is happening you need to work with lighter weights. Otherwise the constant pushing together of the vocal folds will damage your voice.

So if the attention is *not* on the throat *where* is it? It is on some point in the breath support system in the lower half of the body. Where exactly is a matter of personal preference, of what works best for each particular actor. Moreover, it may change depending on the particular role and on the demands it makes.

This work is very easy to do and does not involve you thinking technically during performance. Again it will be covered later in the book.[5]

A last word

Throughout the writing of this book I have continually questioned whether practical voice work can be satisfactorily conveyed through the written word. When I am working with a student I don't go through a set pattern of exercises starting at 'A' and working through to 'Z'. I start from where they are and work according to their needs. With the book, however, I have had to cover all possibilities, which has meant a fair amount of exercises and explanation. I have kept these as clear and straightforward as possible but, nevertheless, the book may feel daunting at times. My advice, therefore, is to approach the book very lightly and trust yourself to find what you need.

Voice work does not need to be a chore nor a daunting, impossible task. See it as explorative, playful skill-building. Children learn a huge amount in the first five years of their life and they learn most of it through play. They have huge curiosity and enjoy learning and, since they don't have any idea of how much there is to learn, they remain undaunted.

Remember, if you wanted to climb Everest you would get nowhere by standing and looking at a picture of Everest thinking 'It's far too high and

5 See pages 86–95 and 99–116.

hard to climb'. You would get on much better if you started rock climbing classes and practised when you could, in a way that you really enjoyed. Gradually you would find yourself doing harder and harder climbs until the idea of climbing Everest was not so remote. We all have our Everests and if we start working in a way we enjoy, not being put off by the enormity of the task, we will conquer them.

2

Body Work

Why do it at all?

Unless we have a specific problem at birth, we all start life with bodies that are aligned, balanced and at ease. As a result we can breathe and make sound fully and freely.

As life goes on we acquire tensions and habits that take our bodies away from their natural states. As a result our breath and voice often lose their fullness and freedom.

Working on the body is, therefore, the quickest way of working on the voice. Although it may seem a slow and frustrating way to start, it will make the rest of the work much quicker and easier.

Objections to body work

'People don't have perfect posture in real life. If I learn to stand and move well I won't look real anymore and I'll lose my individuality'

It is true that few of the characters that actors portray have so-called perfect posture. But body work is not about creating *one* posture or *one* way of moving, it is about finding balance and ease, freedom and flexibility. By working on the body to release personal, habitual posture, the actor opens up the possibilities of what they may play, both physically and vocally.

'Working on my body makes me self-conscious. It doesn't loosen me up, it makes me stiffer'

It is not working on the body as such, or indeed on the voice or anything else, which makes us self-conscious. It is our *attitude* to that work. If we are judgmental and distrustful of ourselves, then, when we start to do any work that focuses on ourselves, we will feel inhibited.

Self-consciousness is judgmental monitoring of ourselves. However, if we swap tense judgement for relaxed attentiveness, if we are softly curious rather than harshly critical, then, we can work and find an ease with ourselves that allows us to move forward.

'I'm hopeless at body work, so what's the point? I don't want to be that sort of actor anyway'

Nobody is hopeless at body work. It is true we are not all cut out to be dancers or mime artists or acrobats but these are specific physical skills, whereas a free and balanced body is possible for us all: it is how we began, just take a look at any two-year-old. So it is not a matter of conforming to some external norm but of regaining the grace and ease our bodies were always intended to have. Becoming more ourselves not less. Whatever '*sort*' of actor one is or intends to be, a performance cannot be alive and flexible if the body is sluggish or stiff!

'I have a physical disability, all this focus on body work excludes me!'

Not at all, we all have a different range of abilities physically. I have worked with actors with profound disabilities, but never has it been a case that they couldn't do the work. They worked at finding balance and ease, freedom and flexibility in their own terms. If the principles of an exercise are understood it can always be adapted to work for individuals with different needs.

'Body work does relax me, but I can't use it. I can't go on stage that relaxed!'

Obviously stage performance requires energy. Relaxation needs to be paired with dynamism. This work is all about finding ease physically in whatever you do, so that, however hard you are working, whatever extraordinary demands your performance may make on you, you always have space and flexibility to perform without physical or vocal strain or fatigue.

SO, LET'S GET STARTED

What are you actually getting up to physically?

So many of our habits are unconscious. We are often not aware of tension building up, we are just aware of the result – fatigue or pain. At other times we are aware of the tension but can't work out how to release it, because we are not really clear enough as to how exactly it is building up.

The following exercise is about noticing your particular physical tension patterns, where the tension starts and how it builds. Once you have this awareness it is much easier to stop tension patterns developing.

Keep your focus light and easy and avoid trying too hard. The theatre director, Declan Donnellan, makes a useful distinction between unhelpful and helpful focus. Rather than *'concentrating'* he encourages his actors to *'pay attention'*. I love this. It is so much lighter. Try concentrating on an activity and, then, try paying attention to the same activity and you'll notice the difference.

Body review

To make you consciously aware of unconscious tensions

We are going to start with a body review. I would like you to look at two situations: firstly, one where you feel nervous, uncomfortable and awkward; secondly, one where you feel confident, comfortable and at ease.

Reviewing how your body feels in these two situations will give you a chance to become more specifically aware of where in your body your tensions lie and how they accumulate in a difficult situation.

This exercise is best done with a partner.

> **Note**
> Releasing tension in your body does not stop you from playing characters that are nervous, uncomfortable or ill at ease. It simply allows you to do so with more versatility.

- *Decide on your two situations. Start with the nervous, uncomfortable or awkward situation.*
- *Stand or sit – depending on what you would have been doing in the situation. Have your partner stand or sit to the side of you, looking at you.*
- *Close your eyes and focus on the situation where you feel uncomfortable.*
- *Your partner goes through the list of body parts below and you describe how each body part feels, using whatever words or images come. For example: 'tense', 'loose', 'heavy', 'light', 'clenched', 'easy'. There's no need to be technical. It is just a question of how it feels to you. Obviously, some parts of the body may feel fine, while other parts may have no particular sensation at all. Simply describe what you notice. Your partner writes down what you say, using only the words that you use.*
- *Throughout the list keep re-imagining the situation as strongly as you can.*

- *Here is the list. Always work from the feet upward. Obviously, if you have sensations in parts of the body not specifically mentioned here, then please add those. This list is just a guideline.*

  Feet

  Ankles

  Lower legs

  Knees

  Upper legs

  Hip joints

  Buttocks

  Belly

  Spine

  Rest of the back

  Ribs

  Chest

  Shoulders

  Shoulder joints

  Upper arms

  Elbows

  Lower arms

  Wrists

  Hands and Fingers

  Neck

  Head

  Face

  Jaw

  Lips and Tongue

- *Once you have gone through the whole list, shake out and, then, move on to the second situation. Don't discuss the list at all at this point.*
- *Again, close your eyes and focus on the situation. Your partner goes through the list again and you describe how each part feels now. Once you have finished, shake out as before.*
- *Now, look at the first list. Where is it in your body that you tense in the nervous, uncomfortable or awkward situation? Try going back into that state and*

exaggerating the tension you feel so that you can bring it more into your consciousness. Try to feel where the tension starts. Experiment with how it might be affecting your breath and voice.

- *Once you have explored the tension in this situation, shake out gently to relax the body.*
- *Then, look at the second list to see if there are any parts of your body that are tense even in the confident, comfortable, easy situation?*

These areas are important because they tend to act as 'seed beds' or 'springboards' from which tension can easily and quickly arise and build once you are in a stressful situation. It is good to work towards releasing these areas. The more at ease you are ordinarily, the easier you will find it to maintain ease in difficult situations

There is no need to repeat this exercise regularly, but you can use it whenever you want to explore what is going on physically and vocally in any situation. Paying attention allows you, to a degree, to become your own teacher and guide.

NOW TO WORK

There are four areas of work I want to look at:

Release and Redirection removes habitual tensions and re-balances the body and so brings flexibility and ease.

Centring and Grounding creates a secure base and so brings stability and balance, which, in turn, enables further release of tension.

Toning and Alignment develops appropriate use of physical and mental effort and continues the re-balancing work and so brings energy and alertness.

Cardiovascular Exercise builds physical fitness and so brings strength and stamina.

Release and Redirection

This work is firstly about letting go, about allowing tension in muscles to release. Muscles take longer to relax than they do to tense, so, it is important to rest in each position for some time or, if it is a movement exercise, to move slowly and smoothly to give the muscles a chance to undo.

It is also important to allow the breath to be as free as possible, so, every so often, check that you are releasing your breath rather than holding it. There is no need to worry about the in-breath – as long as you are letting go of the out-breath the in-breath will take care of itself.

The redirection part of the work is about mentally directing the body to lengthen, widen and open. This enables the body to begin to re-balance and re-align. Remember – the more precise your image and the more you trust this image to work, rather than 'consciously doing', the better the results you will achieve.

Stretching

To release pent-up energy and tension.

It is often difficult to go straight into still relaxation work, so it can be useful to start with some stretches. The ones below are based on a set of Shiatsu exercises.[6] They not only give a physical stretch; they also balance the energy.

If you find you have a great deal of pent-up energy you might want to start with a couple of minutes brisk walking on the spot, really swinging your arms and lifting your legs, before you move on to the stretches.

Rest comfortably in each stretch position and let gravity and the out-breath do the work. This will give you a far deeper and healthier stretch than all the forcing in the world. Forcing only tenses muscles further.

Stretch I

Opening the Chest

- *Stand with your toes turned slightly inwards.*
- *Comfortably link your thumbs behind your back. As you breathe out, lift your arms away from your body behind you, allowing your chest to open. (See diagram 1a.) Rest in this position for a few breaths. Then, bring your arms down.*

6 Shiatsu is based on the same Oriental Medicine system as Acupuncture. Shiatsu literally means finger pressure. In a Shiatsu session the practitioner gently leans with his/her fingers or palms, elbows, knees or feet on the meridians – energy lines in the body – and in so doing stretches these meridians and balances the energy. The Shiatsu exercises similarly stretch the meridians and balance the energy. To find out more about Shiatsu contact the Shiatsu Society on 01788 555 051.

- *Again lift your arms away from your body, allowing your chest to open, then leaving your arms in this position, lean forward from the hips, as far as is comfortable, keeping the legs slightly bent. (See diagram 1b.)*

- *Rest in this position for a few breaths, keeping the legs soft but straight and the neck relaxed so the head is dropped. Then, come out of the position slowly and easily on an out-breath, with the head coming up last.*

Stretch 2

Stretching the front of the body and the front of the legs

- *Stand facing the wall. Raise one arm above your head and rest your hand flat on the wall for support. (See diagram 2a.)*

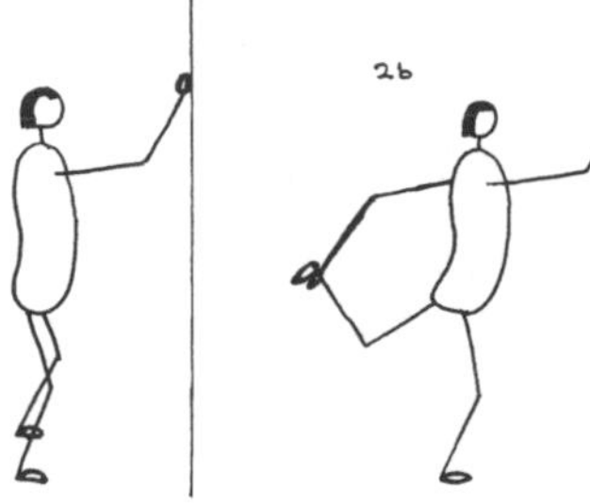

- *On the out-breath, lift your opposite foot behind you and grasp that ankle with your free hand. (See diagram 2b.)*
- *Think of supporting your ankle with your hand rather than pulling the leg up and back.*
- *Breathe in and, then, on the next out-breath, move your thigh back and up, taking care to keep it parallel with the other leg. Then, gently arch your back and look at the ceiling. (See diagram 2c.) This will give you a stretch through the whole of the front of your body, on the raised leg side.*

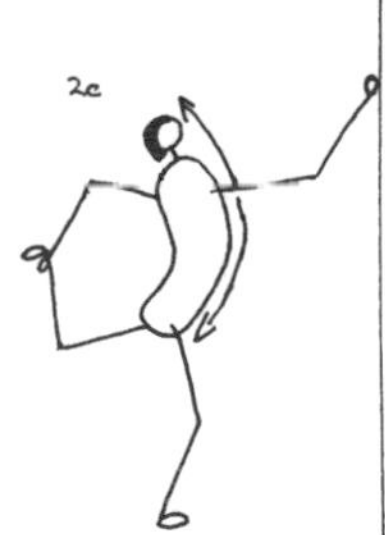

- *Rest in this position for a few breaths and, then, come gently out of the position on an out-breath.*
- *Then, repeat with the other hand against the wall and the other leg raised behind.*

Stretch 3

Opening the hips and stretching the lower back

- *Sit on the floor with your legs bent and the soles of your feet together. (See diagram 3a.) If it is difficult to sit up in this position, place one or two cushions under your bottom.*

- *Then, bring your feet as close to you as is comfortable, whilst still keeping the soles together and the spine long.*
- *Hold your toes loosely and lean forward from your hips keeping the back straight and the shoulders relaxed. Let the elbows move outwards and down towards the floor as the arms bend. (See diagram 3b.)*

Don't worry if you can't lean forward very far. Many people are tight in the lower back and hip area, so, just do what you can without force. Cushions really will help if you are finding it difficult. Then, as time goes by and the lower back becomes looser you may find you no longer need them.

- *Rest in this position for a few breaths and, then, come gently out of the position on an out-breath.*

Stretch 4

Stretching the back of the body and the back of the legs

- *Sit on the floor with your legs stretched out in front of you. Again, sit on a cushion if necessary. As you breathe out raise your arms up above your head, keeping your shoulders and shoulder blades gently dropped as you do so. End up with your arms in line with your body, palms facing each other. (See diagram 4a.)*
- *Breathe in in this position and, then, stretch up and forward from your hips, keeping your back long, your shoulders soft and your shoulder blades dropping gently down your back. Take care to bend from the hips rather than the waist and keep your head in line with your body. (See diagram 4b.)*

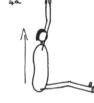

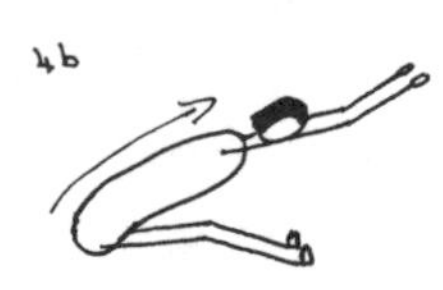

- *When you have stretched as far as is comfortable, rest in the position for a few breaths, imagining your fingers are gently reaching out to the far wall, while your back continues to lengthen, your shoulders to soften and your shoulder blades to gently drop down your back.*
- *Then, come gently out of the position on an out-breath.*

Stretch 5

Stretching the upper back

- *Sit cross-legged on the floor. Again, on cushions if necessary.*

❍ *Cross your arms over your upper-body and hold your upper arms with your hands as if you are hugging yourself. (See diagram 5a.) Then, as you breathe out, curl forward from your hips, keeping your bottom in contact with the floor or cushions. (See diagram 5b.)*

❍ *Rest in this position for a few breaths, making sure you can breathe easily, then come gently out of the position on an out-breath.*

Stretch 6

Stretching the sides of the body

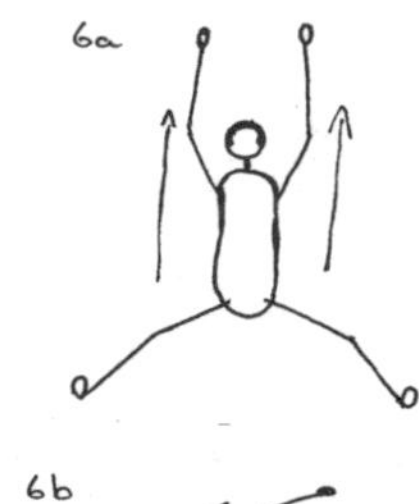

❍ *Sit with your legs stretched out in front of you and as far apart as is comfortable. Again, sit on a cushion if it is difficult to sit upright. (See diagram 6a.)*

❍ *As you breathe out, raise your arms above your head, keeping the shoulders soft and the shoulder blades gently dropping down your back. End with your palms facing forward. Then, turn to face your left leg.*

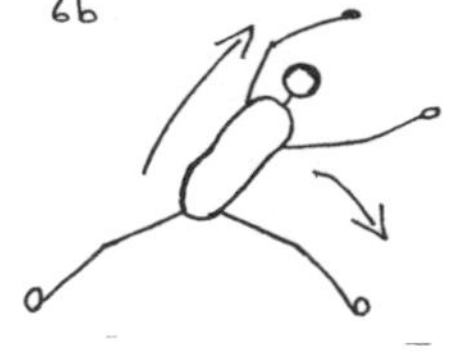

❍ *Breathe in in this position, then, on the next out-breath, from the hips lean over the right leg, looking at your left shoulder as you do so. (See diagram 6b.) You will feel the stretch in the left side.*

❍ *Rest in this position for a few breaths, then come gently out of the position on an out-breath.*

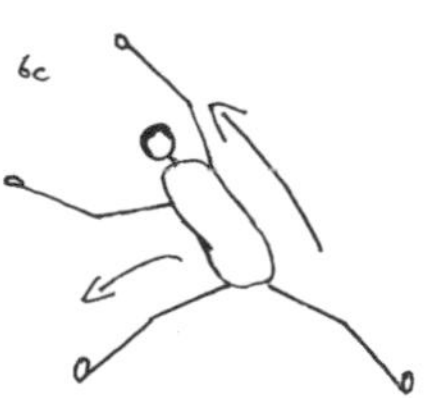

❍ *Repeat on the other side. (See diagram 6c.)*

Putting the stretches together

Once you've learnt the stretches they shouldn't take long to do, just a few gentle breaths in each position. Always rest, lying on the floor, for a few breaths after you have done the stretches.

Release and redirect

To allow release of tension and to begin to rebalance and realign the body

This is an excellent and safe exercise. It gives your body a chance to release from its habitual tensions: to lengthen, widen and open and to return to its natural ease and balance.

As you do the exercise, resist the temptation to bully your tension away. Relaxation and release are achieved through letting go. You can't force them. The more you rest and give up your weight to the floor and allow yourself to let your breath go, the easier you'll find it.

I suggest you read through this exercise first. Then, put the bulleted instructions in parts 2,3 and 4 onto a tape, so you can do the exercise without having to refer to the book.

Part one – Resting in the Alexander position

We are going to use a position from the Alexander Technique.[7] This involves lying on the floor on your back, with your head on a couple of books and your legs bent, so that your feet are flat on the floor. (See diagram 7a.)

There is a natural curve in the small of the back, so this area will not be flat on the floor. Bending the legs helps to lengthen the lower back and so will avoid any excess arching.

Your head needs to rest on enough books so that your chin is slightly lower than your forehead. (See diagram 7a.) This helps the back of your neck to lengthen.

Some people feel a little constricted in the throat, at first, with their head on the books. However, if you avoid pulling your chin into your chest and instead imagine the back of the neck lengthening this sense of constriction will go in time.

- *Lie on the floor in the Alexander position as described.*
- *Check that your legs are parallel, so your knees are in line with your hips and your feet are in line with your knees.*
- *Rest your hands on your belly, with your elbows well away from your sides so that your shoulder blades move out away from your spine. Also, check that there is plenty of space under your armpits.*

7 The Alexander Technique is a training in good use of the body. It was developed by FM Alexander as a result of vocal difficulties he was having when giving professional recitals of dramatic pieces in Sydney at the end of the last century. If you would like to know more about the technique have a look at Michael Gelb's book *Body Work*. Or contact the Society of Alexander Teachers on 020 7284 3338.

Part two – Directing the body to release and balance

You are going to let your attention direct your body into a more relaxed and balanced state. Don't worry if your body does not respond, just keep imagining the ease and relaxation you want and ignore the tension.

- *Start with your feet.*
- *Imagine the soles of the feet softening and spreading and really resting on the floor.*
- *Imagine the toes uncurling and spreading.*
- *Imagine the sides and the top of the feet softening and spreading.*
- *Imagine space and a feeling of fluidity and expansion in the ankle joints.*
- *Imagine the muscles of the lower leg softening.*
- *Imagine space and a feeling of fluidity and expansion in the knee joints.*
- *Imagine the knees floating towards the ceiling.*
- *Imagine the muscles of the upper leg softening.*
- *Imagine space and a feeling of fluidity and expansion in the hip joints.*
- *Imagine the hips opening, sinking into the floor and widening across the floor.*
- *Imagine all the muscles in the groin area softening.*
- *Imagine the belly muscles softening, first, on the surface and, then, deep inside.*
- *Imagine the buttock muscles softening.*
- *Focus on the spine. Imagine the spine lengthening from the tailbone up to the top of the neck.*
- *If it helps, imagine a spiral of energy moving gently up and down inside the spine connecting and lengthening it.*
- *Focus on the rib cage, which extends from just above waist level to just below shoulder level and encircles the whole upper body.*
- *Focus on the back of the ribs, where they join the spine. Imagine space in the joints there, a sense of fluidity and expansion.*
- *Picture the ribs fanning out across the back and then curving round the sides of the body. Picture the upper ribs connecting to the breastbone while the lower ribs connect with each other via cartilage and the bottom two ribs float freely.*

- *Imagine the whole rib cage being able to stretch open and then relax again as it might on a deep and satisfying yawn.*
- *Imagine the lower rib cage, from just below the breastbone down to the waist stretching open and relaxing even more on a deep and satisfying yawn.*
- *Focus on the area between the shoulder blades and the spine. Imagine that area softening, opening and widening. Imagine the shoulder blades moving away from the spine.*
- *Focus on the chest. Imagine the chest area softening, first around the breastbone area and then right out into the corners of the chest.*
- *Imagine the shoulders opening, sinking into the floor and spreading across the floor.*
- *Imagine space and a sense of fluidity and expansion in the shoulder joints.*
- *Imagine the muscles in the upper arms softening.*
- *Imagine space and a sense of fluidity and expansion in the elbow joints.*
- *Imagine the muscles in the lower arms softening.*
- *Imagine space and a sense of fluidity and expansion in the wrist joints.*
- *Imagine the palms softening and the backs of the hands softening. Imagine the fingers softening and spreading. Imagine space and fluidity in the finger and thumb joints.*
- *Imagine the hands becoming heavier and really sinking into your body.*
- *Let your attention move back up your arms and across your shoulders to your neck.*
- *Imagine your neck spine growing up out of the rest of your spine. Imagine your neck spine lengthening and all the muscles in the back of the neck softening.*
- *Focus on the muscles just below the base of the skull, either side of the top of the spine. Let these muscles soften and lengthen. Have a feeling of fluidity, expansion and space here.*
- *Imagine all the muscles of the scalp softening.*
- *Imagine the muscles of the face softening and the face opening.*
- *Imagine the forehead spreading and softening.*
- *Imagine the eye area softening. The eyelids softening and the eyeballs softening.*
- *Imagine the cheeks and nose softening.*

- *Imagine the jaw softening and releasing.*
- *Imagine under the chin softening.*
- *Imagine the inside of the mouth softening.*
- *Imagine the tongue softening. The tip of the tongue softening. The front of the tongue softening. The middle of the tongue softening. The back of the tongue softening.*

Part three – Releasing inner tension

Now imagine that there is a tube, which runs from your lips back along your mouth and down through your throat, your chest and your belly all the way to the anus (See diagram 7c.)

Note

There is a sense of connection between the throat and the anus. This may sound mad, but if you don't believe me try tightening your anus and see what happens to your throat! Also, remember that people the English would describe as tight-lipped, the Americans describe as tight-assed!

Remember to relax your anus again, if you tighten it!

- *At first it may be hard to imagine the tube at all or there may be whole parts of it that seem completely blocked. Just keep working with the idea of the tube opening and clearing.*
- *If it helps, imagine that a gentle spiral of energy is moving up and down this tube opening it up and clearing it out.*

Part four – Centring your attention

- *Move your hands so that they are resting over your navel, if they are not doing so already. Make sure your elbows are still resting on the floor. If this is not possible place a cushion under each elbow.*

- *Focus your attention where your hands are.*
- *Imagine that the breath is gently filling into and emptying from your belly where your hands are. Do not consciously move your belly, just focus on the idea of it moving: gently rising as it fills and falling as it empties.*

Don't worry if you feel that the breath is more in your chest, ignore that and just focus on your belly and in time the breath will drop. Also, let the ribs do as they like. Keep all your attention on your belly where your hands are.

❍ *Rest for a few minutes, keeping your attention on the movement of breath in the belly. Don't judge your breath, or try to control it or change it. Just let it be. Your attention may well wander, so just keep gently bringing it back to rest on your belly and the idea of breathing from there.*

❍ *Gently rest at the end of the exercise, forgetting about your breath altogether.*

❍ *Then, on an out-breath open your eyes and slowly look around to reorient yourself.*

Note

Once you have a good sense of lengthening and widening on the floor, you can take that sense into standing and sitting and even into particular character's postures. For example, if you were playing Richard III, once you had found the posture for the character you could then think of lengthening and widening in that position. This will not change it externally, but it will ease the position for you so that it is easier to maintain and to breathe freely. As a result, this allows more flexibility vocally, physically and mentally.

If you can find 15 minutes as regularly as possible to do this exercise, it will allow deep release of habitual tensions and make the rest of the physical and vocal work easier to do.

Ankle rotations

To release tension in the ankles, small of the back, and neck

Tension works up the body, therefore, tension in the ankles, knees and hips can profoundly affect the rest of the body and many breathing and postural problems are the results of such tension. In order for us to rest and be at ease the ankle, knee and hip joints need to be loose.

This simple exercise releases the ankles and can help to keep the small of the back and the neck more relaxed and fluid. It is amazing how tightness in the ankle can lock up so much of the back. Of course, you do not always have to do the exercise lying down as I describe here; you could do it while you were sitting on the tube, train or bus.

8

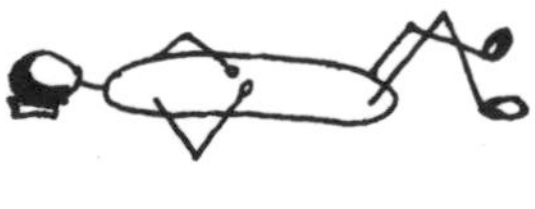

❍ *Staying in the Alexander position* (see *page 24*)*, lift one leg and cross it over the other so the lower part of the crossed over leg hangs loose.* (*See diagram 8.*)

- *Rotate the ankle slowly and smoothly four times in one direction, imagining that you are oiling the joint and making it more fluid. Check that you are not holding your breath.*
- *Then, rotate four times in the opposite direction.*
- *Repeat with the other leg crossed over.*
- *Rest in the Alexander Position for a few seconds.*

Pelvic rounds

To free up the pelvis, lower back and neck

We will look at loosening the knees later. Now, we are going to look at freeing up the hips so that the pelvis and lower back can move freely.

This also helps to free the small of the back and the neck. In fact, this exercise gives a wonderful massage to the whole spine. It is based on a Feldenkrais exercise.[8]

Remember to gently breathe out and loosen your jaw while doing this exercise. It is very easy to hold your breath and clench your teeth, especially at first. Also, remember to move as slowly and smoothly as you can, so the muscles have time to release.

- *Start by lying on the floor in the Alexander Position as in the earlier exercises. (See page 24.) However, remove the book from under your head and let your head rest on the floor.*
- *Focus on your sacrum, which is the bony base of the spine, just below the small of the back.*
- *It is slightly curved and you are going to work with that curve rocking up and down and side to side to loosen up the whole pelvis and lower back area.*
- *Without taking your weight off the floor, gently tilt your pelvis forwards and up until the small of the back is flat on the floor. (See diagram 9a.)*

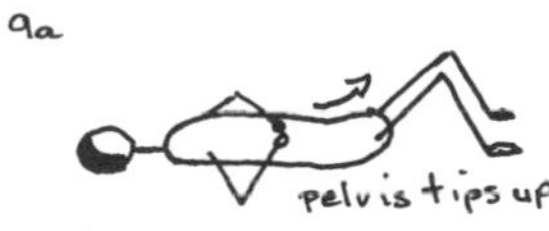

- *Then, again without taking your weight off the floor, gently tilt your pelvis back and down until the small of the back is fully arched away from the floor. (See diagram 9b.)*

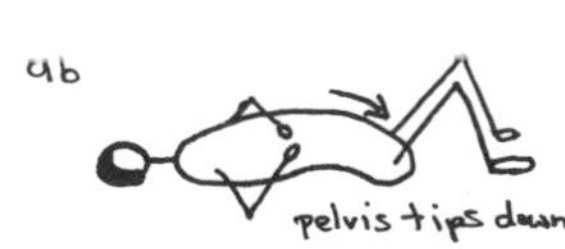

8 Moshe Feldenkrais created a whole series of exercises, which build body awareness, flexibility, co-ordination and ease. For more information refer to his book *Awareness Through Movement*. To find out more look at Feldenkrais Guild UK: www.feldenkrais.co.

- *Rock back and forth several times from the flattened to the arched position.*
- *Once you are happy with the movement repeat it a few more times keeping the belly and buttock muscles and the hip joints as loose as possible. Also, remember not to hold your breath or clench your jaw.*
- *Then, rest in the Alexander position for a few breaths.*
- *Then, rock from side to side of the bony base of spine. This is a tiny rock from side to side of the bone. It is not rocking from one side to the other of the whole bottom.*
- *Then, rest, again, in the Alexander position for a few breaths.*
- *Now, you are going to circle round the bony base of the spine. Start by tilting the pelvis, as before, so that the small of the back is flattened into the floor. Then, circle round to one side; then circle down until the small of the back is fully arched away from the floor and then circle up to the other side and then circle on up until the small of the back is flat on the floor again.*
- *Once you have a sense of the movement, circle four times slowly and smoothly in one direction and, then, four times slowly and smoothly in the other direction, remembering to breathe freely. The less force you use and the more you imagine gently massaging your whole back the better.*
- *Once you have finished, rest in the Alexander Position.*

Shoulder blade lift and drop

To release the whole shoulder area

Having focused on freeing the lower body we will now focus on releasing the upper body. This is an excellent exercise for releasing tension in the shoulder and neck area. It is based on a Pilates exercise.[9]

- *Lie on the floor in the Alexander Position.*

9 Pilates is a system that encourages good alignment and use of the body. It was developed in the early 20th century by Joseph Pilates, who was influenced by many different approaches including yoga, gymnastics, skiing, self-defence, dance, circus and weight training. Fundamentally, Pilates work encourages good alignment and use of the body. An excellent book on the subject is *The Official Body Control Pilates Manual* by Lynne Robinson, Helge Fisher, Jaqueline Knox and Gordon Thomson. Also you can visit their web site on: www.bodycontrol.co.uk.

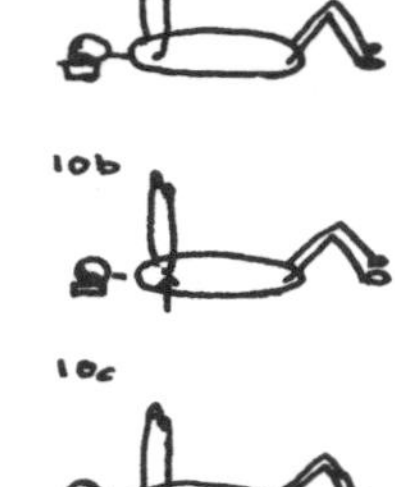

- *Breathe out and, keeping your shoulder blades resting on the floor, let your arms float up until they are directly above your shoulders, with your hands hanging loosely from your wrists. (See diagram 10a.)*
- *Breathe in while resting in this position, then, breathe out and keeping the arms softly straight (i.e. don't lock the elbows), lift the shoulder blades off the floor and, then, drop them back onto the floor. (See 10b and 10c.)*
- *Repeat this lifting and dropping several times as you breathe out imagining your shoulder blades sliding down your back slightly as you do so.*
- *Rest again on the in-breath, then lift and drop the shoulder blades on the out-breath.*
- *Repeat this whole sequence two more times and, then, on the third out-breath let the arms gently drop to the floor.*

Slow neck rolls

To release the neck

Now we are going to focus a little more on the neck and on releasing the tension there.

This exercise will also help to remove jaw tension.

- *Lie in the Alexander position as before, with the book under your head.*
- *Imagine there is a lead weight in the back of your head. Imagine that the lead weight rolls over towards your left ear and in so doing rolls your head over to the left side.*
- *Then, imagine the lead weight rolling back to the centre and, then, over towards your right ear, taking your head with it so that your head rolls back to the centre and, then, across to the right side.*
- *Repeat this rolling of the head from side to side, breathing out as you roll and breathing in as your head rests at each side.*

Spine peel

To connect with the spine and to increase its flexibility

This exercise is excellent for helping you to get in touch with your spine and to increase its flexibility.

- *Start in the Alexander Position, but without the book under your head.*
- *Starting at the base of your spine peel each vertebra off the floor one by one, breathing out as you do so.*
- *As you bring the base of your spine off the floor, the small of your back will flatten into the floor. Then, the small of the back will peel off the floor followed by the upper back, until you are resting on your shoulders. (See diagram 11a.)*

> **Note**
> Doing this exercise, you may not be able to peel your body very far initially, so simply go as far as you safely and comfortably can.

- *Breathe in while resting on your shoulders and, then, as you breathe out place each vertebra back onto the floor starting from shoulder level and working down to the base of the spine. (See diagram 11b.)*

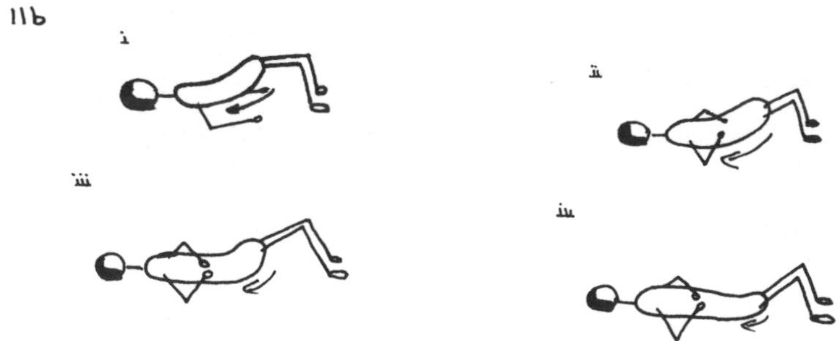

Take your time with this exercise, really visualising each vertebra peeling up off the floor and down onto it. Also, check that you are releasing your breath rather than holding it.

Curve/arch

To stretch and release the spine and increase its flexibility

This exercise continues to work on the spine, stretching and releasing it and increasing its flexibility. It also continues to release the hips and pelvis.

It is best if you can do it the first few times with a partner. The idea is to really start all the movement from the hips and then work up the spine vertebra by vertebra, so the head is always the last part to move.

- *In one movement roll sideways from the Alexander Position, onto your hands and knees. Avoid rolling onto your belly and, then, scrambling up onto all fours. Just roll straight over onto your hands and knees.*
- *Make sure that your knees are directly under your hips and your arms under your shoulders. Have your arms fairly straight, but your elbows loose and unlocked.*

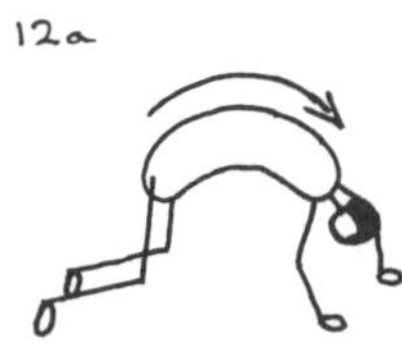

- *Go into a curve so the middle of your back is high and the bottom and head are low. (See diagram 12a.)*
- *Get your partner to place their hands on your hips and start to tilt your hips so that your bottom comes up and the small of your back goes down. Allow the rest of the spine to follow, so that the area between the shoulder blades arches down, the upper spine and neck lengthen and the head finally lifts, without scrunching the back of the neck. (See diagram 12b.)*

- *Once you are fully in the arch position, your partner again places their hands on your hips and starts to tilt the hips in the opposite direction, so that your bottom drops and the small of your back comes up. Allow the rest of the spine to follow, so that the area between the shoulder blades curves up, the upper spine and neck lengthen and the head finally drops. (See diagram 12a.)*
- *Repeat the arching and curving several times with your partner helping you to start from the hips each time and helping you to work up the spine vertebra by vertebra. Your partner can place their fingers on each vertebra to help you further.*
- *Check that both you and your partner are releasing your breath, rather than holding it, while you do this exercise.*
- *Once you have finished this exercise, roll back over into the Alexander Position and rest for a few breaths.*

Once you feel well connected to your spine and find it easy to start from the hips and move vertebra by vertebra, then, you can work with this exercise on your own.

Getting up

To maintain the release as you come to standing, so that you don't just revert to old habits

❍ *Start on your hands and knees. (See page 33 for instructions as to how to roll from Alexander Position onto hands and knees.) Curl your toes under and walk your hands back to just in front of your knees. (See diagram 13a.)*

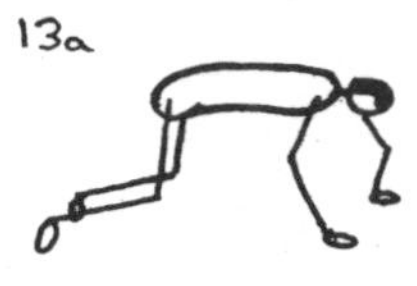

❍ *Rock your weight back until it is all on the balls of your feet and then straighten your legs so your heels drop on to the floor, your bottom goes up and your upper body hangs over. (See diagram 13b.)*

❍ *Then, roll up gently, vertebra by vertebra, from the base of the spine, until you are standing upright. (See diagram 13c.) Keep the neck, shoulders and arms relaxed throughout and keep the chin on the chest until your whole body is upright.*

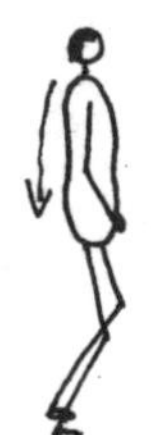

Exploring standing – I

Why a stable neutral helps your body, breath and acting

We will look at standing in more detail later. I would just like to set out a few essentials here. Standing with feet parallel and hipbone width apart is most stable. The hipbones to which I am referring are the knobbly ones on the front of the body. The feet need to be in line with these bones and the weight needs to be evenly distributed between each foot and between the heels and balls of the feet.

❍ *Try standing in this way and see how it feels.*

❍ *Then, try standing with your feet together. Can you feel that this is less stable and that it closes off the lower belly? Can you feel how it restricts your breath?*

- *Now, take your feet wider apart than hipbone width. Can you feel how this affects your lower back causing it to arch more?*

> **Note**
>
> A character may have a wider or narrower stance than the neutral stable position. That is fine. The point is to be able to release from a particular stance back to neutral when not playing the character. This means there will be less likelihood of injury as time goes by and that you will not be imprisoning yourself into only playing one sort of character.

- *Now return to hipbone width. Can you feel that this is more stable and allows the breath to be freer?*

Exploring standing – 2

Free ankles, knees and hips are crucial for free breath and instincts

Next you need to check that the ankle, knee and hip joints are loose. If these joints tighten up they lead to tension in other parts of the body, whereas if they stay loose they help the rest of the body to relax.

- *Try tightening the ankle, knee and hip joints and see what that does to the body and breath.*
- *Then, try relaxing the same joints and see how the body feels.*

If you usually lock your ankle, knee or hip joints, it can feel very shaky and quite weak when you unlock them. If this is the case, keep imagining all the weight in your body pouring down through your legs into the floor. This will give you a feeling of strength but without the previous tension.

Exploring standing – 3

Lengthening and widening will help your stage presence

You have already explored lengthening and widening on the floor and I have mentioned that it brings ease to the body and breath. It also brings presence, helping you to fully inhabit your space.

- *Focus on the spine and imagine the tailbone dropping to the floor while the top of the spine and the crown of the head float up towards the ceiling, so the spine lengthens in both directions.*
- *Then, focus on your buttocks and shoulder blades and imagine them gently dropping down your back as your spine lengthens even further.*

❍ *Then, focus on the hips and shoulders and imagine them opening and widening. Remember not to stiffen the spine or pull the shoulders back just imagine the lengthening and widening and trust that it will happen.*

Putting the 'Release and Redirection' section together

Obviously the first few times you do this section it may take quite a while but eventually it could all be done in 28 minutes as follows:

Stretches	*6 minutes*
Release and Redirect	*14 minutes*
Ankle Rotation	*1 minute*
Pelvic Rounds	*1 minute*
Shoulder Drops	*1 minute*
Neck Rolls	*1 minute*
Spine Peel	*1 minute*
Curve/Arch	*1 minute*

Centring and Grounding

Now you have started to release it is important to find easy support for the body so you won't be tempted to tighten up the ankles, knees or hips in order to support your self.

Centring and Grounding are about finding support through resting and letting go, rather than through holding and fixing.

Most of the time we hold ourselves up off the floor. Tightening ankles, knees, hips, buttocks and stomachs and heaving up chests and shoulders. It's an awful lot of work and it also lifts our centre of gravity, which makes us more likely to lose our balance.

❍ *Try tightening up the ankles, knees and hips. Then, tighten the buttocks and pull in the belly a little more and lift your chest and tighten your shoulders. How does it feel? Pretty uncomfortable and not very restful and yet it is often what we do.*

Centring allows us to let go of all this tension and really rest in our body, with a lower centre of gravity. It gives us a sense of internal support, Grounding also allows us to release tension and really rest on the ground. It gives us a sense of *external* support.

Learning to be centred and grounded will help you to produce your best work even in stressful situations.

Centring – I

To help you explore the sensation of being on or off centre

We are going to start by exploring centring and the creation of internal support.

The following exercise allows you to explore for yourself the difference between being out of your centre and being in your centre. It is a matter of attention, since attention directs energy.

You need a partner to help you explore this exercise.

- *Stand with your partner to the side of you. Check that your knees are soft rather than locked. Place all your attention in your forehead. Focus solely on your forehead. Take as long as you need to do this.*
- *Once you are ready, let your partner know. They, then, push you gently but firmly, first from one side and then from the other. You both simply note what happens.*
- *Then, after you have again checked that your knees are soft rather than locked, focus all your attention on your belly just below your navel and let that area relax. It is helpful to place your hands over your navel to help you focus there. Also, it can help to focus on the gentle movement of the breath in the belly. Again, take as long as you need to do this.*
- *As before, once you are ready, let your partner know. Again, they push you gently but firmly, first from one side and then the other. Again simply note what happens.*
- *What differences do you notice? Do you feel more stable and yet more flexible when your attention is in your belly? Do you feel heavier and yet lighter when your attention is in your belly? Do you feel clearer in the head when your attention is in the belly? All the above are the results of being centred, which is what begins to happen when you focus on your belly.*
- *Your partner may also have noticed a difference: finding you more stable and yet flexible when your focus was on the belly.*

Don't worry if you don't notice much at first or if you have a completely different experience from the one I described. Simply note any change and also be aware of where you find it easier to place your attention.

If you find it easier to place the attention in the forehead, it may be that that is where you tend to focus generally. Certainly, if you find you get nervous or excited very easily or find yourself easily knocked off balance, either mentally or physically, it may well be that your focus is mostly in your upper body, anywhere from your chest upwards. Some people even notice that their focus is above their head or way out in front of them!

If you find it easier to focus your attention on your belly, it may be that you are already centring to a smaller or greater degree. Certainly, if you find that you can stay quite composed and relaxed even when nervous and that you don't easily get knocked off balance, it may well be that your focus is more often in your belly.

❍ *Try the exercise again with you now pushing your partner.*

You do not need to keep practising this exercise. It is a one-off to let you have an experience of being in and out of centre.

Centring – 2

To help you centre your energy and breath, so you can work from a place of greater balance. To help you prepare for stressful situations

Once you have a sense of centring by placing your attention in your belly, you can practise on your own. You can do this anywhere. I find it particularly useful to practise when standing waiting – for a train, a bus, in a queue – or when travelling. It can be done either sitting or standing. It is also excellent to do just before an interview or audition.

❍ *Stand, or sit, with your feet parallel and hipbone width apart. Let your feet really rest on the floor and let the soles soften and spread. Let your ankle, knee and hip joints soften. Imagine your spine lengthening, your shoulder blades dropping gently down your back and your hips and shoulders widening.*

❍ *Place your hands over your navel and gently begin to rest your attention there on the gentle movement of the breath.*

❍ *Don't try to push the attention or breath down. You may feel the energy or breath in your chest or the head congested and racing. Register these sensations but don't try to change them or indeed to keep your focus on them. Simply rest your attention on the belly where your hands are and on the movement of breath there.*

❍ *Start by doing this for a minute at a time and then begin to do it for longer and longer periods of time. It is natural for the mind to wander, just keep bringing it back to focus on the belly as soon as you notice it has wandered.*

Practise this as often as you can so that in time it becomes habitual.

Grounding – figure of eight

To increase flexibility in ankles, knees and hips and to exercise your leg muscles so they properly support you

Now that you have some sense of internal balance and support we will look at grounding, at really allowing yourself to rest on the floor and be externally supported.

This exercise will help you to become more aware of your legs and how they can work to support you. It really helps me to ground myself and I have found it has helped a lot of actors I have worked with.

- *For this exercise stand with your feet a little wider than hipbone width apart. Let your ankles, knees and hips soften, your spine lengthen and your hips and shoulders widen.*
- *Then, hang over loosely from your hips. Keep the hip, knee and ankle joints soft. Let the arms and head hang freely. Relax your feet and spread your toes.*
- *First, just get comfortable in this position, keep softening and releasing any holding, especially in the feet, legs, shoulders and neck. Imagine the weight of your body pouring down through your legs and feet into the floor and keep imagining your legs softening and your feet spreading.*

14a

- *Now imagine a figure-of-eight shape lying sideways, flat on the floor, with each of your feet in each half of the eight. (See diagram 14a.)*
- *Focus on your hips and let your hips move round that figure-of-eight shape. (See diagram 14b.) Let your weight move from one foot to the other as you do so.*

14b

- *As you move around the figure-of-eight shape you will feel your legs really taking the weight of your body. Keep them soft, keep spreading and softening your feet and keep a sense of fluidity in the ankle, knee and hip joints, as if all your weight is still pouring down through your legs into the floor. Also, check that you are releasing the breath rather than holding it.*

14c

- *Having gone one way four or five times, go the other way an equal amount of times. (See diagram 14c.)*
- *Then, rest, hanging over, for a moment before coming up slowly. Once up, pay attention to how your legs feel. Usually this exercise gives you more sense of your legs and gives you a feeling of being far more rooted.*

❍ *Even if you only feel slightly more grounded stay with the feeling for a moment. Really register it so that your body has a good sense of how it feels. The more you do this exercise and return to this groundedness, the easier it will be to access this feeling when acting and going about your daily life.*

Grounding – pressing, squatting, bouncing, jumping

To release leg tension and encourage you to use your legs more appropriately to support you, so giving you a feeling of being more grounded

All of these activities help you to feel more grounded. Try them all and see which you find most useful.

Pressing Tension in the back of the body literally holds us back. It stops us from resting in the present. In Shiatsu, and the Chinese philosophy of medicine on which it is based, the back is considered to relate to the past, to our past experiences and beliefs, while the belly area is considered to relate to the here and now, to our present experiences. By releasing the tension in the back, and so releasing old patterns and attitudes that may be holding us back, we are able to rest in our bodies and become more grounded and present.

Pressing – I

To release tension in the back and the back of the legs

I find this is an excellent exercise for releasing the back and letting the energy drop. It is a quick but effective way to ground yourself before an audition or rehearsals or performance. It is also a good exercise to start the day with, after some gentle stretches. It is a powerful exercise so you only need to do it three or four times.

❍ *Stand, as before, with your feet hipbone width apart and parallel, your ankle, knee and hip joints softening, your spine lengthening and your hips and shoulders widening.*

❍ *Then, again, hang over from your hips. This time bend your legs until your finger tips comfortably make contact with the floor. If this is not possible use a block or low stool to rest your fingers on. (See diagram 15a.)*

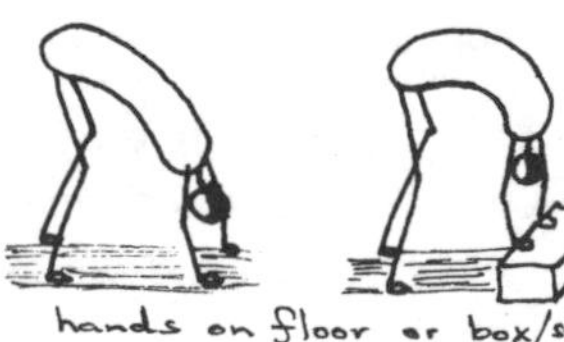

- *Then, while you breathe out easily, press into the floor with your heels so that your bottom moves up towards the ceiling and your legs softly straighten, while your upper back and head drop down a little and your fingertips remain in contact with the floor. (See diagram 15b.)*

- *Although it is fine to feel some stretch in the back of your legs, make sure that you don't force or strain.*
- *At the end of the out-breath let yourself drop back into the start position with your legs bent and let the breath come in of its own accord. Don't suck it in.*
- *Repeat this exercise three or four times, then, slowly roll up to standing. Notice how your legs feel.*

Pressing – 2

To release the back and calves

This exercise is excellent for stretching the entire back from shoulder to heel. It is particularly useful whenever you feel yourself pulling back from a situation or when you feel stuck and unable to make any progress. In these cases you may find it useful to repeat this exercise regularly through the day. Then, after a few days, you may notice a shift.

- *Stand facing the wall, with your palms flat against the wall and your arms straight, with the elbows soft. Have your feet hipbone width apart and parallel.*
- *Step straight back with your left leg until it is just beyond the point where you can place your left heel flat on the floor. (See diagram 16a.)*

- *Drop your upper body from the hips and ease the weight backwards so that the left heel touches the floor. This will give a gentle stretch in the left calf. Make sure there is no strain. (See diagram 16b.)*

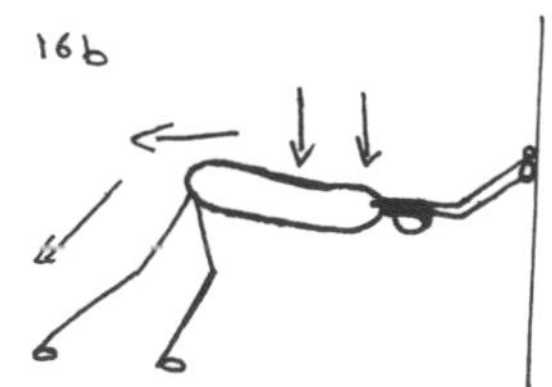

- *Rest in this position for three to four breaths and then repeat with the other leg.*
- *Again, once you have finished the exercise notice how your legs and, indeed, the rest of the body feel.*

Squatting I find squatting very useful for grounding when working on text. It really helps the weight to drop. I often ask actors to speak text in this position and then once they feel well grounded to slowly come up to standing while continuing to speak the text. If this feels hard on your knees you can have a chair either side which you can hold onto with one hand to support you.

Squatting – 1

To release muscles in the lower back and legs and help you feel your weight more

- *Try squatting, keep your legs as relaxed as possible, with your hips soft and open. It's unlikely that the whole of your feet will be on the floor, unless you squat all the time, so just rest on the toes and balls of your feet letting them soften and spread. Also, let your belly be soft.*
- *Keep your back as straight as possible so any bending occurs at the hips not the waist. (See diagram 17.)*

- *Really rest in this position; keep softening the legs and buttocks and belly and imagine the breath and energy dropping down into the belly. Never force the breath or energy down.*
- *Then, gently come up to standing. Again, notice how you feel. You may be more aware of your legs and of the weight in the lower half of your body.*

Squatting 2

To help you rest into your body and feel your weight

This is an excellent exercise to do with text. You need a sturdy door on a sturdy frame with sturdy door handles!

- *Hold on to the door handles, then bend your knees so that you are in a semi-squat position. Keep your spine long so you are bending at the hips not the waist and imagine your hips and bottom are being pulled away from the door. Also, imagine the hips and bottom sitting down slightly while the spine lengthens forwards and up. (See diagram 18.)*

- *Keep your feet well planted and spread and then move side to side and back, continuing to drop the weight into your feet as you do. Check that you are releasing your breath rather than holding it.*
- *As before, notice how your legs and body feel when you stop.*

Bouncing Gentle bouncing helps you to feel your weight more and can be very useful for keeping the ankles, knees and hips loose if you have a habit of holding and fixing. Again it can be a very useful way to work with text.

Bouncing

To loosen the ankles, knees and hips and discourage tension in those joints

- *Stand with your feet hipbone width apart and parallel. Check that your ankle, knee and hips joints are loose. Imagine your spine is lengthening and your hips and shoulders widening.*
- *Then, gently bounce by bending and straightening the legs a little. Don't stick the bottom out behind or the pelvis out in front. Keep the legs soft throughout and the spine lengthening so you're not slumping the body. (See diagram 19.)*

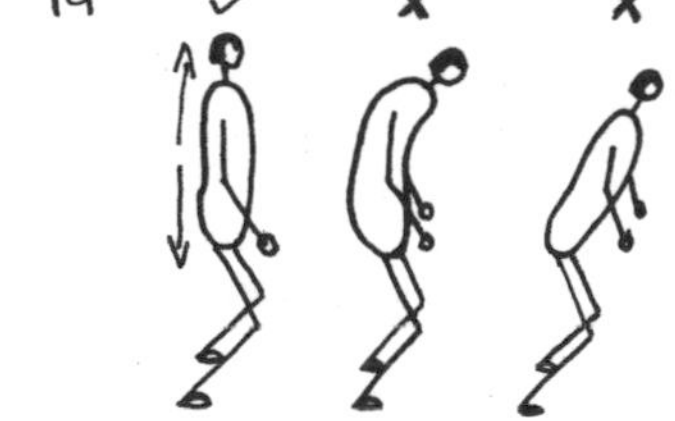

- *While you're bouncing keep your belly and buttocks loose and imagine that you're oiling the ankle, knee and hip joints. Again, when you stop, pay attention to how your body feels.*

Jumping Like bouncing, jumping gives you a good sense of weight. However, it should be avoided if you have any problems with your knees. Also, don't practise this exercise on a concrete floor, or one that is similarly hard. Wooden floors are best for jumping.

Jumping

To help you be more at rest in your body and feel a sense of weight

- *Stand with your feet one-and-a-half to two hipbone widths apart. Bend your knees as much as is comfortable and make sure your knees are over your toes. This is vital to insure against knee injury. Keep your torso upright so you don't stick your bottom out. (See diagram 20a.)*

❍ *Without straightening your legs do small, gentle, easy jumps, really softening into the floor as you land. (See diagram 20b.) Keep the belly, especially the lower part, soft and also the buttocks. Let the spine continue to lengthen.*

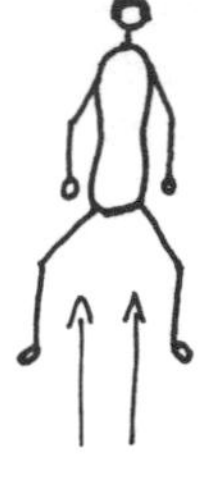
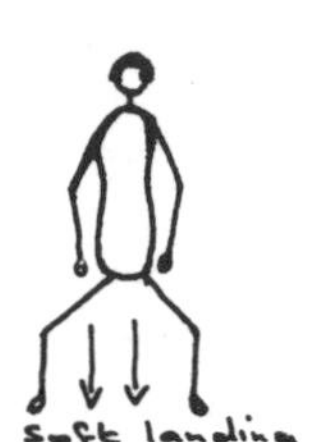

❍ *Repeat four or five times. Then, again, notice how your body feels.*

This is also a good exercise to do with text.

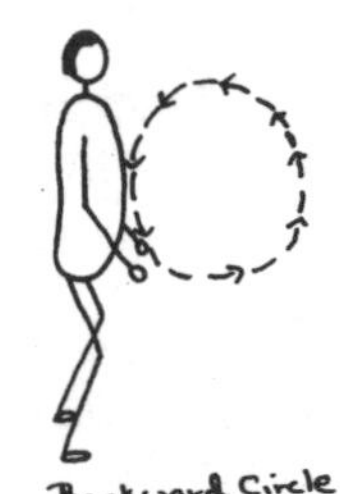

Grounding and Centring – the Backward Circle

The Backward Circle is a movement in Tai Chi. (See diagram 21a.) I also learnt to work with it when training as a Shiatsu practitioner. It is a wonderful centring and grounding movement that really helps to connect the voice and prevent pushing and straining.

Comparing forward and backward circles

To feel how these circles affect the body, breath and mind in different ways

❍ *Stand, as before, with your feet parallel and hipbone width apart, your ankle, knee and hip joints loose and your spine lengthening and hips and shoulders widening.*

❍ *Check that you are releasing the breath rather than holding it as you do the forward and backward circles. Also, check that the knees stay loose.*

❍ *Imagine that you have a large beach ball in front of you. To make a forward circle: start by bringing your hands up the front of your body to shoulder level, then reach your arms out in front of you, as if over the top of the beach ball and, then, take your arms down round the front of the ball to hip level and then, in towards your body. (See diagram 21b.) Repeat this forward circle about ten times, then, stop and see how it feels.*

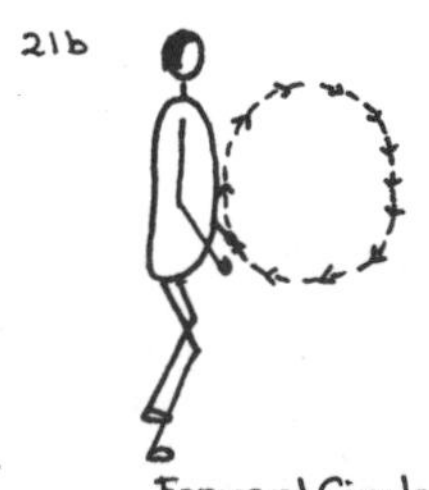

❍ *Where do you feel the energy? How does your head feel? Usually the forward circle brings the energy up into the chest or head or even way out in front of you. It can make the head feel busy and full.*

- *Now try a backward circle. Start by taking your hands away from your body at hip level, as if reaching out underneath the beach ball, then bring your arms up round the front of the ball to shoulder level and, then, bring your hands in towards your body and take them down to your hips. (See diagram 21a.) Repeat this backward circle about ten times and then stop and see how that feels.*

> **Note**
>
> The forward and backward circles remind me of different kinds of present giving. When we are unhappy about the present we have given someone we usually lean forward and thrust it at them. However, when we are happy with the present we usually lean back very slightly and offer the present in a very open way.
>
> When we present ourselves and our work on the backward circle there is an ease and openness that makes both our work and ourselves engaging. The listener or audience is reassured by our ease and has space to receive us in the way they wish. So practise the Backward Circle regularly.

- *Where do you feel the energy now? How does your head feel now? Usually the backward circle helps the energy to drop. You may feel more centred and more rooted. Yet, at the same time you may feel taller and lighter. Your head may feel clearer and stiller.*

Backward circle arms

To help you centre and ground your energy

This is an excellent exercise to practise on a daily basis, at first silently and later with sound and text. It can revolutionise your voice work and yet it is so simple. It is also a great exercise to do before and during rehearsals and performance to keep your energy and voice centred. Whenever you do the exercise always give it your full attention and work with respect, because then it can have a very strong and positive effect.

- *Stand, as before, with your feet parallel and hipbone width apart, your ankle, knee and hip joints loose and your spine lengthening and hips and shoulders widening.*
- *Make a gentle backward circle with your arms, breathing in as your arms go out away from you and up and in towards you and, then, breathing out as your arms drop back down to hip level. Then, rest in this position and wait for the next in-breath to come.*
- *Stand for a moment and let the energy settle.*

> **Note**
>
> If you find yourself getting over-excited when you talk and you end up rushing and saying all kinds of things that you didn't mean to, then you can make small backward circle gestures with your hands as you talk. I find this enormously helpful for keeping me grounded when I'm excited and it can be a particularly helpful device in auditions to stop you spouting rubbish!

Putting the 'Centring and Grounding' section together

When you initially go through this section, as with the previous one, it may take some time. However, once you have worked through the exercises, you can do the centring exercise out and about as you go through the day, so you only need a couple of minutes each day to do whichever grounding exercises you find most useful.

The rest of the grounding exercises can be used when and where you need them and can form part of your personal rehearsal work.

So, added to the releasing and redirecting work this gives you a 30-minute session.

Toning and Alignment

The centring and grounding work provides stable foundations on which the rest of the body work can be built. Mostly we're going to look at alignment work here but I'd like to talk a little about tone first.

Tone

In order to stand or move with ease you need tone – both physical and mental.

Tone is a readiness, an aliveness. There is no extraneous effort in tone, nor any sluggishness.

Physical tone may be easier to understand than mental tone. Toned muscles are those which have an elasticity, they are alive and active. They are neither tight nor floppy. Such muscles are strong but flexible. They give us energy with which to complete tasks.

Mental tone is an elasticity of the mind: an alertness, an ability to pay attention, to focus, to be awake and present. In a way mental tone is bounce or spring in the 'muscles' of the mind.

Physical and Mental tone are inextricably linked. Sometimes if we are feeling sluggish and we go for a brisk walk or play a physical game or do some exercise we feel not only physically more alive but also mentally more alert. Here physical tone brings mental tone.

From the opposite end if we are engaged in a physical activity and begin to flag we can find physical energy by focusing our mind on the task in hand, by strengthening our resolve.

The link is vital and powerful. If we continually tell ourselves 'I'm exhausted', 'That's too much for me', 'I'm not up to that' then we will deplete our physical energy. Equally, if we have a slumped, under-energised posture this will lead to a feeling of mental fatigue.

Does this matter? Yes, because it is when we feel under-energised that we start to push, to try too hard. We sense that we don't have the energy we would like to have to do the work, so we overcompensate.

I saw this happen time and time again at the RSC. An actor would feel tired when they came in for the evening's performance. Obviously, this would concern them because they did not wish to give a tired un-energised performance, so they tended to overwork and sometimes this resulted in vocal strain.

Apart from vocal strain, over-effort can lead to a great deal of overacting and shouting. It can lead to a performance that is so busy that there is no room for the audience to enter the experience. Over-effort also bars us from our instincts, because we are too busy *doing* to be aware of them and let them guide us.

When we start to make an effort we lose all our ease and flexibility, we are pressed up hard against the task and we cannot easily change direction. Whereas when we are toned, we have an easy energy, an alertness, a readiness, which gives us space to jump in any direction. As Hamlet says 'the readiness is all'.

So Physical and Mental tone are a must. In fact, they are our birthright. We start out with an abundance of Mental and Physical tone. That's why children are so indefatigable!

Physical tone Brisk walking, running, skipping, swimming, rowing, dancing, trampolining, playing sports: all of these activities can be good for muscle tone, if they are engaged in fully, but with ease. Force and over exertion lead nowhere.

If you want to spend the least amount of time and make sure you tone all the muscles, you may prefer to do specific toning exercises. A good fitness instructor would be able to help you with these. You need to make sure you work all the sets of muscles equally so you achieve and maintain the delicate balance of the body. Remember that you want to keep flexible and the exercises should not involve force. You should be able to breathe in and out fairly normally throughout and never feel you are straining or holding your breath.[10]

Yoga and martial arts can also improve muscle tone and might appeal to you more. The trick is to find what suits you.

Mental Tone Before we look at developing alertness and readiness, try an experiment to see what your mental tone is like – sluggish, tight or easily alert?

Examining your mental tone

To discover the state of your mental tone!

- *Recall a time when you felt uninspired, perhaps when you felt bored or depressed, or completely unmotivated. Let yourself really tune into the feeling physically and mentally. Then ask yourself: 'what does this energy feel like? Is it a familiar energy you often feel or one you rarely feel?'*
- *Next, recall a time when you felt wired up, tense and stressed. Again, let yourself really tune into the feeling physically and mentally. Again ask yourself: 'what does this energy feel like? Is it a familiar energy you often feel or one you rarely feel?'*
- *Then, recall a time when you felt very interested in a person or project; a time when you also felt confident about your abilities and the likely success of the relationship or project. As before, let yourself really tune into the feeling physically and mentally. As before, ask yourself: 'what does this energy feel like? Is it familiar or unfamiliar?'*
- *Then, ask yourself which of the three energies feels most familiar? Do you habitually find yourself somewhat disinterested or conversely somewhat tense or do you find yourself alert and easy?*

You may feel these are stupid questions and that, obviously, you feel disinterested when a situation is uninteresting, stressed when a situation is stressful and interested when a situation is interesting.

However, often we get into a habit of approaching situations in a certain way irrespective of the situation and what is more we don't even know we are doing it! So explore again and ask yourself what is my tendency? Do I approach situations with an easy alertness and interest or do I approach situations either with disinterest or tension?

10 Heavy weightlifting is a bad idea for anyone, but especially for actors and singers. Apart from the loss of flexibility, there can be harm to the vocal folds, since they press hard against each other when we strain. To avoid this make sure that you can always breathe in and out easily and that the breath is never held. If you can't do this the weight is too heavy for you at this time.

The important point here is that these various mental approaches have a huge effect on your vocal work. As I have pointed out earlier mental sluggishness leads to physical sluggishness and mental tension leads to physical tension. Equally mental alertness and interest lead to physical alertness and engagement and provide a huge reservoir of easy energy.

So just practise being interested!

Exercising the interest muscle

To develop a mental approach that will give you mental and physical energy

- *If you have a tendency towards mental sluggishness, notice how you approach each task or situation in the day and where you find you approach it with boredom, fatigue, disinterest or dread, gently drop that approach and instead imagine being interested. It is as if you have an 'interest muscle' you can exercise and strengthen.*
- *If your tendency is towards mental tension, before you can work on strengthening your interest you need to practise centring so that you can allow your mind to rest. So, as you approach each situation, let your breath out gently so you are not holding it and gently rest for a moment to release at least some of the tension. Then work on strengthening the interest as above.*

Alignment

Now that you have the tools – physical and mental tone – to help align the body and return it to its natural balance, we can start to work.

Sacrum whoosh

To explore how the base of the spine moves and supports the rest of the spine, releasing energy and power

The sacrum is the bony base of the spine. It actually consists of five vertebrae, which are fused together. Place your finger on your tailbone and then run it upward along your spine for about three inches. The area that you have run your finger over is the sacrum.

This exercise helps you to understand how the movement of your upper body is powered from the sacrum and pelvis. It is vital to loosen and awaken this lower area since it acts as the support on which the rest of the spine can build.

Stage one

You need a partner for this exercise. Also you might want to record the bullet points so you can do the whole exercise without stopping.

- *Stand, as before, with feet hipbone width and parallel, your ankle, knee and hip joints soft, your spine lengthening and your hips and shoulders widening.*
- *Imagine the soles of the feet softening and spreading.*
- *Check the weight is equally distributed between both feet and between the balls and heels of each foot. If you're not sure shift the weight from side to side and backward and forward so you get a sense of equal weight.*
- *Check again that the ankle, knee and hip joints are loose and, then, drop over from the hips as far as you comfortably can. Re-check that the ankle, knee and hip joints are still loose and that the feet are still parallel, hipbone width apart and soft and spread.*

- *Check that the body, arms, head and neck are all soft and hanging.*
- *Your partner then places one hand on your sacrum and the other arm across your belly. (See diagram 22a.)*

- *Leaving the arm across the belly inactive, your partner firmly, though not forcefully, pushes your sacrum down and forward in a backward circle, while you focus on allowing your ankles, knees and hips to yield and your thighs to move forward. (See diagram 22b.) As a result you will, hopefully, find yourself standing upright.*

- *If your partner cannot move you it will be due to tension in the ankle, knee or hip joints, so really loosen these joints.*
- *Repeat this exercise three times so you have a chance to feel what is going on.*
- *Do you notice that if you stay relaxed you automatically come upright when your partner pushes your sacrum? (See diagram 22c.) Do you notice how bringing your sacrum into place moves the rest of your spine into place? Do you also notice how you feel? Usually this exercise brings energy and leaves you feeling more awake, more alert.*
- *If you can't be moved it will be due to tension in the ankle, knee or hip joints. Move on to the next stage, as this will explore tension in these joints and how it affects the body's freedom and flexibility.*

Stage two

- *Hang over, as before, but this time mentally hold in the ankle, knee and hip joints so they don't give way when your partner pushes your sacrum down and forward in the backward circle.*
- *If you truly hold, your partner will be unable to move you. Yet it does not take much physical effort on your part. That is why we often are unaware of tension and how it is locking us up.*

Why does this matter? Well, when you fix any joints in the body, however lightly, you stop free physical flow. You can no longer simply respond to an impulse, to move you have to unlock the joints first and by that time the impulse may have passed. Nor does it end there. This physical unresponsiveness leads to mental unresponsiveness. If you want to be able to fly with your instincts you need to release your joints!

Obviously, as with all the work in this book you can't think about loose joints on stage or even in rehearsal. That is why building a habit of all the joints being loose as you go about your daily life is so important. Then, if you do take on some tension in the joints for your character you won't find yourself getting completely locked up.

Stage three

- *So, now try the sacrum whoosh again, this time allowing your ankle, knee and hip joints to be as soft and loose as possible.*
- *Try this a few times really exploring what is going on in the joints. Do you have a tendency to hold in all the joints or just in the ankles, knees or hips? Imagine the joints expanding and becoming more fluid and then try again.*
- *Can you feel that the whole movement has more freedom and flow now?*
- *Once you have finished come up to standing and see how you feel. Are you more awake, more alert? I find that engaging the sacrum really wakes me up.*

You can do the 'sacrum whoosh' for yourself, once you have worked on it with a partner, although it is never quite so much fun! Start hanging over, as described above. Place the backs of your hands on your sacrum and gently give yourself a push.

I find it very useful to do this exercise three times whenever I feel a little dull or weary.

Spine roll

To raise your awareness of your spine and begin to feel it building up vertebra by vertebra from the base

When the sacrum properly engages, as we have been practising above, it provides support for the rest of the spine. Now that we have explored that support, we are going to look at aligning the rest of the spine, building up vertebra by vertebra.

By working with a partner initially this exercise allows you to connect with each vertebra in your spine, so that it is easier to come up vertebra by vertebra starting from the tailbone and working up to the top of the neck without missing out any section of your spine.

Again you might find it useful to record the bullet points.

- *Stand, as before, with feet hipbone width and parallel, your ankle, knee and hip joints soft, your spine lengthening and your hips and shoulders widening. Imagine the soles of the feet softening and spreading.*
- *Again, check the weight is equally distributed between both feet and between the balls and heels of each foot. Again, shift the weight from side to side and backward and forward so you get a sense of equal weight.*
- *Drop over from the hips as far as you comfortably can. Re-check that the ankle, knee and hip joints are still loose and that the feet are soft and spread.*
- *Check that the body, arms, head and neck are all soft and hanging.*
- *Start by moving the sacrum down and forward in a backward circle, as you did in the previous exercise, keeping the ankle, knee and hip joints soft.*
- *Then, begin to slowly roll up the spine vertebra by vertebra until you are standing. As you do this get your partner to work up your spine touching each vertebra firmly as you build it on top of the one below. (See diagram 23.)*

- *Get your partner to check that parts of your spine do not get missed out and that your chin stays on your chest until the whole of your body is upright.*

- *Repeat several times so you get a chance to really connect with the spine.*
- *Once you have explored the spine roll with a partner and have a good connection with your spine and know that you are coming up vertebra by vertebra then you can practise on your own, visualising the vertebrae building one on top of the other.*
- *It's good to do this exercise three of four times in a row and really pay attention to your spine. Try doing this exercise regularly, after you've done the centring and grounding.*

Lining up

To practise finding and sustaining alignment

This is a very good exercise to practise in queues, when on the tube, train or bus, anywhere you have to stand and wait. In fact it's much better to practise in real-life situations because you want the posture to become habitual, you don't want to have to think about it.

You might want to practise initially at home with the bullet points below recorded so you get the order clear in your mind. Then, you can practise wherever and whenever you are waiting.

We are going to line up the whole body so each part is resting directly above the part beneath.

- *Stand with your feet hipbone width and parallel. Check the weight is equally distributed between both feet and between the balls and the heels of the feet. Check that the ankle, knee and hip joints are loose.*
- *Close your eyes, if possible.*
- *Imagine the ankle, knee and hip joints softening and the weight of the body pouring through the legs into the feet, which are softening and spreading into the floor.*
- *Imagine the hips resting on the legs directly above the front of the ankles.*
- *Imagine the hips opening and widening.*
- *Imagine the buttocks gently dropping.*
- *Imagine the base of the spine dropping towards the floor and the rest of the spine lengthening upwards.*
- *Focus especially on the spine between the shoulder blades and imagine that lengthening upward even more while the buttocks and base of the spine continue to drop, so that there is a sense of lengthening in the small of the back.*

- *Imagine the ribs floating directly above the hips.*
- *Imagine the shoulders floating directly above the ribs.*
- *Imagine the shoulders opening and widening and the shoulder blades dropping gently down your back, as your neck lengthens up out of your body.*
- *Let the arms hang free.*
- *Imagine the head floating on top of the neck, directly above the shoulders and slightly lifted from the crown.*
- *Rest easily for two or three minutes in this position, checking that the breath is free rather than held. Keep the position easy and relaxed. It still needs to feel like you!*

The wide arm – anti-slump and anti-head poke – exercise

To open up the chest, lengthen the upper spine and bring the head into line with the body

This exercise really opens the upper chest area. It is also the best exercise I know to stop the upper back slumping, the shoulders rounding and the head poking forward. It also helps the ribs to move freely and is great for building energy and stamina and for developing the breath.

Again you may want to record the bullet points.

- *Stand as before, with feet parallel, soft and spread, ankles, knees and hips soft, hips over the front of the ankles, buttocks and sacrum dropping gently, spine lengthening, ribs over the hips, shoulders over the ribs, with shoulder blades gently dropping, and head over the ribs and shoulders.*
- *While imagining your shoulder blades dropping down a little further let your arms float out to the sides until they are at shoulder level. Keep the shoulders relaxed and lowered and the palms facing forwards. (See diagram 24.) Think of the arms spreading sideways rather than of lifting them. They will get less tired that way. Also, keep letting the shoulder blades drop gently down your back.*

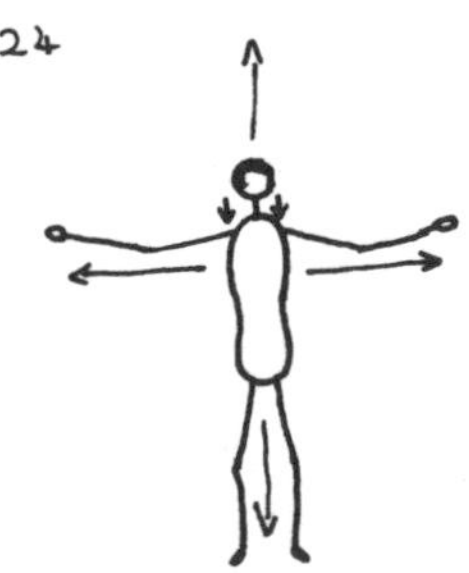

- *Check that the arms are directly in line with the shoulders so the back and front of the body are equally open.*
- *Check that the ankles, knees and hips are loose and that you are not arching your back. Think of the base of the spine dropping towards the floor and the top of the spine lifting towards the ceiling.*

- *Now keep thinking of the spine lengthening, the hips and shoulders widening, the buttocks and shoulder blades dropping and the arms spreading. Keep the rest of the body soft.*
- *The arms get tired very quickly, but try, without torturing yourself, to keep them there as long as you comfortably can. The more you mentally direct the spine to lengthen and the shoulders to widen and the arms to spread the easier it will be.*
- *Then, still thinking of your shoulders widening and your arms spreading wide, lower the arms and feel the openness across the chest.*
- *Repeat this exercise three times.*

Putting the 'Toning and Alignment' section together

As with previous sections this one may take a while to work through initially but in the end it should be possible to work through it in 5 minutes, or less, not counting the physical toning exercises you might do. So added to the previous two sections it will give you a 35-minute session.

As soon as you have done the centring and grounding work go straight into three sacrum whooshes, followed by three spine rolls and then three wide arms and finish with a minute of lining up.

Cardiovascular Exercise

Why do actors need to be fit? Fitness brings energy. Without this energy as I've mentioned previously, we may push, which tires the body and the voice and robs acting of all its subtlety or we may just be under-energised and the work becomes dull.

I should make it clear that by energy I am not referring to the hyped-up manic activity that is sometimes seen. That is effort dressed up as energy and it's very tiring to watch as well as to do. I am talking about an easy aliveness, which allows great variety, subtlety, wit and invention.

Cardiovascular exercise keeps you fit and helps whether you have too much energy or too little. If you have too much it uses some of it up. If you have too little it stimulates the body's systems and finds you some!

Obviously, it's important to exercise at a rate and to a degree that's safe for you. If you are in any doubt ask a doctor. Brisk walking is excellent, as is swimming. With running you need to check you have good shoes and watch the knees, running on a hard surface can be punishing. I run on a bouncer,[11] which is like a mini trampoline, and is much less hard on the knees.

Rowing is good all-round exercise and it's the only machine I ever really enjoyed at the gym. Dancing is great as well. The important thing is to find something you actually enjoy. I find it very hard to exercise for exercise sake, so, I have started to leave home earlier and walk for half an hour or so and then catch the bus or train.

As with all the exercises mentioned in this chapter you need to choose what suits you. The important point with cardiovascular exercise is to do it for long enough to increase your heart rate and keep it at a safe increased level for 20 to 40 minutes.[12] If you are not sure what is safe for you check with your doctor or a sports specialist. When exercising your breath should not be forced and you should not feel faint or dizzy or sick. If you do feel any of these you should stop immediately.

Note
If you haven't exercised for a while start with something gentle like walking or swimming.

It is not productive to be over-ambitious. Work out what is the least you can do to gain the results you want. That way you're more likely to stick at it.

Note
It is a good idea to work physically, regularly, for a couple of weeks before you move on to the next chapters. This will give you an excellent foundation on which to build the rest of the work.

11 This is a small trampoline, also known as a 'Rebounder'. Doing any work on it is excellent for balance and, therefore, for voice work because as we find more balance we are able to let go of more tension.

12 Some exercise experts say that this can be broken down into 10-minute sessions, which can be done at various points in the day.

Putting the Whole Chapter together

You can do all the exercises at once if you prefer or split them up. I've suggested an order below. The dotted lines shows where you could divide the exercises. I've also included some guidance as to timing.

The whole set could be done in one session, or in two or three separate sessions. This is practicable and I find that the energy it gives means I get more done in the day. So in the end it can save time.

However, if what is set out below just looks too daunting then simply work on what you can. There is no point in forcing or overburdening yourself. This chapter is designed as a springboard to get you started and to give you an understanding of what work is necessary and why. Hopefully, it will have given you a framework within which you can decide what work you specifically need. If you understand the thinking behind the work you can find your own route, so, as always trust your instincts.

❍	*Warm-up stretches*	*2 minutes*
❍	*Warm-up into cardiovascular exercise*	*4 minutes*
❍	*Cardiovascular exercise*	*20/40 minutes*
	Total time	*26-46 minutes*

....

❍	*(Add 2 minutes of warm-up stretches if doing this session separately)*	
❍	*Physical Toning exercise*	*20 minutes*
❍	*Warm-down stretches*	*3 minutes*
	Total time	*23-25 minutes*

....

❍	*Release and Redirection*	*28 minutes*
❍	*Grounding Exercises*	*2 minutes*
❍	*Alignment Exercises*	*5 minutes*
	Total time	*35 minutes*

3

Breath and Support

As the body becomes more at ease, with all the joints loosening, the spine lengthening and the hips and shoulders opening and widening, it is much easier to breathe and for the support muscles to work effectively.

Free breath and strong support can bring power, energy and ease. I find them exhilarating to work on, especially support.

Before we start the exercises, I want to review how breath and support work, so that you have a clear sense of what is going on and, consequently, of what you are exercising and why.

BREATHING IN

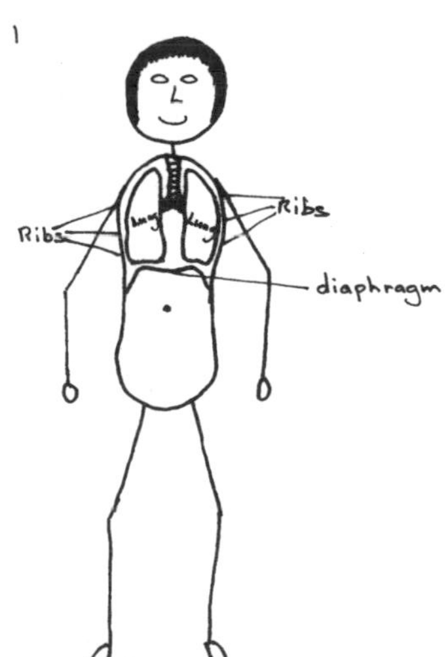

The diaphragm and ribs are responsible for breathing in. They form the floor and walls of the chest cavity. (See diagram 1.) The diaphragm moves down and the ribs move out as you breathe in. (See diagram 2.)

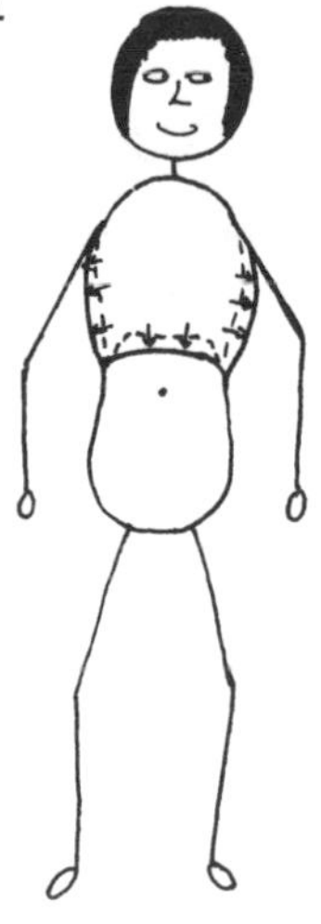

The *inner* lining of the diaphragm and ribs and the *outer* lining of the lungs are held together by a layer of moisture, which allows them to slide against each other but not to be pulled apart.

Consequently, when the diaphragm moves down and the ribs move out, the lungs are stretched downwards and outwards, in other words, they are expanded and opened.

The pressure in the lungs is, then, less than the pressure outside the lungs and air rushes in to equalise.

Think of a plastic washing-up liquid bottle that is almost empty. You squeeze it to get the last drop of liquid out. Then, when you stop squeezing and the bottle expands the liquid is drawn back in. In the same way, when the lungs expand the air is drawn in.

So breath doesn't have to be sucked in!

True, the rib and diaphragm muscles are working, but they are designed to do this, so extra effort around the face, neck and shoulder area is *not* helpful.

What *is* necessary is to strengthen the diaphragm muscle and the muscles that move the ribs and we will look at exercises to do this later.

How the diaphragm works on the in-breath

The diaphragm is a large muscle, which, as I mentioned earlier, forms the floor of the chest cavity. It is attached to the lower edges of the rib cage.

When the brain sends the message that we need to breathe in, the diaphragm contracts and flattens somewhat. (See diagram 2, previous page.)

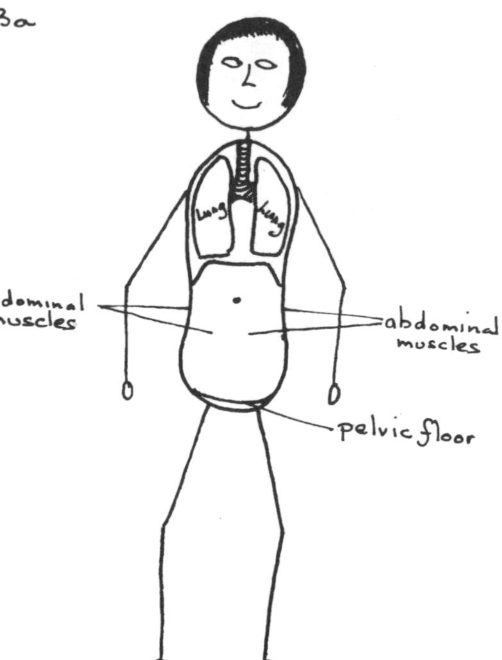

The diaphragm is the most important muscle of respiration. It is responsible for 60 to 80 per cent of the in-breath, so it is vital that this muscle is able to move appropriately.

Helping and hindering the diaphragm

In order that the diaphragm can flatten and breath can be taken deep into the base of the lungs, it is important that the abdominal and pelvic floor muscles relax on the in-breath. The abdominal and pelvic floor muscles form the walls and floor of the abdominal cavity, which sits underneath the chest cavity. (See diagram 3a, 3b, 3c.) If the abdominal and pelvic floor muscles do not relax on the in-breath the organs inside the abdominal cavity cannot get out of the way of the descending diaphragm and so a full and deep breath cannot be taken.

- *Try squeezing your belly as tightly as possible and then breathing in. You'll notice that it is fairly impossible to breathe low. All the breath is pushed up into the chest.*
- *Release your belly and, now, try squeezing your pelvic floor muscles as tightly as possible. To do this, imagine squeezing those muscles between your legs from your pubic bone back to your anus.*
- *Try to breathe in again. You will be able to get a fuller breath than when the whole belly was tight, but you may feel a stiffness in your lower belly and, also, in your neck and throat.*

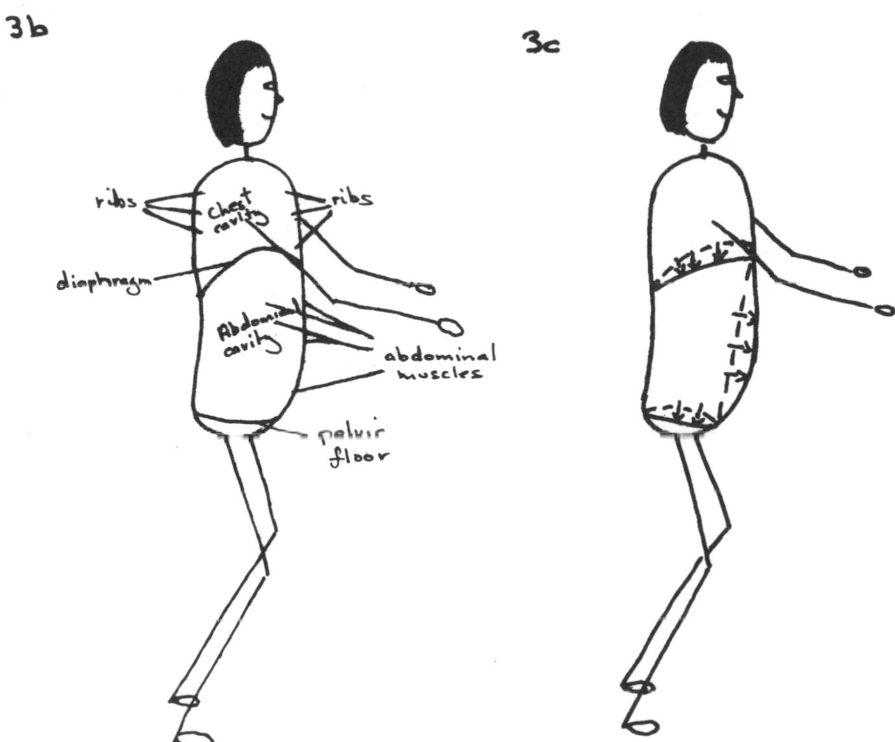

It is important to learn how to release the abdominal and pelvic floor muscles so that the diaphragm is free to move fully and the breath can be easy and deep.

How the ribs work on the in-breath

When breath is efficient the lower ribs move outward and upward, rather like the handles on a bucket. (See diagram 4.)

> **Note**
>
> *Top chest or clavicular breathing:* when the breath is less efficient the upper ribs tend to move more, causing the chest to lift. This kind of breathing is called 'top chest breathing'. If your chest lifts and your belly pulls in as you breathe in then it is likely that you are top chest breathing. This kind of breath can also cause backache.

The short muscles in the back,[13] between the spine and the back ribs, are believed to play an important part in moving the ribs. Certainly I find the more focus there is on the back of the ribs the easier it is to achieve efficient and effective rib movement.

Helping and hindering the ribs

In order that the ribs can move easily and fully the out-breath needs to be fully released and the posture needs to be long and wide.

If there is tension in the body, and the out-breath is therefore not releasing fully, or if the posture is slumped or over-erect, the working of the rib muscles will be hindered.

- *Try tensing the muscles in your back and, then, breathe in. Can you feel how the ribs are locked by the tension in your back?*
- *Now try slumping your spine and, then, breathe in. Can you feel how little rib movement is possible and how all the breath seems to be forced down into the belly?*

13 The levatores costarum muscles.

❍ *Now arch your back and puff your chest out and breathe in. Can you feel that the back ribs can't move at all and that the breath has come up high into the chest?*

It is very good to practise the behaviour you don't want. It allows you to be more aware and understanding of how your body works.

BREATHING OUT

On the out-breath the diaphragm relaxes upwards and the ribs relax downwards and inwards, thus compressing the lungs and causing the air to flow out. (See diagram 5.)

This happens quite naturally, so, there is no need to push the breath out.

So are there any muscles which can usefully work on the out-breath?

Yes, in fully connected and committed speech the abdominal and pelvic floor muscles are gently but firmly working. The pelvic floor muscles make an upwards movement, while the abdominal muscles make an inwards and upwards movement and in this way they act upon the diaphragm assisting its movement upward as it relaxes. (See diagram 6.)

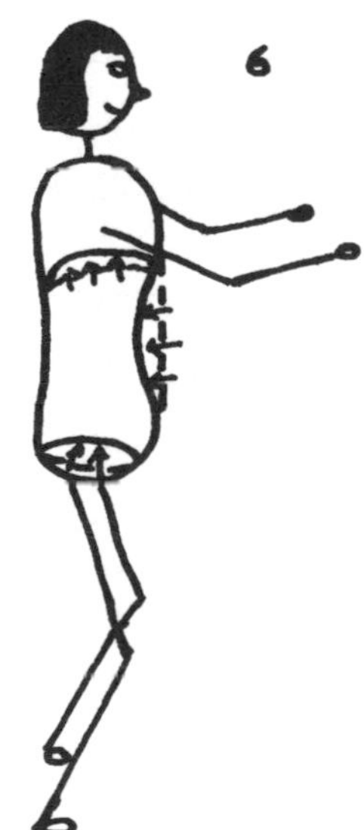

It is helpful to think of the body as a tube of toothpaste and of the breath as the toothpaste. Engaging the abdominal and pelvic floor muscles on the out-breath is like gently squeezing the base of the tube in order to get the toothpaste, or in this case the breath, to come out of the top of the tube.

The abdominal and pelvic floor muscles do not need to be pumped or pushed forcefully. It is simply a matter of mentally engaging with them to encourage them to do the work they are designed to do.

I'll describe in detail how to engage the abdominal and pelvic floor muscles appropriately later in the chapter (see pages 74-76). It is not at all difficult once you get started and it's a great deal of fun and gives you a real feeling of power and connection.

The important point to remember here is that, while the abdominal and pelvic muscles need to be *involved* in the out-breath for fully connected speech and song, they do not need to be over-worked, which they sometimes are.

Having enough breath

Keeping the spine long and the hips and shoulders wide, whatever position your body is in, will stop the body collapsing and so help the breath to release more slowly.

Note

When you are on stage, or indeed in rehearsals, you shouldn't be thinking about keeping your spine long and hips and shoulders wide. That would be catastrophic nonsense. The exercises later in this chapter will show you how to work to incorporate this length and width so it becomes natural and automatic.

So, there is no need to hold the breath back by fixing the ribs or narrowing the throat.

In addition to lengthening and widening, there are points on the abdominal muscles that can be focused on to help sustain the breath. I find working with these points excellent for giving me a sense of control over the out-breath and for enabling me to release any holding in the throat.

I will explain how to work on these points later in the chapter in the section on sustaining the breath (see pages 93-96). For now, simply remember to let the out-breath go, easily and freely without any holding back, and don't worry how long or short the breath is.

Note

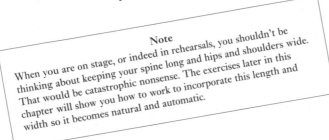

Rib Reserve is the practice of holding the ribs open and just moving the diaphragm and belly as you breathe in and out. It is considered to allow a quicker and more flexible in-breath and to give sustaining power and richness of tone. Some actors have found that it works well for them.

The problem with rib reserve is that it can create tension and holding. Anyone who has tension problems generally, and a tendency to hold back the breath, should certainly avoid it, at least until they have remedied these tendencies.

Good posture, with a long spine and open hips and shoulders naturally engages the muscles between the ribs. This, together with active, engaged abdominal, pelvic floor and 'go slow' muscles, encourages the ribs to stay more open and so produce a more organic and flexible Rib Reserve, and, of course, we will explore all of these skills during this chapter.

Outwards and inwards not up and down

One of the major causes of breath releasing too fast from the body is what I call 'up and down' breathing, where the chest lifts on the in-breath and falls on the out-breath.

This is rather like squeezing toothpaste out from the top of the tube.

Two things happen if you do this, firstly the air at the top of the lungs comes out very fast because it is very hard to control the large amount of bone in the chest. Secondly, a great deal of air gets trapped inside and there's no way of getting it out.

The natural breath is an outward and inward breath, with nearly all the movement occurring below armpit level.

There is a *sense* of soft expansion in the chest, because the lungs come right up to the second rib, just below the collarbone. However, neither the in-breath nor the out-breath ever begin in the chest. Also, the shoulders, breastbone and collar bone stay soft and still, neither lifting on the in-breath, nor dropping on the out-breath.

Support

'What on earth is 'support'?' It is the *way* the out-breath is handled to provide power for the voice. A constant stream of air at a consistent pressure is needed, with increases in pressure for higher and louder sounds.

This constant pressure is created by the abdominal and pelvic floor muscles, working *in conjunction* with the coming together of the vocal folds.

Imagine a ping-pong ball resting on top of a column of air. That air has to be at a certain pressure to keep the ball afloat. If the pressure lessens the ball will sink nearer the ground, if the pressure stops altogether there is no column of air and the ball falls to the ground. If you want the ball to go higher you have to increase the pressure.

In the above example the air pressure is created, maintained and increased *only* by the activity of the abdominal and pelvic floor muscles.

However, in the case of the voice, the vocal folds come together, so creating resistance to the upcoming air stream and in doing so they assist the creation, maintenance and increase of air pressure.

The important point to understand here is that the out-breath does not solely control breath pressure muscles. So whilst it is vital to have a sense of engaging with the abdominal and pelvic floor muscles, it is a waste of time squeezing them like mad.

Note

The whole breath and support system can seem complex and bewildering. But your body was designed to work like this. All it needs is to be reminded. All you need to do is let go of the less helpful habits you have acquired along the way and then strengthen the system you were born with. That way it will become as easy and natural as . . . well, as breathing!

SO LET'S GET STARTED

As in the body chapter, we are going to look at what you are actually doing. This will save so much grief and frustration later.

Breath review

To find out how you breathe

Explore the following questions lying down, sitting, standing and walking.

Approach this work with the curiosity of an explorer, rather than with an attitude of judgement. Be fascinated by what you do, rather than critical of it. You will find out far more this way.

- *Where does your in-breath start? In the middle of the body or the chest?*
- *Where does your out-breath start? From the belly or the chest?*
- *Does any part of your body tense when you breathe in? The chest, shoulders, neck, head or back?*
- *Does any part of your body tense when you breathe out? The throat, shoulders, neck or head?*
- *Does your spine or collarbone lift as you breathe in or drop as you breathe out?*
- *Do you hold your breath between breathing in and breathing out?*
- *Do you wait for the next in-breath to come naturally or do you suck it in immediately you have breathed out?*

You do not need to ponder over what you are doing or worry about it. Just be aware what is going on and take that awareness into the exercises. Remember awareness itself triggers change.

NOW TO WORK

We are not going to work with sound at all in this chapter, just breath. We will add the sound in the next chapter, so have patience – it will be worth it in the end!

Again, we are going to work slowly, taking one area at a time until we have explored all the areas we need.

If you are a beginner Work on each area until you feel comfortable and then move onto the next one. No area need take more than twenty minutes to work through initially and once you are comfortable with a particular area, the work there can usually be reduced to no more than five minutes.

At the end of the chapter I have put all the work together into a shorter session that you can use as a warm-up as you move into exploring the areas in the next chapter. In this way you will not be faced by an ever-expanding session.

You might find it helpful, after you have explored each exercise once, to read carefully through the instructions again and, then, draw yourself a simple picture or diagram that summarises the whole exercise. This will help to make the learning more organic and, also, it could mean that you end up with just a page or two of simple pictures or diagrams covering all the exercises in the book, which would be much simpler to take in and to carry around!

If you have more experience You might wish to quickly read through the chapter and then focus on the exercises you think will help you.

Each section's title tells you what the exercises in that section aim to achieve.

Freeing and Centring the Breath

This area is vital. It releases the body *and mind* from the habits that inhibit the breath. If you take the time to explore the work in this area you will find it speeds up all the later work on breath and support. Again, it is a question of slower is faster.

Using the breath's natural energy Much tension and effort is caused in breathing because we don't use the breath's natural energy. We start to breathe in before the body is ready. Then we start to breathe out before the body has finished breathing in. It is rather like going surfing and then not waiting for the big wave to surf on.

If you breathe out fully, but without force, and then wait, *really wait,* without holding, until the body wants to breathe in, you will find there is an energy available, which you can ride on. Equally, if you allow the body to keep breathing in until it wants to move onto the out-breath, you will find there is a natural release of the out-breath.

This is not about having a long out-breath or a large in-breath it is about allowing *your body* to breathe rather than you bullying it around. At first you may find this hard to do but, if you trust the exercises and yourself, with time you will find it easier and easier and again it will save you so much time, energy and effort in the long run.

Freeing the breath

To release holding and tension in the breath

This exercise is excellent for freeing up the breath. It stops you from holding your breath, which is why I like to start with it. It gets the whole breathing system working and releases a great deal of tension, which makes the following floor exercises much easier.

You can return to this exercise again and again and it is an excellent way to keep the voice free when working on text.

- *March easily but fairly energetically, swinging the arms freely from the shoulder joints and lifting and dropping the legs freely from the hip joints. Check that there is no tension or excess effort.*
- *Keep the torso upright and stable, imagining the spine lengthening, the hips and shoulders widening, the buttocks and shoulder blades gently dropping and the joints loosening as you march and swing. (See diagram 7.)*

- *Then, blow out on an easy relaxed 'ffff', still imagining your spine lengthening and swinging your arms and legs freely. Keep blowing firmly but without force until the breath has comfortably finished. Then, still swinging, let the new breath come in as and when it feels like it.*
- *You may find you use up your breath very fast. That is fine. Just check your spine keeps lengthening on the out-breath.*
- *Do this exercise for two or three minutes and, then, rest in the Alexander Position* (see page 24) *before moving onto the next exercise.*

Note

Floor work: the body operates differently – in terms of breath and support – when we are lying down and when we are standing. This leads some people to argue that floor work is, therefore, not particularly helpful. However, it is easier to relax when lying on the floor and to eliminate postural habits both of tension and collapse.

Once a new habit of maintaining a relaxed and stable posture while breathing has been established on the floor, it is then easier to transfer this postural habit to sitting and standing and the changes in breath and support can take place naturally because the body is more balanced and at ease.

Centring the breath

To anchor the breath in the centre of the body

This exercise allows the breath to settle and return to centre. It is a vital 'building block' exercise for everyone, but is particularly helpful for those who 'top chest breathe'.[14]

We are going to focus on the breath filling and emptying from the area just above the navel. This is the hub or centre of the breath, where the breath starts.

We are going to work with a couple of images here because they will really help you to reconnect with your natural breath and avoid any force.

- *Imagine that you have a nose with large nostrils deep inside the body, just above navel level, through which the breath flows in easily and freely.*
- *Then, imagine this nose turns into an open mouth on the out-breath and that the breath flows out easily and freely through this mouth.*

Note

Breathing in through the nose: I am always being asked 'Should I breathe in through my nose or my mouth?' When you breathe in through your nose two things happen: firstly the air is cleansed, warmed and moistened; secondly the ribs are stimulated to move. So breathing in through the nose is beneficial. However, when breathing to speak, breathing through the nose is simply not quick enough. So, when practising breathing exercises breathing in through the nose is helpful, but, when breathing for speech breathe in through the mouth.

14 See page 62 for an explanation of Top Chest Breathing.

I know these images may sound stupid but they work. They allow you to keep your attention in the centre of your body and they offer the quickest way to reconnect with the movement of the diaphragm.

We're going to practise the exercise lying down.

- *Lie in the Alexander position (see page 24) with your hands just above your navel. Centre your attention where your hands are.*
- *Then, take the time to re-imagine the nose deep inside the body just above navel level through which you breathe in. Imagine that it has large nostrils so that the air can flow in easily.*
- *Then, imagine the nostrils turning into an open mouth, deep inside the body, and the breath freely sighing out through that mouth. Keep the images light and simple, there is no need to see the nostrils or mouth in detail!*

Note

Whenever you are doing breathing work it is always a good idea to start by breathing out, even if you feel you have hardly any breath. If you start by breathing in you are likely to take an effortful breath whereas if you start by breathing out you can then wait for the impulse to breathe in and ride on that energy.

- *Gently sigh out any breath you have through the imaginary open mouth. Then, rest and wait for the impulse to breathe in. There is no way you can miss it, so simply trust and wait.*
- *When you feel the impulse to breathe in there is no need to consciously 'do' the breathing. Simply imagine the breath streaming in through the nostrils, deep inside the body, just above navel level and let the breath move the body.*
- *Then, once the breath has flowed in, imagine it flowing out on an easy sigh, through the open mouth deep in the body just above navel level.*
- *Practise this exercise for a minute, really waiting for the impulse to breathe in and, then, receiving that in-breath through the 'central nostrils' and, then, allowing that breath to sigh out through the 'central mouth'.*

Releasing the breath – I

To reconnect with the natural rhythm and release of the breath

There is a moment when the in-breath reaches its peak and tips smoothly over into the out-breath, rather like a wave builds and then breaks. However, often we start to breathe out before our body has finished breathing in and so we lose the natural release.

So, we are going to practise letting the in-breath find its natural rhythm, so that the out-breath can be fully and naturally released.

Note

Many actors worry about allowing their breath to find its natural rhythm: 'I haven't got time to wait around for the breath on stage. I need to get on with it!' I know you do, but cutting off your in-breath and, as a result, not being able to freely release your out-breath is not the way to go about it. If you practise these exercises and build up a habit of released breath then you won't have to worry about your breath on stage and it will respond to your needs freely and quickly.

While it is important to wait for the impulse to breathe out there is no holding or stopping between the in-breath and the out-breath. The in-breath reaches its peak and, then, flows straight into the out-breath without a pause. The transition does occur slowly, rather like a 'slow melt', but there is never a complete stop.

Holding the breath interrupts the flow not only of the breath but also of the body and the mind. Think of the times when you hold your breath – in fear, anxiety, amazement, over concentration – all these are moments of suspension, of stopping, from which we need to release before we can continue.

Many people get into a habit of holding their breath for much of the time and this not only causes a huge amount of voice problems but also acting problems. There can be little spontaneity or flow of ideas, images or instinct when the breath is held.

❍ *Repeat the last exercise, waiting for the impulse to breathe in, then, letting the breath flow in freely through the 'central nostrils'. Continue to let the breath flow in for as long as it wants, simply watching for the moment when the in-breath chooses to 'melt' into the out-breath.*

Note

Breath holding exercises: I know that there are breathing practices, in yoga and other traditions, where there is holding between the in and out-breath and that such exercises are used to balance energy. I have no quarrel with these exercises as long as you learn them properly from someone fully qualified to teach such exercises.

It is important that any breath holding which takes place is achieved through holding the ribs open and the diaphragm flattened not by constriction in the throat. Some speech and singing teachers will use breath-holding exercises to strengthen the ribs and diaphragm and encourage slow release at the start of the out-breath and they can be effective. So, if such exercises work for you, fine – just check your throat is completely free or you will be storing up trouble for later.

- *Then, let that out-breath sigh out freely though the open 'central mouth', as before.*
- *Practise the exercise, as described above for a minute or two. Never take the length of the in-breath for granted. It may change on every breath. Simply keep watching for the moment when the in-breath chooses to 'melt' into the out-breath.*

Releasing the breath – 2

To more fully release the out-breath and so free and energise the whole system

Fully releasing the out-breath galvanises the whole breathing system, making it much easier to breathe in. Also, the more fully the breath is released the more fully the voice and also the thoughts and feelings of any character you are playing can be released. Holding back the breath will hold back your performance and is likely to cause vocal fatigue and strain.

It is helpful to work with a feeling of letting go or of melting or of softening as you breathe out to help the breath release more fully and to avoid either holding back or pushing out.

- *Repeat the previous exercise again, waiting for the impulse to breath in, then, letting the breath flow in through the 'central nostrils' until it wants to melt into the out-breath and, then, sighing out through the 'central mouth' with the feeling of completely letting go; of softening, melting and emptying.*

Once you have worked through the last three exercises separately and are happy with each one, you can then simply practise the third exercise – Releasing the breath – 2, since that incorporates the earlier two.

Opening the throat

To begin to create space in the back of the mouth and the throat and so enable freer release

This exercise is based on the Alexander Technique's 'Whispered Ah' and is excellent for beginning to open up the throat and jaw area so that the breath can be more freely released.

It is very important to keep the breath as light as possible, without any rasping quality. That is how you can tell your throat is open. If you find it difficult to find a quiet breath, imagine you are breathing onto a pair of glasses in order to clean them. This usually does the trick.

The smile is also very important because it helps to lift the cheekbones and create more space in the back of the jaw. It also helps the jaw to stay open while you breathe out. Keeping the smile warm and sincere stops the face muscles from stiffening up.

- *Staying in the Alexander position, with your hands resting just above your navel, slide your lower teeth forward until they are level with your upper teeth. Imagine the back of your neck lengthening as you do this.*
- *Smile a warm sincere smile, with the lips lightly closed, and breathe in through your 'central nostrils'.*
- *Keep smiling and, then, open the mouth until there is a finger's width between the top and bottom teeth and breathe out almost silently from your 'central mouth'.*
- *Check that you flow smoothly from your in-breath into your out-breath without any holding.*
- *Repeat the exercise four or five times, smiling warmly throughout, checking the gap between your teeth when you open your mouth and breathing out almost silently.*

Putting the 'Freeing and Centring the Breath' section together

Initially it is important to take your time to work through this section. However, once you are comfortable with these exercises, you only need to do *Freeing the breath*, *Releasing the breath-2* and *Opening the throat*. Since each one need take no more than two minutes, that gives you a total session of six minutes.

Developing the Out-Breath

So far we have looked at freeing the breath, at releasing some of the tension that inhibits natural, easy and centred breathing. That work is rather like returning to neutral, stripping away less helpful habits so that we have solid foundations on which to build.

We are now going to look at how to use the out-breath effectively. We are going to focus on the abdominal and pelvic floor muscles and explore what they *naturally* do when we breathe out more *dynamically*. We will then look at how to harness that *natural* activity so that we can access it whenever we wish.

This work is excellent for taking the attention and effort away from the throat. It also helps the in-breath because, as I mentioned earlier, the more fully you breathe out the easier it is to breathe in

Although the abdominal and pelvic floor muscles engage most effectively when we are standing, I, nevertheless, find it worthwhile to start the work on the floor in the Alexander Position. This ensures that the spine stays long and the hips and shoulders stay wide while the belly muscles engage and release. Once this habit has been set up it is much easier to transfer this to standing.

Because we now want to work more dynamically we are going to *blow out* gently but firmly and consistently, rather than sighing out. This will naturally begin to engage the lower abdominal, and later the pelvic floor, muscles, as you will see. By engagement I mean *appropriate* muscle activity. When muscles work appropriately there is no tension or force. The muscles simply do their job.

Also, we are going to move the attention down to the area just *below* the navel and imagine that we are blowing from there because, although the abdominal and pelvic floor muscles are designed to support the breath, less helpful postural habits and tensions can result in us becoming disconnected from these muscles, leaving the breath unsupported. By working with the image of blowing from the area just below the navel we reconnect with the lower abdominal and pelvic floor muscles, so ensuring that they re-engage and *do* support the breath and voice.

Engaging the abdominal muscles

To explore how these muscles work on a dynamic out-breath and to build the habit of connecting with and engaging them

We are going to start by focusing just on the abdominal muscles.

❍ *Lie in the Alexander Position. This time, place your hands just below the navel. Again, centre your attention where your hands are.*

❍ *Then, blow gently, but firmly and surely, imagining that you are blowing from the area just below your navel. Obviously, you will be blowing out through your lips, but let them take care of themselves while you keep your focus below the navel, on the image of blowing from there. Keep blowing right to the end of your comfortable breath with full commitment but no effort.*

- *At the end of the out-breath let the belly area relax and wait, as usual, for the impulse to breathe in. This impulse may come more quickly now that you are breathing out more dynamically, but it may not, so have no expectations just watch out for the impulse to breathe in and, then, let the breath flow in, as before.*
- *Repeat this exercise a few times and notice what happens in the area just below the navel.*

Can you feel that area being pulled in and slightly up as you blow out? The more you blow out with sureness and commitment, but without force, and the more you focus on the area just below the navel the more likely this 'natural pulling in' is to occur.

- *Play with this exercise for six more breaths, really focusing on the idea of blowing out firmly and surely from the area just below the navel and really waiting for the in-breath.*

Keeping long and wide while breathing out dynamically

To keep the body stable and easy while the abdominal muscles engage

Now that you have begun to reconnect with the abdominal muscles, we are going to focus on keeping the spine long and the hips and shoulders wide while blowing out. This is vital, it avoids the 'up down breathing' I talked about earlier in the chapter and frees the belly muscles to engage more effectively. Don't skip over this part of the exercise because developing the habit of staying long and wide while breathing out dynamically will solve a myriad of problems.

- *Again, lie in the Alexander Position with the hands over the area just below the navel and centre your attention where your hands are.*
- *Again, blow gently, but firmly and surely, with the image that you are blowing from the area below the navel. Again, keep blowing right to the end of your comfortable breath, with full commitment but no effort, and, then, relax the belly and wait for the impulse to breath in, letting the in-breath flow in as and when it wants to.*
- *Repeat this three times imagining the spine lengthening as you blow. Then, repeat the exercise three times imagining the hips widening as you blow and, then, repeat it three times imagining the shoulders widening as you blow.*

If you repeat this exercise regularly you will build up the habit of lengthening and widening as you breathe out so that it becomes automatic. Then, you will find that your breath lasts much longer, even though you are releasing it freely rather than holding it back.

Adding the pelvic floor muscles

To explore how the pelvic floor muscles work on a dynamic out-breath and to build the habit of connecting with and engaging them

Now the abdominal muscles have begun to engage we will focus on the pelvic floor muscles as well.

- *Again, lie in the Alexander Position with your hands just below your navel and centre your attention where your hands are.*
- *Blow, as before, firmly and fully. In the first half of the breath focus on the image of blowing from the area below the navel, as before. Then, as you come to the second half of the breath, mentally reach down into the lower belly and the floor of the body, between the legs, for more breath, as if you are mentally scooping the breath up from those areas.*
- *As always, relax the belly at the end of the out-breath and wait for the in-breath to flow in by itself.*
- *Repeat this exercise a few times and see what happens.*

Can you feel the muscles lower down in the belly and the pelvic floor engaging? The movement is quite subtle and occurs deep inside the body rather than on the surface. Often, it is happening but we are just not used to placing our attention on that area of the body and therefore we don't notice it. If you really can't feel anything check the following:

- *Are you tensing anywhere above the armpits? If so, try again, imagining the area above the armpits softening and opening as you blow and mentally reach down.*
- *Are you blowing with full commitment and firmness? If not the brain and body will be less dynamically engaged and so the muscles in the lower body will work less. So try again and blow with great sureness right to the end of the comfortable breath.*
- *Is your attention really on your lower belly and pelvic floor? Often we miss what is happening because we are not used to being so subtly aware of our bodies. If necessary, squeeze and release the lower belly and pelvic floor muscles deep inside to help bring the attention there.*

However you are finding this exercise move onto the next one since they make a pair. Then, you can work on them together. Although the work may feel complicated and unnatural at present, remember that the lower belly and pelvic floor muscles are designed to work in the way described above. So, if you keep playing with the idea of mentally scooping down for breath, you will find that, in time, the muscles will engage and you will notice them doing so.

Releasing the lower abdominal and pelvic floor muscles

To relax the abdominal and pelvic floor muscles so that the in-breath can flow in easily and the muscles are available to engage again on the next out-breath

In the last exercise I suggested relaxing the belly at the end of the out-breath and, for some, this thought may be enough to release the lower belly and pelvic floor muscles. However, for others, especially those who perhaps unconsciously hold the lower belly and pelvic floor muscles tight most of the time we need to work a little more specifically to achieve full release. This release is important for two reasons: firstly, it allows a deep and full in-breath to occur easily and quickly; secondly, it allows the muscles to be ready to re-engage on the next out-breath. Too often the reason that an actor's breathing goes haywire during rehearsal or performance is because the lower belly and pelvic floor muscles don't release and it becomes harder and harder to find the breath needed and there is less and less sense of support. So learning to release these lower belly and pelvic floor muscles is vital and brings immense freedom and ease.

- *Lie in the Alexander Position with the hands just below the navel. Again centre your attention where your hands are.*
- *Blow fully and firmly as before. Again, in the first half of the out-breath, focus on the image of blowing from just below the navel. Then, again, as you come to the second half of the breath, mentally reach down into the lower belly and the pelvic floor for more breath.*
- *At the end of the out-breath pause for a moment so that you can feel where the muscles have naturally contracted in the lower belly and floor of the body and, then, let those muscles release.*
- *Play with this exercise a few times taking time in the pause at the end of the out-breath to really register and connect with the muscles in the lower belly and floor of the body that have contracted. The more you register these muscles and connect with them the easier it will be for your brain to work out which nerves it needs to send a message down in order for those muscles to release.*

If you are able to release these muscles you may notice that a new breath pours in immediately.

Note

But what about waiting for the impulse? Because you have used the out-breath more dynamically the impulse to breathe in can occur much more rapidly – indeed as soon as you release the lower belly and pelvic floor muscles. So, although everything is happening much quicker the principle has not changed. The breath is still coming in when it wants.

It is important to check that the in-breath is occurring naturally as a result of the release and that you are not thinking 'Oh, I've released, now I need to breathe in'. The in-breath always looks after itself.

That is fine. If it doesn't, don't worry. It can take a while to really get in contact with the lower belly and pelvic floor muscles and fully release them. It is best to focus deep inside the body and imagine the muscles releasing there rather than on the surface. Also, pausing for that moment at the end of the breath to contact the muscles is very helpful.

We will be looking at this exercise standing up later in the chapter. This is usually much easier because you have gravity on your side. As I mentioned earlier the reason for working on the floor is to check that you can stay long and wide while engaging and releasing the belly and pelvic floor muscles.

Putting the 'Developing the Out-Breath' section together

Once you are comfortable with the exercises in this section you can put them together into one exercise, *Long and wide – engaging and releasing*, as follows.

- *Lie in the Alexander Position with the hands just below the navel.*
- *First, think of lengthening and widening.*
- *Then, blow out from just below the navel, mentally reaching down in the second half of the breath for more air.*
- *Then, release the lower belly and pelvic floor muscles at the end of the out-breath and allow the in-breath to flow in by itself.*
- *Work on this combined exercise for two minutes.*

This combined exercise added to the exercises from the previous section will give you an eight-minute session.

Developing the in-Breath

Now we have explored and developed the out-breath we will return to the in-breath and look at developing that. Work on the in-breath needs to be effective but unforced. There is no point getting a great deal of diaphragm and rib movement if excess effort and tension accompany it. So, again, we are going to use simple images to *guide* or *stimulate* the desired movement and so avoid all unnecessary effort, while successfully leading to increased expansion.

It is very important, when working on the in-breath, to check that you really let it take care of itself, while you simply direct it by focusing on the image. So, we are going to use the sighing out-breath rather than the more dynamic blowing out-breath and at the end of *every* out-breath I want you to *wait* for the impulse to breathe in so you can ride on the breath's natural energy. When that impulse occurs allow the breath to come in in its own time while you simply imagine *receiving* it.

Expanding the central breath

To stimulate the beginning of greater diaphragm and rib movement

As in the *Centring the breath* exercise we are going to focus on the area above the navel where you can feel the main movement of the diaphragm and ribs. This exercise really helps the diaphragm and rib movement to start in the right place and the right way. It forms a great foundation on which to build the rest of the diaphragm and rib work.

- *Lie on the floor in the Alexander position, as before.*
- *Place your hands just above the navel as you did in the Centring the breath exercise.*
- *Imagine a wide belt stretching all around your body from navel level to breastbone level. It is a good idea if you focus on the inside of the belt, since this helps to prevent any forcing when you breathe.*
- *Sigh out any breath and imagine the belt relaxing inwards. Then, wait for the impulse to breathe in. Then, let the breath flow in, imagining the back of the belt expanding, then, the sides and lastly the front. Then, sigh out and imagine the belt gently releasing inwards again.*
- *Repeat this exercise for one to two minutes, remembering to focus on the expansion starting in the back of the belt.*

Engaging the rib muscles in the back

To enable the ribs to move easily and effectively

Now that we have got the centre expanding we are going to focus on the movement in the back of the ribs.

As I mentioned earlier, the rib muscles in the back are largely responsible for moving the rib cage. If they move, the rest of the rib cage will follow.

We are going to work with a towel in this exercise. The towel helps the part of the spine to which the ribs are attached to stay long and relaxed and allows the back to stay open, so avoiding tension in the back as you explore the rib movement there.

- *Take a towel and fold it so it is the length of your forearm, wrist to elbow. (See diagram 8a.) Roll the towel up as tightly as you can so it will not squash flat. Then put some elastic bands around it to keep it in shape.*

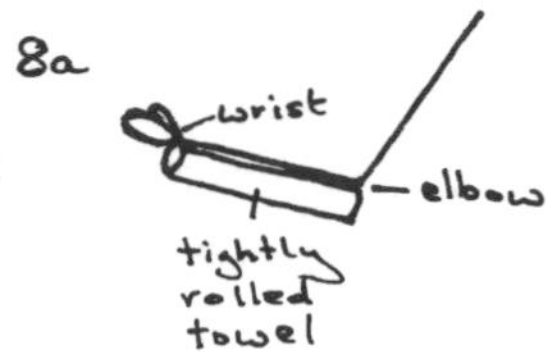

- *Lie on the towel so it runs along the part of your spine to which your ribs are attached. The towel should only be under the 'rib spine', not under the small of the back or the neck. (See diagram 8b.) This is why it is important that the towel is the right length.*

- *Have your legs flat on the floor and your head resting on the floor rather than on books. As usual your hands are resting over your navel.*
- *Focus on your 'rib spine' for the moment. Your 'rib spine' runs from just above waist level to just below shoulder level. Imagine there is a row of noses running up either side of your spine from waist to shoulder level. Rest with this image for a few moments.*
- *Then, sigh out and wait for the impulse to breathe in. When the breath starts to flow in imagine it entering through the noses from the waist up. As always there is no need to consciously 'do' anything. Just focus on the image and let the image move the muscles.*
- *Also, as usual, don't worry if the movement is small at first, the more you pay attention to the movement and feed it by focusing on the image the more the movement will grow.*
- *Play with this exercise for about a minute.*

You can repeat this exercise with the image of noses stretching up the sides of the body from waist to armpit level.

The 'n' breath

To strengthen and extend the diaphragm breath

Now that the muscles in the back are beginning to engage freely and effectively, we are going to focus a little more on the diaphragm movement.

We are going to use the image of a three-dimensional 'n' inside the lower body. Imagine the top of the 'n' stretching across the centre of the body just above navel level and the 'legs' of the 'n' stretching all the way down to the base of the buttocks. (See diagram 9.)

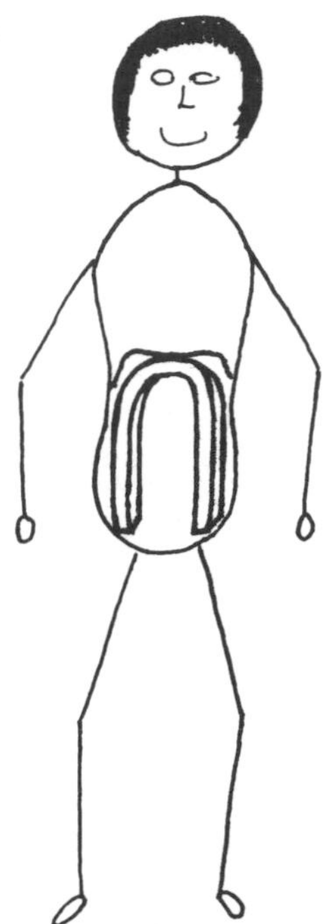
9

We are going to focus on the breath starting deep inside the centre of the body above the navel as we did in the Centring the breath and the Expanding the centre breath exercises.

- *Lie in the Alexander Position as before, with the hands resting just above the navel. I find this image helps the sense of expanding outwards as well as downwards and prevents the centre of the belly from over protruding.*
- *Place your attention deep inside your body and imagine the three dimensional 'n', with the top stretching across the centre of the body and the 'legs' stretching down to the base of the buttocks.*
- *Sigh out and wait for the impulse to breathe in as you did earlier. When you feel the impulse and the breath begins to flow in, imagine it filling across the top of the 'n' and, then, down its 'legs'.*
- *At first it may hardly fill down at all, but if you really work with the image you will eventually begin to have a sense of filling all the way down to the base of the buttocks.*
- *Remember not to actually consciously 'do' it. Let your imagination guide the movement.*
- *Play with this exercise for a minute or two, remembering always to sigh out easily on the out-breath and, then, to wait for the impulse to breathe in.*

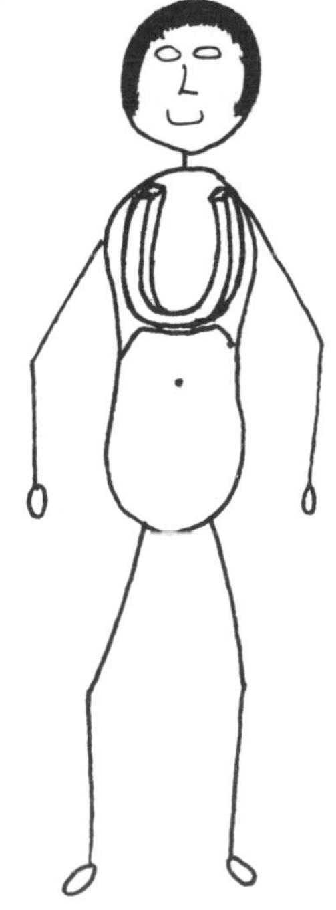
10

The 'u' breath

To strengthen and extend the rib breath

Now we are going to focus on the rib movement using the 'u' breath, which is the partner to the 'n' breath.

Imagine a three-dimensional 'u' deep inside the upper body, with the bottom of the 'u' stretching across the centre of the body just above navel level and the 'arms' of the 'u' stretching up through the upper body to just below the shoulders. (See diagram 10.) As with the 'n' breath I find the 'u' breath helps the outward expansion. Also, it avoids any tendency to heave the breastbone during the in-breath.

Again, we are going to focus on the breath starting above the navel level, deep inside the body, just as you did when working with the 'n' breath.

- *Lie in the Alexander Position as before, with the hands resting just above the navel.*
- *Place your attention deep in your body just above navel level, and imagine the three dimensional 'u' with the base stretching across the centre of the body and the arms stretching up through the ribs to just below shoulder level.*
- *Sigh out and wait for the impulse to breathe in, as you did earlier. When you feel the impulse and the breath begins to flow in, imagine it filling across the base of the 'u' and up its 'arms'.*
- *At first it may hardly fill up at all, but if you really work with the image you will eventually begin to have a sense of filling all the way up to armpit level and possibly even to the underside of the shoulders.*
- *Again, remember not to actually consciously 'do' it. Just imagine the breath filling into the 'u' and let that guide the movement. There should be no tension or effort in the upper body and the shoulders particularly need to stay wide, soft and dropped.*
- *Play with this exercise for a minute or two, remembering always to sigh out easily on the out breath and, then, to wait for the impulse to breathe in.*

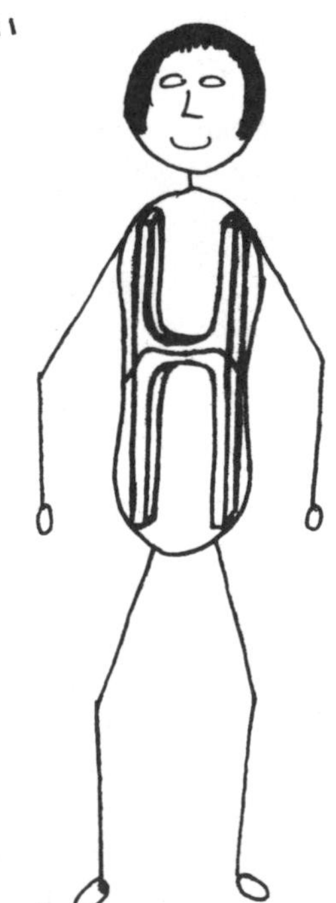

11

The 'H' breath

To balance, strengthen and extend the diaphragm and rib movement

Once you feel that the 'n' and 'u' breaths are equally strong, try putting them together to form the 'H' breath. (See diagram 11.)

- *Lie in the Alexander Position as before, with the hands resting just above the navel.*
- *Again, place your attention deep in your body just above navel level, and imagine a three dimensional 'H' with the middle stretching across the centre of the body, its 'legs' stretching down through the buttocks and its 'arms' stretching up through the rib cage.*

- *Sigh out and wait for the impulse to breathe in, as you did earlier. When you feel the impulse and the breath begins to flow in imagine it filling first across the middle of the 'H' and, then, down its 'legs' and up its 'arms'.*
- *At first, you will probably need to work on a 'my turn your turn' basis where you imagine filling down a little and, then, up a little. Don't worry if the breath stops and starts. It can take the brain a while to re-co-ordinate the diaphragm and rib movement, especially if you have been in the habit of letting one dominate.*
- *Play with this exercise for a minute or two, remembering always to sigh out easily on the out-breath and, then, to wait for the impulse to breathe in.*

If you work patiently with this image, trusting it to stimulate the desired movement of the diaphragm and ribs and avoiding physically pushing, then, in time, this complete filling from the centre will become habitual. So that when you are using the breath more dynamically, as you do in supported speech, and you release the lower belly and pelvic floor muscles at the end of the out-breath, the in-breath will easily and naturally fill the whole body.

Putting the 'Developing the In-Breath' section together

Once you are happy that the ribs and diaphragm are working in a balanced way, you only need to work for two minutes with the final exercise in this section. So, this, added to the exercises from the previous sections, will give you a total session of ten minutes.

Bringing the Work off the Floor

Now that we have explored freeing and centring the breath and developing both the out-breath and in-breath on the floor, we are going to bring that work off the floor, since, on the whole, you don't get to act lying down!

We are going to work against the wall, so that we can continue to build the habit of lengthening and widening. It is much easier to check that the back is not collapsing and narrowing when in this position. Really allow the parts of your back touching the wall to rest against it as you work, especially the upper back.

The small of the back naturally curves in and so won't be flat against the wall, in the same way that it was not flat on the floor. To avoid excessive curving imagine the base of the spine dropping towards the floor whilst the rest of the spine lengthens towards the ceiling.

Engaging and releasing against the wall

To practise engaging and releasing the lower belly and pelvic floor muscles in an upright position

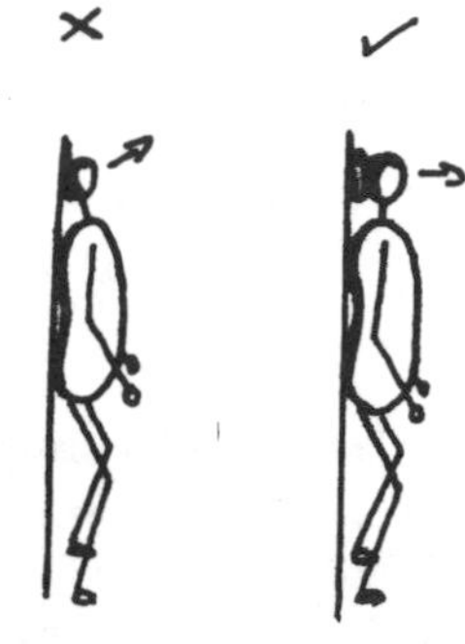

- *Stand with your back against the wall. Your feet need to be an inch or so from the wall; they also need to be parallel and hipbone width apart. Bend the knees very slightly and let your back rest against the wall as if you were lying on the floor. If you had a lot of books under your head when you were lying on the floor you will probably need a cushion behind your head when against the wall so that you don't end up shortening the back of your neck. (See diagram 12.)*
- *Place your hands just below the navel, as for the earlier engage and release exercises. Then, imagine the spine lengthening, the hips and shoulders widening, the buttocks and shoulder blades dropping gently down your back and the ankle, knee and hip joints loosening.*
- *Blow fully and firmly from the area below the navel, as before. In the first half of the out-breath again feel the area below the navel being pulled in and slightly up, then, as you come to the second half of the breath, mentally reach down into the lower belly and the pelvic floor for more breath.*
- *At the end of the out-breath again pause for a moment so you can feel where the muscles have naturally contracted in the lower belly and floor of the body and then, let those muscles release. As before, the in-breath will flow in quite naturally by itself.*
- *Play with this exercise for a minute or two remembering not to consciously 'do' the in-breath but rather to let it take care of itself.*

Adding the 'H' breath

To practise full, balanced diaphragm and rib movement, as well as engaging and releasing the lower belly and pelvic floor muscles, in an upright position

Now we are going to add the 'H' breath to the above exercise so that we put together a total blueprint of dynamic breathing.

- *Stand against the wall as before, with your hands below your navel.*
- *Again, blow fully and firmly from the area below the navel. As before, in the first half of the out-breath feel the navel being pulled in and slightly up, then, as you*

come to the second half of the breath, mentally reach down into the lower belly and the pelvic floor for more breath.

- *At the end of the out-breath, again, pause for a moment so that you can feel where the muscles have naturally contracted in the lower belly and floor of the body and then let those muscles release.*
- *As the breath begins to flow in, focus deep in your body, just above the navel, and imagine the three dimensional 'H' filling first across its middle and then down its 'legs' and up its 'arms' – just as you imagined it filling on the floor. Remember, of course, not to consciously 'do' the breathing but rather to use the image to stimulate the diaphragm and rib movement.*
- *Play with this exercise for a minute or two, working calmly and feeling that you have plenty of time to go through each part of the process. If you work in this way you will 'programme in' this pattern of breathing so that eventually it becomes habitual.*

Once you feel happy about releasing the lower belly and pelvic floor muscles you can leave out the pause at the end of the out-breath and simply allow these muscles to release as soon as you reach the end of the out-breath. Do check, however, that if you do this you are really releasing and not just pushing the lower belly area out.

Engaging, releasing and the 'H' breath away from the wall

To put the whole dynamic breathing process together away from the wall

We are going to practise the above exercise away from the wall now. However, to keep working on avoiding collapsing and narrowing, I would like you to hold a chair above your head! Holding the chair above your head activates the upper spine and lifts the chest. Also, the whole upper body has to find a balance and stillness so that the chair can be held. (See diagram 13.) As a result the belly is freed to engage and release as it was designed. Obviously, it is important to work with a light chair that you can easily pick up without hurting your back and that is not too tiring to hold above your head!

13

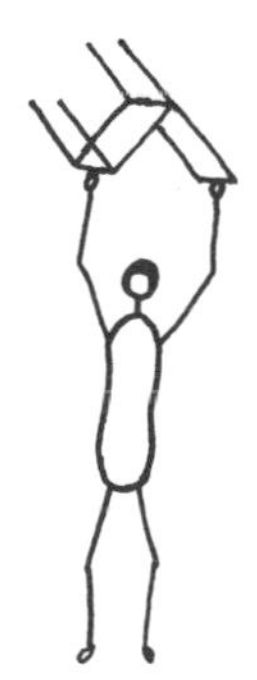

- *Once you have lifted the chair up above your head, check that you are standing with your feet parallel and hipbone width apart and your knees soft. Imagine the spine lengthening, the hips and shoulders widening, the buttocks and shoulder blades dropping gently down the back and the ankle, knee and hip joints loosening. Keep the elbows soft.*

- *Blow fully and firmly from the area below the navel, as before. Again, in the first half of the out-breath feel the area below the navel being pulled in and slightly up, then, as you come to the second half of the breath, mentally reach down into the lower belly and the pelvic floor for more breath.*
- *At the end of the out-breath, either pause for a moment, so you can feel where the muscles have naturally contracted in the lower belly and floor of the body, and then let those muscles release or release them as soon as you reach the end of the breath, whichever you find easier and more helpful.*
- *As the breath begins to flow in, again focus deep in your body, just above the navel, and imagine the three dimensional 'H' filling first across the middle and, then, down and up its legs as you did against the wall. Remember, again, not to 'do' the breathing but rather to use the image to stimulate the diaphragm and rib movement.*
- *Work with this exercise for a minute or two.*

Putting the 'Bringing the Work off the Floor' section together

I suggest that you work on the whole Engaging, releasing and filling exercise for three minutes. Work for a minute in the Alexander Position, then, for a minute standing against the wall and, then, for a minute holding the chair above your head. Together with the exercises from the previous sections this will give you a total session of thirteen minutes.

Building the Support Energy

Now that we have laid down the blueprint for dynamic breathing we get to the really fun work. It is my favourite. I realised a long time ago that simply relaxing an actor just doesn't work. Performing does require effort. The question is what sort of effort? The answer is the kind of effort any well-trained athlete uses. That is good muscle effort as opposed to push and strain. In the first chapter I talked about the link between mental and physical bounce. Now we are going to use mental bounce to create physical bounce in the support muscles. So, here goes.

'Diaphragm bounce'

To experience the links between mental and physical bounce and develop an energy in, and sense of support from, the diaphragm

It was Kristin Linklater, in her book 'Freeing The Natural Voice', who first got me excited about the 'bounce' potential of the diaphragm. She talked about it being like a trampoline, which I think is an excellent image and one that I have used ever since.

The diaphragm is the first port of call in our tour of the support system in the lower body. We are going to start by exploring what the diaphragm feels like when it is under or over-energised.

Stage one – Establishing the silent pant

- *Stand with the feet parallel and hipbone width apart, the spine lengthening, the hips and shoulders widening and all the joints loose.*
- *Pant gently, thinking of the spine lengthening as you do so. Don't worry if it is not very regular, as long as you are not collapsing your spine as you pant, you will find it becomes more regular with gentle practice.*
- *As you pant put your attention inside your body just below your breastbone.*
- *Do you get a sense of the diaphragm moving up and down as you pant? Don't worry if you can't feel very much at present, just go with whatever you can feel however unsure you might be about it.*
- *Now try panting as silently as possible. This ensures that your throat is open. It is this silent pant that we will use in all the panting exercises.*

Don't pant for longer than a minute at a time because you are not getting an appropriate exchange of air and carbon dioxide when you pant. Also, if you pant for too long the diaphragm may tighten up.

Stage two – how mental energy affects muscular activity

Now we are going to explore how different mental states affect the way the diaphragm works.

- *Imagine that you feel very unconfident and tentative about panting and pant with this attitude. Do you feel what happens to the panting, how it becomes less even and has less energy?*
- *Now imagine that you still feel unconfident about panting or that you feel too tired to pant, so to compensate you are going to try very hard. Pant with this attitude. Do you notice what happens to your panting now? Do you notice how it becomes tighter and that other parts of the body start to tense?*
- *Now imagine that you feel quietly confident about panting and interested in doing so. Pant with this attitude. Do you notice what happens to your panting now? Can you feel that it is easier, that the body is relaxed and free? Can you also feel that there is more energy or 'bounce' in the movement?*

Obviously, it is this last version of panting on which we want to build, not just in the panting work but in all the support work.

Stage three – increasing the mental bounce to increase the physical bounce

- *Now we are going to explore how we can increase the physical bounce by increasing the mental bounce. As you pant again try the following attitudes and see which one gives you the most bounce:*
  - *Playful and teasing, perhaps as if you have an amazing secret*
  - *Flirty, as if you were flirting with someone you really liked whom you knew liked you*
  - *Coolly confident, as if very sure of and pleased with yourself, but very laid back at the same time*
- *Using whichever attitude gives you the most bounce, regularly practise panting for no more than a minute so you can get used to this energy in the middle of your body.*

Notes

Using the 'Diaphragm bounce' to prepare for high-energy scenes: this exercise is an excellent one to do just before you go on stage if you have a high-energy scene. It allows you to find a great deal of energy without tightening up.

Pant silently with ease and sureness for about 30 seconds. Then, place the feeling you wish to take on stage with you in the centre of the panting area and continue to pant for about 30 seconds, keeping the rest of the body relaxed.

Using the 'Diaphragm bounce' to take your attention away from your throat: panting is also excellent for taking your attention away from your throat. By focusing on the area where you feel the panting and imagining talking from there you can really begin to connect with your breath so it supports your voice properly. It is much easier, far more useful and far less wacky than you might think! I find it particularly helpful when an actor has a cold, since it takes the focus back to the centre of the body and the support muscles.

Again, pant silently with ease and sureness and imagine that your throat or mouth is in the panting area and that you talk from there.

Using the 'Diaphragm bounce' to find energy for performance and rehearsal: also, if you are tired or haven't had a chance to warm–up before rehearsing or performing it is much better to find some energy this way than by forcing. I do voiceover work and sometimes the sessions are booked for early in the morning so I always pant silently on my way there, for 30 seconds to a minute, using whichever attitude – cheeky, flirty, coolly confident – seems most helpful to me at the time.

The diaphragm bounce is very useful, as I have pointed out, to help take the attention away from the throat and build a sense of bounce in the body. Now, however, we are going to focus on the abdominal muscles, which support the breath and voice.

Abdominal bounce I – The lower belly bounce

To engage the belly area, just below the navel, and feel a sense of support from there

We are going to use the same sense of 'mental bounce' with the belly as we did with the diaphragm. The belly support is vital for healthy and dynamic voice use and we began to explore engaging the belly in the last chapter. The belly will naturally come into play if you work with sureness and interest, using the playful, teasing, flirty or coolly confident attitude you used in the last exercise.

- *Stand with the feet parallel and hip bone width apart, the spine lengthening, the hips and shoulders widening and all the joints loose, as before. Again, place your hands just below your navel.*
- *Say 'sh' firmly as if you were telling someone to be quiet. Repeat this a few times, firmly, confidently and a little sharply.*
- *Do you notice what happens? Can you feel the belly area just below the navel being pulled in and even, perhaps, slightly up? You don't need to consciously pull it in. If you say the 'sh' with sufficient firmness, letting your spine stay long, the belly will automatically be engaged. Don't worry if it's a small movement. Again we can build on that.*
- *If you really aren't getting anywhere, try the exercise holding a chair above your head, as you did earlier in the chapter, this usually does the job.*

> **Note**
>
> *About the belly pushing out rather than pulling in:* sometimes the belly goes the other way, that is, it pushes outwards on the 'sh'. There are two main reasons for this in my experience: firstly, a collapsed spine and secondly, too much effort. If the spine is collapsed it constricts the abdominal area and stops the muscles there working appropriately. If there is conscious effort to move the belly the message often gets sent to the wrong muscles and the belly ends up pushing out instead of going in.
>
> So you need to let the spine lengthen and then replace all conscious physical effort with a good dose of mental bounce.

- *Once you have a sense of the belly being pulled in start to make the 'sh' more bouncy. Again, think of flirting or teasing if it helps and also of speaking from the area just below the navel, as if your mouth is there and each 'sh' is bouncing up from there. This may sound crazy but it does work – we'll look more closely at this idea in the next chapter.*

❍ *As with the panting, practise this exercise regularly for no more than a minute.*

Abdominal bounce 2 – The 'oomph points' bounce

To explore, connect with and strengthen the other support points in the abdomen

This exercise is based on the research and teaching of Janice Chapman, an excellent singing teacher I worked with many years ago.

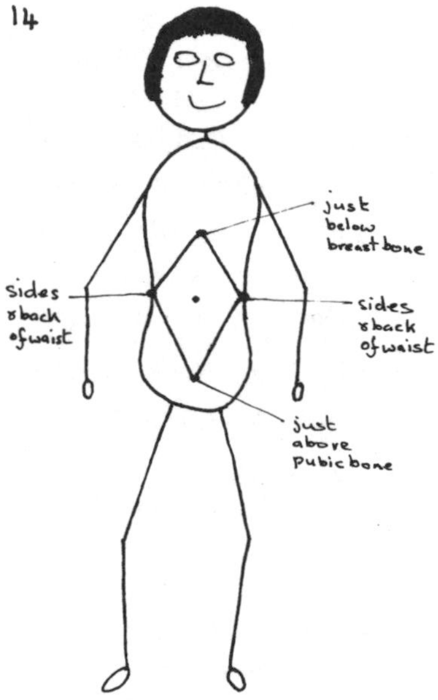

Imagine a diamond shape surrounding the centre of the belly. The top point of the diamond is just below the breastbone. The bottom point is just above the pubic bone, and the side points, which wrap around the body somewhat, are on the sides and the back of the waist. (See diagram 14.)

Whereas the centre of the belly, that is the area just below the navel, goes in when we breathe out or make sound, the points of the diamond go out. Meribeth Bunch, a specialist in vocal anatomy, uses the following wonderful analogy to clearly explain what is occurring.[15] Imagine a balloon. If you press one side of the balloon in, the area above and below and either side of where you have pushed in will bulge out, because the balloon is a closed space so its contents cannot leave but can only be displaced. The abdominal area is also a closed space and its contents similarly can only be displaced.

> **Note**
> Whereas the balloon's content is air, the content of the abdomen is not air, even though it can sometimes feel like it! The contents of the abdomen are the various organs, blood vessels and so forth.

15 Meribeth Bunch is the author of *Dynamics of The Singing Voice,* an excellent book on vocal anatomy for those who would like to go into more detail.

I call these points of the diamond the 'oomph' points because they give such energy, power and strength to the voice. Focusing on them will really give you somewhere to 'oomph' from and will take all the effort away from the throat.

We will work through each point in turn, discovering how they work. Here we will simply work with breath, but in the next chapter we will look at how these muscles work to support sound and speech.

❍ *As with previous exercises, stand with the feet parallel and hipbone width apart, the spine lengthening, the hips and shoulders widening, the buttocks and shoulder blades dropping gently and the ankle, knee and hip joints loosening as you work on each point.*

The top-of-the-diamond bounce

❍ *The first point we are going to focus on is the one just below the breastbone. Place your thumb there quite firmly and say 'psh – psh' with great sureness, as if you were shooing away a cat. Repeat this a few times.*

❍ *Can you feel the area under your thumb bounce out? As always don't worry if it is a tiny movement – that's enough to build on.*

❍ *If you can't feel any movement first check that your thumb is in the right place, which is on the soft area just below the breastbone. Then, check that you are touching the point firmly enough. Also, check that your spine isn't slumping and finally make sure you say 'psh – psh' with a lot of firmness and bounce.*

❍ *Once you have found the point and got it moving practise for 30 seconds on 'psh – psh' with a lot of mental bounce and as much playfulness and ease as possible.*

Note

If you get a lot of throat tension, the top-of-the-diamond point, just below the breast bone, is a very good focus point. It really helps to take the attention off the throat and to open it.

The bottom-of-the-diamond bounce

❍ *The second point is just above the pubic bone. Place your fingers there, again touching firmly, and, as before say 'psh –psh' several times.*

❍ *Can you feel the area under your fingers bouncing out slightly? Again, don't worry if the movement is only tiny.*

❍ *Again, if you can't feel anything, go through the usual checklist. Are your fingers in the right place – just above the pubic bone? Are you touching the point firmly enough? Is your spine long? Are you saying the 'psh – psh' with sufficient bounce?*

- *Once you have located the point and got it moving, practise for 30 seconds on 'psh – psh' again with a lot of mental bounce and as much playfulness and ease as possible.*

The sides-of-the-diamond bounce

As already mentioned, the diamond is not flat. Instead, it curves round so that the side points are on the sides of the waist and on the back of the waist, on the big muscles either side of the spine. We will look at the sides and the back separately.

Sides-of-the-waist bounce

- *Place your hands on the sides of your waist. Make firm contact but keep the shoulders relaxed. Again say 'psh – psh' surely and firmly several times.*
- *Can you feel the area under each hand bounce out? As usual, don't worry if the movement is only tiny.*
- *Again, if you can't feel anything, go through the usual checklist. Are your hands in the right place – exactly on the waist rather than a little higher or a little lower? Are you touching the sides of your waist firmly enough? Is your spine long? Are you saying the 'psh – psh' with sufficient bounce?*
- *Once you have located the movement, practise for 30 seconds on 'psh – psh' again with a lot of mental bounce and as much playfulness and ease as possible.*

Back-of-the-waist-bounce

- *Place the backs of your hands on the back of your waist. Make firm contact but keep the shoulders relaxed and don't arch your back. Again say 'psh – psh' surely and firmly several times.*
- *Can you feel the area under your hands bounce out? As usual, don't worry if the movement is only tiny.*

- *Again, if you can't feel anything, go through the usual checklist. Are your hands in the right place – exactly on the back of the waist? Are you touching the back of the waist firmly enough? Is your spine long? Are you saying the 'psh – psh' with sufficient bounce?*
- *If you are still having no luck, try leaning forward from the hips, with your back rounded. (See diagram 15.)*
- *Often there is movement in the back but the stronger inward movement of the belly distracts you. So just keep focusing your attention on your back and saying 'psh – psh' with lots of mental bounce and eventually you will pick up on the movement there.*

❍ *Once you have located the movement, practise for 30 seconds on 'psh – psh' again with a lot of mental bounce and as much playfulness and ease as possible.*

Putting the 'Building the Support Energy' section together

Once you feel you have connected with all the points, then, it is just a matter of regularly doing no more than 30 seconds to a minute working in each place to build the connection with these points and get them to engage firmly and energetically. Therefore, the whole section can be worked through in two and a half to five minutes.

This work, together with the exercises from the previous section will give you a session of no longer than 18 minutes.

Note

All the activity you have discovered in the muscles in this last section is natural. The body is designed to work this way. In fact, that is true of every exercise in this chapter. All you are doing is paying attention and sending mental directions to remind the body of what it already knows. So, once you have practised, forget about what you have done completely and trust that because you are reminding the body regularly, and because what you are practising is what the body is designed to do anyway, it will begin to do it.

Sustaining the Support and the Breath

The work above deals with *initial* support: with supporting the *start* of the breath from the healthiest place in the healthiest way. Obviously, support needs to be sustained throughout the breath, since this provides a constant supply of breath at a consistent pressure rather than a breath supply that tails away.

We have already looked at one way of engaging some of the support muscles to sustain the breath. The mental reaching down in the second half of the breath does this, engaging as it does the lower abdominal and pelvic floor muscles. (See '*Long and wide – engaging and releasing*' page 78.) Now we are going to look at how the diamond points can work to sustain the support.

'Oomph points' sustain

To keep the points of the diamond engaged throughout the out-breath

Top-of-the-diamond sustain

❍ *Stand, as always, with the feet parallel and hipbone width apart, the spine lengthening, the hips and shoulders widening, the buttocks and shoulder blades gently dropping and the ankle, knee and hip joints loosening.*

- *Reconnect with the point just below the breastbone by placing your thumb there again and saying 'psh – psh' surely and firmly a few times.*
- *Now, say 'psh – psh' again but this time continue the final 'sh' until you run out of breath.*
- *What happens to the area under your thumb? Does it stay out or does it move back in? Often, at first it relaxes back in, which is fine. But we want to explore that point staying out until the end of the breath, since this helps to sustain the support.*
- *So, try again, imagining the area under your thumb continuing to move out as you continue to 'sh' out. It won't necessarily move out any further, but imagining it moving out stops it from collapsing back in. Obviously, as always it is important that you don't consciously push this point out, just trust your imagination to bring about the desired result.*
- *At the end of the out-breath allow the area under your thumb to relax.*
- *Play with this exercise for no longer than a minute, each time imagining the area under the thumb moving out on each out-breath and allowing that area to relax at the end of the out-breath.*

Bottom-of-the-diamond sustain

- *Again, stand with the feet parallel and hipbone width apart, the spine lengthening, the hips and shoulders widening, the buttocks and shoulder blades gently dropping and all the ankle, knee and hip joints loosening.*
- *Reconnect with the point just above the pubic bone by placing your fingers there again and saying 'psh – psh' surely and firmly a few times.*
- *Now, say 'psh – psh' again continuing the final 'sh' until you run out of breath.*
- *What happens to the area under your fingers? Does this point stay out or does it move back in?*
- *Try again, imagining the area under your fingers continuing to move out as you continue to 'sh' out. As with the first point, it won't necessarily move out any further but, again, imagining it moving out stops it from collapsing back in. Obviously, as before, it is important that you don't consciously push this point out, but rather that you work with your imagination to keep the point engaged.*
- *At the end of the out-breath allow the area under your fingers to relax.*
- *Play with this exercise for no longer than a minute, imagining the area under your fingers moving out on each out-breath and allowing that area to relax at the end of the out-breath.*

Sides-of-waist sustain

- *Reconnect with the sides of the waist by placing your hands there again and saying 'psh – psh' surely and firmly a few times.*
- *Now, say 'psh – psh' again continuing the final 'sh' until you run out of breath.*
- *What happens to the sides of your waist? Do they stay out or do they move back in?*
- *Try again, imagining the sides of your waist continuing to move out as you continue to 'sh' out. As with the earlier points, they won't necessarily move out any further, but as before, imagining it moving out stops it from collapsing back in. Obviously, it is again important that you don't consciously 'do' anything but, rather, that you let it do itself.*
- *At the end of the out-breath allow the areas under your hands to relax.*
- *Play with this exercise for about a minute imagining the areas under your hands moving out on each out-breath and allowing that area to relax at the end of the out-breath.*

Back-of-waist sustain

- *Again, stand with the feet parallel and hipbone width apart, the spine lengthening, the hips and shoulders widening, the buttocks and shoulder blades dropping and the ankle, knee and hip joints loosening.*
- *Reconnect with the back of the waist by placing the backs of your hands there again and saying 'psh – psh' surely and firmly a few times.*
- *Now say 'psh – psh' again continuing the final 'sh' until you run out of breath.*
- *What happens to the back of your waist? Does it stay out or does it move back in?*
- *Try again, imagining the back of your waist continuing to move out as you continue to 'sh' out. As with the other two points, it won't necessarily move out any further but, as before, imagining it moving out stops it from collapsing back in. Obviously, it is again important that you don't 'do' anything but rather that you let it do itself.*
- *At the end of the out-breath allow the areas under your hands to relax.*
- *Play with this exercise for about a minute imagining the areas under your hands moving out on each out-breath and allowing that area to relax at the end of the out-breath.*

Putting the 'Sustaining the Support and the Breath' section together

Once you are comfortable with the exercises in this section they need take no longer than a minute each, which makes this another five-minute section.

This section, together with all the previous sections, will, therefore, give you a session of approximately twenty-three minutes.

Putting the Whole Chapter together

Below is a summary of a shorter fifteen-minute session. I suggest you work on this once you feel happy with the individual elements of the chapter. It is only a guideline. Feel free to ignore it and put the exercises from this chapter together in your own way. My advice would be to keep the session short – no more than twenty minutes – that way there is more chance you'll do it!

Note

The page numbers refer to the original exercises in case you want to refresh your memory. Obviously, you do not need to do the exploratory parts of the exercise each time, simply work through as suggested at the end of the relevant exercise or section.

Warm-up (1 minute)

Freeing the breath (68)

Floor work (4 minutes)

Releasing the breath – 2 (72)
Opening the throat (72)
Long and wide – engaging and releasing (78)
H breath (82)

Standing (10 minutes)

Engage and release against the wall (84)
Adding the 'H' breath against the wall (84)
Engaging, releasing and the 'H' breath holding a chair (85)
Diaphragm bounce (86)
Abdominal bounce 1 – The lower belly bounce (89)
Abdominal bounce 2 – The 'oomph points' bounce (90)
'Oomph points' sustain (93)

4

Breath into Sound: Supporting the Voice

The last chapter explored breathing and support: where and how they happen most effectively. This chapter looks at converting breath into sound and speech and supporting that sound and speech effectively. We will explore both initiating and sustaining sound and speech in a way that is connected and healthy, so developing vocal strength, flexibility and subtlety.

How we make sound

Before we start that work, I would like to briefly describe how sound comes about.

When we decide to make a sound the brain sends a message to the vocal folds telling them to come together to form a light closure across the larynx. The breath, flowing up from the lungs, builds up underneath the lightly closed vocal folds until the pressure is great enough to cause the vocal folds to open. As the breath flows through the opening the pressure reduces and, so, the folds come together again.

This closing and opening of the vocal folds happens very rapidly and, as a result of this rapid opening and closing, the vocal folds are set in vibration. The vibrating folds, in turn, set the breath, escaping through them, in vibration and sound is produced as a result.

Trusting your throat to get on by itself

All of the above activity happens without us needing to consciously direct it. However, as I mentioned earlier, the *knowledge* that the sound is made in the throat can lead us to put unhelpful attention, and, therefore, effort there. I will talk about the *helpful* attention we can pay to the throat area, to open it, in the next chapter. In this chapter I would like you to *ignore your throat completely*, trusting it to get on by itself, and focus on whatever part of the body the particular exercise is engaging.

Remembering the mental bounce

If you work with mental bounce, as described in the earlier chapters (pages 9, 85-86) the support muscles *will* engage. So, remember to use the feelings of sureness and interest, of playfulness, flirting and teasing to galvanise your body's natural support activity.

Initiating Sound

All of these exercises are best done upright – either standing or sitting – because the support muscles work much better in this position. If you have a tendency to slump the spine and poke the head forward or to over-arch the back, work against the wall as you did in the previous chapter. This helps you to monitor the back and head without tension. (See diagram on page 84 to remind yourself of the position.)

If you are sitting make sure that your feet are flat on the floor and that your spine is erect without the small of your back over arching. Think of the buttocks and sacrum dropping slightly to prevent over-arching. (See diagram opposite.)

We are going to take each of the support points we explored in the last chapter and add sound, working with the *idea* of speaking from whichever point we are focusing on. This may sound rather stupid, but imagining that you are speaking from a certain point helps you to *connect* with that point so that the muscles there engage effectively and the co-ordination of breath and sound is easy and seamless.

Initially, we are going to work with sounds and simple words and phrases so you can get a feeling of connection with and support from each point. Later in the chapter we will look at practising with text.

Bouncing sounds, words and phrases from the diaphragm

To build a sense of connection with the diaphragm when making sound and speaking

Again, we are going to start with the diaphragm because I find focusing on it is an excellent way of taking the attention away from the throat and beginning to create a sense of vocal connection and energy.

Stage one – Bouncing sounds from the diaphragm

- *Stand, as before, with the feet parallel and hipbone width apart, the spine lengthening, the hips and shoulders widening, the buttocks and shoulder blades dropping and the ankle, knee and hip joints loosening.*
- *Reconnect with your diaphragm by panting silently, with good mental bounce, as before.*
- *Now, imagine that you have a mouth in the panting area and that you speak from there. Pant with this image, for a short while.*
- *Now, stop panting and with great sureness and mental bounce, again imagining you are speaking from your panting area, say 'Hoo Hoo'. As always there is no need to consciously 'do' anything with your diaphragm, just put your attention there and work with plenty of mental bounce and it will do what it needs to do.*

> **Note**
> The diaphragm will work in a slightly different way when you are making sounds from the way it did when you were panting so there is no need to try and reproduce the panting feeling. Just focus on the idea of the sound coming from the panting area.

- *Repeat this a few times, working quietly but with lots of bounce, keeping the 'Hoo Hoo' fully voiced rather than whispered.*
- *Now, bounce the following sequence of sounds from the diaphragm in the same way: 'Hoo Hoo – Hoh Hoh – Hor Hor – Hah Hah – High High – Hey Hey – Hee Hee'*

> **Note**
> If you simply release the belly slightly between each pair of sounds new breath will come in. (See page 77 for work on belly release.) There is no need to make a big deal of this – simply, as much as possible, let the breath take care of itself.

❍ *Play through the whole series of sounds two or three times, each time imagining that you are speaking from the diaphragm area and increasing the bounce and ease.*

Note

'Hoo Hoo to Hee-Hee' sequence: the 'Hoo Hoo to Hee Hee' sequence is one we will use frequently because it allows you to practise supporting a whole range of sounds made in all parts of the mouth, with the tongue and lips in varying positions. Why is this important? Often we naturally find it easier to connect with and support some sounds more than others. Working across a spectrum of sounds allows you to even this out, so that all sounds become supported. Also, you can use the sounds you find easy to connect with and support as a guide to working with the others.

For example, say that you find 'High' the most connected and supported sound you might start with that and then work round the sequence from there. Always keep the sequence in the same order even though you might be starting from a different point in that order.

Hopefully you will now have some sense of speaking from the diaphragm area. However, if you have no idea whether you are or not, don't worry. If the sound feels easy and the throat free, that is fine. There is no need to worry about what is actually happening, let that take care of itself, just continue to focus on the diaphragm area and the 'idea' of speaking from there.

If you do still feel that you are speaking from the throat don't worry about that either. Since you are working quietly and without force you are not going to hurt it. Just keep focusing your attention on the diaphragm area and the idea of speaking from there. In this way you will build up the connection with this area and, if the throat is still troubling you by the end of the chapter, we will look at exercises to release it in the next chapter.

Stage two – Giggling the sounds from the diaphragm

❍ *Giggling helps the throat to open so now repeat the 'Hoo Hoo to Hee Hee' sequence on a giggle, still focusing on the diaphragm. Remember to release and breathe between giggling each sound:*

> *'HooHooHooHooHoo – HohHohHohHohHoh – HorHorHorHorHor – HahHahHahHahHah – HighHighHighHighHigh – HeyHeyHeyHeyHey – HeeHeeHeeHeeHee'*

Stage three – Bouncing words from the diaphragm

❍ *Now, we are going to bounce the following sound/word sequences from the diaphragm in the same way as we did the Hoo Hoo sequence.*

'Nuh-Nuh'	*'Nuh-Nuh'*	*'Nuh-No'*
'Yuh-Yuh'	*'Yuh-Yuh'*	*'Yuh-Yes'*
'Fuh-Fuh'	*'Fuh-Fuh'*	*'Fuh-Fine'*

Note

Make sure you keep your focus on the diaphragm and the idea of speaking from there, rather than letting the attention creep up into the throat to see how that is getting on.

Stage four – Bouncing phrases from the diaphragm

Note

Putting an 'H' before 'I'm' and 'and' helps to keep everything open and connected. There can be a tendency to close the throat on words that begin with a vowel and putting an 'H' in front of such words helps avoid this. We will look at this tendency in more detail in the next chapter.

- *Now, try this sequence, working in the same way, with lots of sureness and mental bounce. Again, remember to release and breathe between each part of the sequence.*

'High-High'	*'High-High'*	*'Hi!'*
'How-How'	*'How-How'*	*'How are you?'*
'High-High'	*'High-High'*	*'HI'm fine thanks!'*
'Hand-Hand'	*'Hand-Hand'*	*'Hand how are you?'*

- *Could you feel a sense of speaking from the diaphragm area? If not have a rest and then try again.*
- *There are two important points to remember: firstly, to really focus on the diaphragm, and, secondly, to work with lots of mental bounce.*
- *So play with the panting until you get a good sense physically of where the panting is happening. Panting with your eyes closed can really help.*
- *Then, play with increasing the mental bounce: think flirty or cheeky as before. This is what spurs the support muscles into action. If there is little or no bounce there will be little or no support.*

Work through the four stages of this exercise regularly spending about 30 seconds on each stage.

Note

Taking this exercise into daily life: because, ideally, you want to speak in this connected way all the time, rather than just on stage, it is good to pant silently for 30 seconds every so often throughout the day to refocus on your diaphragm. Then, simply think 'I speak from my diaphragm', without worrying about how, so that as you speak throughout the day you have a sense of the voice coming from the diaphragm area. There is no need to be over-serious about it, just the lightest thought will do and then as usual let everything get on by itself.

Silent panting with mental bounce– instant energy for quiet work. I spoke in the last chapter about panting with mental bounce to access energy when you are feeling sluggish and in preparation for a high-energy scene. You can also use it to find energy for quiet work when working in a studio space or on television, film or radio.

Pant silently as before and then bounce the sounds as quietly as you can while keeping them fully voiced rather than whispered. Keep increasing the mental bounce but not the volume. This will give you a sense of internal energy, like your own personal dynamo.

The same exercise is also very useful as preparation if you are working with a microphone on stage. A microphone will give you volume but it will not give you energy. Only engaged support muscles can give you energy.

Bouncing sounds, words and phrases from the lower belly

To engage the lower belly muscle support when making sound and speaking

Now we are going to focus on the belly area just below the navel and work through the same sequences of sounds and phrases, as in the last exercise.

- *Stand as before with the feet parallel and hipbone width apart, the spine lengthening, the hips and shoulders widening, the buttocks and shoulder blades dropping and the ankle, knee and hip joints loosening.*
- *Place your hands just below your navel.*
- *Say 'sh' firmly a few times as if you are telling someone to be quiet, just as you did in the Abdominal bounce 1 – lower belly bounce (page 89) in the last chapter. Feel the area just below the navel being pulled in and slightly up.*
- *If you find the belly isn't pulling in and up you can consciously pull the belly in and up, gently but firmly, to help it re-engage. It's helpful to imagine that there are two strings attached to the inside of your belly, just below the navel, and that you pull those strings in and up on each 'sh'.*
- *Imagine that your mouth is now in the area just below your navel and that you speak from there. Say 'sh' a few times with this image.*
- *Now, with great sureness and mental bounce say 'Hoo Hoo'. Can you feel the area below the navel being pulled in and slightly up? If your spine is lengthening*

rather than collapsing and you are using plenty of mental bounce the belly will usually pull in and up quite naturally.

- *Try a few more times increasing the mental bounce each time. Also, remember to work with a sense of the sound coming up from the belly and not with any sense of pushing it down.*
- *Now, bounce the whole 'Hoo Hoo to Hee Hee' sequence feeling the belly pull in and up on each sound:*

  'Hoo Hoo – Hoh Hoh – Hor Hor – Hah Hah – High High – Hey Hey – Hee Hee'

- *Repeat the sequence on a giggle, still focusing on the belly. Remember to release and breathe between giggling each sound:*

  'HooHooHooHooHoo – HohHohHohHohHoh – HorHorHorHorHor – HahHahHahHahHah – HighHighHighHighHigh – HeyHeyHeyHeyHey – HeeHeeHeeHeeHee'

- *Now, bounce this sound/word sequences from the belly in the same way:*

'Nuh-Nuh'	'Nuh-Nuh'	'Nuh-No'
'Yuh-Yuh'	'Yuh-Yuh'	'Yuh-Yes'
'Fuh-Fuh'	'Fuh-Fuh'	'Fuh-Fine'

- *Make sure you keep your focus on the belly and the idea of speaking from there, rather than letting the attention creep up into the throat.*
- *Now, bounce this sequence from the belly, again working in the same way, with a lot of sureness and mental bounce:*

'High-High'	'High-High'	'Hi!'
'How-How'	'How-How'	'How are you?'
'High-High'	'High-High'	'HI'm find thanks!'
'Hand-Hand'	'Hand-Hand'	'Hand how are you?'

Work through the four stages of this exercise regularly spending about 30 seconds on each.

Bouncing sounds, words and phrases from the 'oomph points'

To engage the diamond points when making sound and speaking

Now we are going to work with the points of the diamond (see page 90) in exactly the same way we have just worked with the belly, taking each point in turn and working through the same sequence of sounds and words.

Here is the whole sequence. Work through it focusing on each point in turn: starting with the top of the diamond point – just below the breast bone – then, moving on to the bottom of the diamond point – just above the pubic bone – and, then, moving on to the sides of the diamond points – on the sides and back of the waist.

Remember that the points of the diamond bounce out and that the more you work with mental bounce – with a flirty, teasing or cocky attitude – the more physical bounce you will have.

- *Stand, as before, with the feet parallel and hipbone width apart, the spine lengthening, the hips and shoulders widening, the buttocks and shoulder blades dropping and the ankle, knee and hip joints loosening.*
- *Firmly touch whichever point you are focusing on – use your thumb or fingers to touch the top point, your fingers to touch the bottom point and your hands to touch the side points.*
- *Say 'psh-psh' with sureness and mental bounce as if you were shooing away a cat. Feel the area you are focusing on bounce out.*
- *Then, say 'Hoo Hoo' several times with great sureness and mental bounce and again feel the area you are focusing on bounce out. Also, remember to work with a sense of the sound coming up from the area and not with any sense of pushing it down.*
- *Then, work through the whole 'Hoo to Hee' sequence in the same way, feeling the area your are focusing on bounce out on every sound:*

  'Hoo Hoo – Hoh Hoh – Hor Hor – Hah Hah – High High – Hey Hey – Hee Hee'

- *Then, giggle the sequence, remembering to release and breathe between giggling each sound:*

  'HooHooHooHooHoo – HohHohHohHohHoh – HorHorHorHorHor – HahHahHahHahHah – HighHighHighHighHigh – HeyHeyHeyHeyHey – HeeHeeHeeHeeHee'

  Then, bounce the sound/word sequences in the same way, making sure you keep your attention on the area you are focusing on rather than letting your attention creep up into the throat:

'Nuh-Nuh'	*'Nuh-Nuh'*	*'Nuh-No'*
'Yuh-Yuh'	*'Yuh-Yuh'*	*'Yuh-Yes'*
'Fuh-Fuh'	*'Fuh-Fuh'*	*'Fuh-Fine'*

- *Then, bounce the phrases in the same way, working with lots of sureness and bounce:*

'High-High'	*'High-High'*	*'Hi!'*
'How-How'	*'How-How'*	*'How are you?'*
'High-High'	*'High-High'*	*'HI'm find thanks!'*
'Hand-Hand'	*'Hand-Hand'*	*'Hand how are you?'*

Work through the whole sequence regularly focusing on each point in turn.

Putting the 'Initiating Sound' section together

Once you have learnt the sequence of *Bouncing the sounds*, *Giggling the sounds*, *Bouncing the words* and *Bouncing the phrases*, it need take no longer than a minute to work through each of the six points – *diaphragm, lower belly, top of diamond, bottom of diamond, sides of diamond.*

So, this whole section need take no more than six minutes and is an excellent warm-up for a rehearsal or performance and, indeed, simply for the day! Added to the fifteen-minute session from the end of the last chapter this will give you a twenty-minute session.

Practise the exercises in this section for about a week before you move on to the calling section.

Calling for Greater Energy and Greater Release

Calling is fantastic for engaging the support muscles and finding good, easy energy. Unlike shouting, which usually involves tension, calling encourages good support and release.

I first worked on calling with Janice Chapman, the singing teacher I mentioned earlier, and for me it was a revelation. I was so used to tensing and pushing because I was worried about not having enough energy. Calling both released the tension in my throat, neck and shoulders and galvanised my horribly sluggish body into amazing and enjoyable activity. If you want good, easy support, start calling!

Basic calling exercise

To experience what happens when you call and also to begin to use the calling energy in your sound and speech

We are going to focus on the points at the sides and the back of the waist for this exercise, because I find these points the easiest and most effective to call from.

Stage one – Experiencing what happens when you call

- *Stand, as before, with the feet parallel and hipbone width apart, the spine lengthening, the hips and shoulders widening, the buttocks and shoulder blades dropping and the ankle, knee and hip joints loosening.*
- *Place your hands on the sides of the waist, as you have done before.*
- *Imagine that you have been on holiday for a couple of weeks and that you are feeling very relaxed and chilled out. Suddenly you catch sight of your best friend at the other end of the beach or across the square. You are delighted to see him or her and you call out to attract their attention: 'Hey'.*
- *What happens when you call out easily? If you are not sure repeat the scenario and call out a few more times. The more relaxed and easy you are, while at the same time being delighted and really wanting to attract your friend's attention, the more you will galvanise the body into easy but energetic action.*
- *Can you feel the sides of your waist move out as you call? For me it really does feel as if I am calling from there. Also, I feel an opening in my whole neck and throat area.*
- *If you can't feel anything go through the usual checks. Is my spine lengthening? Are my joints loose? Is there plenty of mental bounce? The more you call with delight and abandon, the more released energy you will get.*
- *Then, repeat the whole scenario with the hands on the back of the waist.*

Stage two – Calling words and phrases

- *Once you have got the idea, try calling the following phrases, first calling with the hands on the sides of the waist and then with the hands on the back of the waist:*

  'Hey!'
  'Hi!'
  'How are you?'
  'I'm fine!'
  'And how are you?'
  'I'm fine too'

- *As always imagine the voice releasing up from the sides or the back of the waist rather than pushing down.*
- *If you feel you are pushing mentally and that you are unable to let the voice release, try imagining you are a little bit drunk. This usually works.*

- *Now, try alternating between calling the words and phrases and speaking them, keeping the same sense of connection with the sides and back of the waist. Of course, there may not be as much movement when you speak.*

Once you have tried both the sides and the back of the waist, you can choose which you prefer to focus on when speaking, depending on which seems to help most.

Working through this exercise regularly will both strengthen the support muscles and build the habit of released energy.

Shouting without strain

To use the calling mechanism and energy for shouting

When we call there is a natural release, whereas often shouting involves much more grabbing and pushing. By this I mean excess tension in the neck and throat. That is what often makes shouting so unpleasant to listen to. So on stage it is a good idea to base any shouting on 'call release' rather than 'grab and push'. This saves both your voice and the audience's ears! Also, it will allow you much more flexibility and subtlety and ensure the audience actually hear what you say rather than turning off to protect themselves from the onslaught.

- *Having warmed up as described in the last exercise, take the text that you might wish to shout and start by calling it easily. For the moment let go of the intention and emotion that might eventually be behind the text and just get used to releasing those lines on a call, from the sides and then the back of your waist. Have your hands on the sides and then the back of the waist as previously.*
- *Once you are comfortable with this and feel you have a good level both of ease and energy, start to add in the intention or emotion you feel might be behind the text. Don't think of shouting instead think of communicating the intention or the emotion by calling from the sides or back of the waist, depending on which place you find it most effective to call from.*

Far from feeling false, I find that working in this way helps the text to be more connected and makes you feel far more powerful and expressive.

If you regularly practise the text in this way, for short periods, you will find that it will become more natural. Then, you might just need to do a quick 'Psh-Psh' or 'Hey-Hey', with your hands on the sides or the back of the waist, just before you go on stage to remind the muscles to engage.

Screaming without strain

To use the calling mechanism and energy for screaming

Unlike shouting, screaming is a natural release. The problem is that screaming is such a spontaneous, unconscious release that we are not aware of what we are doing. Screaming is an immediate instinctive response to an external stimulus. It simply happens. But, particularly in rehearsal, that stimulus is often missing. We know we have to react by screaming but there is nothing to provoke that release so instead we often grab and push.

> **Note**
> If a person is very tense and held, a scream will not be able to naturally release and in the process of screaming they may cause themselves vocal strain. Babies and children, however, unless traumatised, can scream without vocal harm. I remember the child of a friend of mine jumping up and down a staircase, screaming on each step. He was playing and was vocally at ease as he screamed. The only strain that occurred was to our ears; his throat was fine!

In a way you can't practise screaming you have to let it happen. What you can do is prepare by calling.

- *Again, prepare by warming up as described in the basic calling exercise – stage one (page 105).*
- *Then, practise calling the text or sounds you have to scream. Call with great playfulness and delight and bounce so you really wake up and engage the support muscles and the release mechanism.*

Then, forget about the text, or sounds, and focus on what makes your character scream because it is this stimulus, in the end, which will provoke you to release a scream.

Above all don't worry about screaming, that will only make you tense. Practise calling regularly so that you really connect with the waist and, then, trust your body and voice to sort it out.

Putting the 'Calling' section together

There is no need to regularly explore the shouting and screaming unless you need to for a particular play. Simply working on calling will keep you prepared. So just add a minute of calling to the earlier exercises in this chapter. This will give you seven-minute session to add to the fifteen minutes from the end of the previous chapter.

Practise the calling exercises for a couple of days before moving on to the next area.

Sustaining the Sound

Now that we have explored *initiating* the sound from the various support points, we are going to look at *sustaining* that sound from the same points. We are going to start by working with the lower belly and pelvic floor muscles that we worked on in '***Long and wide – engaging and releasing***' (*page 78*).

We are going to work against the wall again so that it is easier to check that you're lengthening and widening rather than collapsing down and in, since collapsing is one of the greatest enemies of sustained sound.

Sustaining the sound by engaging the lower belly and pelvic floor muscles throughout the breath

To practise continuing to engage the lower belly and pelvic floor muscles throughout the sound

- *Stand with your back against the wall, as you have done previously, with your feet a couple of inches away from the wall, parallel and hipbone width apart, with the weight equally distributed between each foot and between the heels and the balls of the feet. Bend the knees very slightly and, again, let your back rest against the wall as if you were lying on the floor. Place a cushion behind your head if necessary, to prevent the back of the neck shortening.*
- *Think of your spine lengthening in both directions, your buttocks and shoulder blades gently dropping down your back and your hips and shoulders widening. Check that ankle, knee and hip joints are loose.*
- *Place your hands just below your navel as before. Again, imagine the spine lengthening and the hips and shoulders widening.*

Stage one – *Sustaining sound from the lower belly*

- *To reconnect with the belly bounce 'Hoo Hoo' a few times, just as you did earlier in the 'Bouncing the sound from the lower belly exercise' (page 107) and feel the area just below the navel being gently but firmly pulled in on each 'Hoo'.*
- *Then, bounce 'Hoo Hoo' again but keep sounding out on the second 'Hoo' for as long as your breath comfortably lasts. Eg: 'Hoo Hoooooooooooooooooo'. As you do so imagine the sound flowing up from the area just below the navel and this area being slowly pulled inwards and upwards as the sound releases.*
- *As always, it is important that you don't consciously do the pulling. If you keep mentally engaged with the idea of the sound flowing up from the belly and of the*

belly, just below the navel, being gently and slowly pulled inwards and upwards as the sound releases, then, the belly will work itself.

Repeat this a few times until it feels comfortable.

Stage two – Sustaining sound from the lower belly and pelvic floor

- *Now, repeat the exercise again, but, this time, in the second half of the breath mentally reach down into the base of the belly and the pelvic floor as if scooping the sound up from there. This mental scooping will cause the base of the belly and the pelvic floor muscles to engage, as we saw in the last chapter.*

- *Repeat this exercise a few times really reaching down mentally for the sound. Check that the spine stays long, especially in the upper back and neck and that the shoulder area stays relaxed and wide, with the shoulder blades dropping.*

- *Now, play through each of the following sounds with the idea of the sound coming first from just below the navel as the belly there is pulled in and up and, then, mentally reaching down into the base of the belly and the pelvic floor for the sound in the second half of the breath:*

  'Hoo Hooooooooo'
  'Hoh Hoooooooh'
  'Hor Hooooooooor'
  'Hah Haaaaaaaaah'
  'High Hiiiiiiiiiigh'
  'Hey Heeeeeeeeey'
  'Hee Heeeeeeeeee'

- *Practise this exercise regularly going through each sound once.*

Sustaining the sound by engaging the 'oomph points' throughout the breath

To practise continuing to engage the diamond points to sustain the sound

We are now going to work with the points of diamond using the same set of sounds. Remember that whereas the belly moves in and up the diamond points move out.

With the belly we worked on sustaining the sound by mentally reaching down into the lower belly and pelvic floor in the second half of the breath. With the diamond points we are going to work on sustaining the sound by mentally directing the diamond point we are focusing on to continue moving out as we continue to release the breath or sound. By mentally directing the diamond points to move out we enable them to stay engaged so they can continue to support and so sustain the breath and voice.

Start by focusing on the top of the diamond point – just below the breastbone.

- *Stand with your back against the wall, as you have done previously, with your feet a couple of inches away from the wall, parallel and hipbone width apart, with the weight equally distributed between each foot and between the heels and the balls of the feet. Bend the knees very slightly and, again, let your back rest against the wall as if you were lying on the floor. Place a cushion behind your head, if necessary, to prevent the back of the neck shortening.*
- *Think of your spine lengthening in both directions, your buttocks and shoulder blades gently dropping down your back and your hips and shoulders widening. Check that ankle, knee and hip joints are loose.*
- *Firmly touch the point you are focusing on – use your thumb or fingers for the top point, your fingers for the bottom point and your hands for the side and back of waist points.*
- *To reconnect with the diamond point you are focusing, bounce 'Hoo Hoo' a few times and feel the point move out on each 'Hoo'.*
- *Then, bounce 'Hoo Hoo' again, but keep sounding out on the second 'Hoo' for as long as your breath comfortably lasts, i.e. 'Hoo Hoooooooooooooooo'. As you do so imagine the point you are focusing on continuing to move out as you sound out.*
- *As always you don't have to consciously 'do' it. If you keep mentally engaged with the idea of the point continuing to move out as you sound out, then, that point will stay engaged throughout the sound.*
- *Remember to let the point relax back in at the end of the breath/sound.*
- *Play through each of the following sounds with the same idea of the point you are focusing on continuing to move out as you sound out. Remember to let the point relax back in at the end of the breath/sound:*

'Hoo Hooooooooo'
'Hoh Hoooooooh'
'I lor I looooooooor'
'Hah Haaaaaaaah'
'High Hiiiiiiiiiigh'
'Hey Heeeeeeeey'
'Hee Heeeeeeeee'

Now repeat the sequence focusing on the bottom of the diamond point – just above the pubic bone – then, on the sides of diamond points – the sides and back of waist.

Putting the 'Sustaining the Sound' section together

In order to save time you can go through the 'Hoo Hoo' sequence once. Focusing on the top point of the diamond for two or three sounds and, then, on the bottom point of the diamond for two or three sounds and, then, on the sides and back of the waist for two or three sounds. Obviously, keep changing which point you focus on for which sound. Done in this way the exercise need only take three minutes, so added to the earlier exercises in this chapter it will give you a ten-minute session to add to the fifteen-minute session from the end of the previous chapter.

Taking the Support Work into Text

Now that you have got used to both initiating sounds, words and phrases and sustaining sounds we are going to look at taking the support work into text.

We are going to start by looking at supporting the *beginning* of each phrase or sentence and, then, we will move onto looking at *sustaining* that support throughout each phrase or sentence.

The technique is exactly as we have been practising throughout this chapter, so you are simply applying what you have already learnt.

Initiating supported speech

Again, we are going to work through the various support points – that is the belly and the diamond points – separately. The reason for this is because it is simpler and allows you to check that all parts of your support system are working. However, in reality all these points work together and having got all the points up and running you can feel free to focus on whichever point you find most helpful, which may change from character to character.

We are not going to work with the diaphragm here. We focused on it earlier because it is a helpful way of connecting the voice. It is a first step on the way to connecting with the abdominal muscles – the belly and the 'oomph points' – which is what we are focusing on here.

Initiating supported speech from the lower belly

To engage the lower belly support muscles as you begin to speak

- *Stand, as before, with the feet parallel and hipbone width apart, the spine lengthening, the hips and shoulders widening, the buttocks and shoulder blades dropping and the ankle, knee and hip joints loosening.*

- *Bounce through the 'Hoo Hoo' sequence, as before (see page 102) to engage the belly muscles:*

  'Hoo Hoo – Hoh Hoh – Hor Hor – Hah Hah – High High – Hey Hey – Hee Hee'

- *Then, take some text and break it down into phrases or sentences that make sense and that can be comfortably said in one breath. I have divided up a speech from 'Stanley' by Pam Gems to give you an idea. The slashes represent the division points.*

  Hilda: You resent them. / You resent the time I spend with them . . . / look at your face. / You . . . who talk and talk and talk of your own family, / your parents, your brothers, your beloved sisters –

- *As we did with the practice phrases earlier in the chapter (page 103) we are going to use the double bounce to begin each phrase. The reason for this is that it ensures that the support muscles engage.*

- *So, double bounce the first sound of each phrase twice, adding an 'h' if the phrase starts with a vowel. Feel the belly muscles engage and move in. Then, say the whole phrase with the same sense of initial bounce or engagement of the belly muscles as you start to speak. Keep your attention on the belly where your hands are and work with plenty of mental bounce and easy sureness. If you are at all tentative the muscles won't engage. Again, I have given an example below.*

  Yuh-yuh Yuh-yuh You resent them

  Yuh-yuh Yuh-yuh You resent the time I spend with them

  Luh-luh Luh-luh Look at your face

  Yuh-yuh Yuh-yuh You . . .

  Hoo-Hoo Hoo-Hoo who talk and talk and talk of your own family

  Yuh-yuh Yuh-yuh Your parents, your brothers, your beloved sisters

It is useful to work through a variety of different texts in this way to build the habit of engaging the support muscles as you start to speak. Also, it is good to regularly work through any text you are going to perform in this way, just to remind your body that this is how you want it to work.

Initiating supported speech from the 'oomph points'

To engage the diamond points as you begin to speak

Now we are going to work in the same way focusing on each of the diamond points in turn. Start, as before, with the top point, just below the breastbone.

Then, moving on to the bottom point, just above the pubic bone. Then moving on to the side points, focusing first on the sides of the waist and, then, on the back of the waist.

Remember that these diamond points bounce out rather than in.

Follow this sequence for each point:

- *Stand, as before, with the feet parallel and hipbone width apart, the spine lengthening, the hips and shoulders widening, the buttocks and shoulder blades dropping and the ankle, knee and hip joints loosening.*
- *First, bounce through the 'Hoo Hoo' sequence to engage the particular diamond point muscles that you are working on.*
- *Then, take each phrase of the text, as you did above. Double bounce the first sound and feel the muscles you are focusing on move out. Then, say the whole phrase with the same sense of the muscles moving out when you start to speak. Again, work with a great deal of mental bounce and easy sureness, with the image of speaking from whichever point you are focusing on.*

Again, work with a variety of texts to build up the habit of engaging the support as you start to speak and work through any texts you are going to perform to remind your body that this is how you want it to work.

Calling the text

To galvanise the support system when you are speaking

Once you are happy with initiating supported speech as described above, then it is really worth working with calling since this encourages the support muscles to engage with even more bounce and gives you a great sense of ease and power, even when speaking quietly.

- *Stand, as before, with the feet parallel and hipbone width apart, the spine lengthening, the hips and shoulders widening, the buttocks and shoulder blades dropping and the ankle, knee and hip joints loosening.*
- *Place your hands on the sides or back of your waist as you prefer.*
- *First, call easily and freely on 'Hey Hey' and feel the support muscles in the sides or back of the waist moving out.*
- *Then, alternate between calling and speaking until you feel there is the same level of activity in and connection with the support muscles in the sides or back of the waist when you talk as you do when you call.*

Sustaining supported speech

Now that you have practised engaging the various support muscles as you start to speak, it is time to practise sustaining that engagement as you continue to speak. We are going to use the same approach as we used for sustaining sound earlier in the chapter (see page 109-112).

Engaging the lower belly and pelvic floor muscles throughout speaking

To practise continuing to engage the lower belly and pelvic floor muscles to support and sustain speech

Again we are going to start with the belly and pelvic floor muscles.

- *Stand, as before, with the feet parallel and hipbone width apart, the spine lengthening, the hips and shoulders widening, the buttocks and shoulder blades dropping and the ankle, knee and hip joints loosening.*
- *To reconnect with the belly sound out on a short 'Hoo' followed by a long 'Hoooooo' as you did earlier (see page 109). Feel the belly begin to be pulled in and up gently but firmly on the first short 'Hoo' and, then, feel the belly continue to be pulled slowly in and up on the sustained 'Hooooo', all the time imagining the sound flowing up from the belly to the lips.*
- *Then, release the belly at the end of the out-breath/sound and let the new breath come in by itself.*
- *Repeat the 'Hoo Hooooooooo' again, mentally reaching down into the lower belly and pelvic floor, to scoop up the sound, on the second half of the breath.*
- *Now, we are going to work with the text in a similar way, bouncing the first sound of the phrase as we have before and, then, flowing straight into the rest of the phrase releasing it on a chant, e.g. 'Yuh-yooo – whooo – tuuulk – aaand – taaalk'.*

> **Note**
> Chanting helps flow and vocal release because by allowing the vowels more time and running one word into the next there is less chance of the breath being held back or stopped.

- *Feel the belly being gently but firmly pulled in on the first bounce and, then, feel the belly continue to be pulled in and up slowly and smoothly as you chant the rest of the phrase. Keep imagining the text flowing up from the belly.*
- *Once you are happy with this, increase the length of the phrase slightly and add mentally reaching down for breath/sound in the second half of the breath.*

- *Remember to release the belly at the end of each breath and to allow the new in-breath to flow in by itself.*
- *Once you are happy with this, alternate between chanting and speaking, keeping the same sense of flow from, and connection with, the belly and pelvic floor when you speak as you have when you chant.*

Again, work with a variety of texts to build up the habit of sustaining the support as you continue to speak and regularly work through any texts you are going to perform to remind your body that this is how you want it to work.

Note

Remember that the more you put your attention on your belly and imagine speaking from there and the more mentally bouncy you are, the more the belly and pelvic floor muscles will engage.

Engaging the 'oomph points' throughout speech

To practise continuing to engage the 'oomph points' to support and sustain speech

Now we are going to work on continuing to engage each of the diamond points. Again, we will start with the top point, just below the breastbone. Then, move on to the bottom point, just above the pubic bone. Then, move on to the side points of the diamond, focusing first on the sides of the waist and, then, on the back of the waist.

Again, follow this sequence for each point:

- *Stand, as before, with the feet parallel and hipbone width apart, the spine lengthening, the hips and shoulders widening, the buttocks and shoulder blades dropping and the ankle, knee and hip joints loosening.*

Note

Remember that imagining these muscles moving further out as you continue to make sound is a device to keep the muscles engaging throughout and prevent them from relaxing back in during the sound. Do, however, remember to release them at the end of the out-breath/sound.

- *First, work with the Hoo Haaaaaa sound, as before, feeling the muscles at whichever point you are focusing on move out as you start the sound and, then, imagining those muscles moving further out as you continue to make the sound.*
- *Then, take the text and bounce the first sound of the phrase, as before and again flow straight into the rest of the phrase, releasing it on a chant.*
- *Feel the muscles at whichever point you are focusing on move out on the initial bounce and then imagine them moving out further as you chant the phrase.*

It is good to work with all the points in turn on a variety of texts, but if you find one particular diamond point is more helpful that would be the one you would focus on when practising a text for rehearsal and performance.

Putting this Chapter together with the previous Chapter

I have taken out the support exercises you did with breath at the end of the first chapter and replaced them with the sounded support exercises that you have done in this chapter. This will give you a twenty-minute session that you can use as a warm-up before exploring the areas in the next chapter.

Note

Again, the page numbers refer to the original exercises in case you want to refresh your memory. Obviously, you do not need to do the exploratory parts of the exercise each time, simply work through as suggested at the end of the relevant exercise or section.

Warm-up (2 minutes)

Freeing the Breath (68)

Floor work (4 minutes)

Centring the Breath (69)

Releasing the Breath – 2 (72)

Opening the throat (72)

Engage, release and 'H' breath (this is not described above as such. It is simply the version against the wall – page 84 – done on the floor)

Standing (14 minutes)

Engage, release and 'H' breath (against wall) (84)

Engage, release and 'H' breath (with chair) (84)

Bouncing sound from the diaphragm (99)

Bouncing sound from the lower belly (102)

Bouncing sound from the 'oomph points' (103)

Calling (105)

Engaging the lower belly and pelvic floor muscles throughout the sound (109)

Engaging the 'oomph points' throughout the sound (110)

5

Releasing the Sound

In the last chapter we ignored the throat and mouth area and focused on the parts of the body that support the sound. Now that we have begun that work, it will be easier to remove any tension in the throat, jaw, tongue and soft palate to allow full vocal release. That is what we will explore in this chapter.

Full vocal release is important not only from a vocal health point of view but also from an artistic point of view. When we allow our voice to release fully and freely we allow our unique response to the text to release. The voice then has a freshness and spontaneity and feels truer both for the actor and the audience.

So this chapter is about *letting go* of any tension that *interferes* with full and free release and, also, about *building* good muscle use that *enables* full and free release.

The enemies of vocal release

Tension in the throat and mouth area has many causes and we will look at these in detail as we go through this chapter, but I would like to talk about a couple of causes now.

The first is lack of trust. This may be lack of trust in our *voice itself* or in the *content* of what we say. The lack of trust causes us to hold in the throat as a way of *monitoring* what is coming out. The voice, then, feels blocked and less powerful and, as a result, we may then push in an attempt to release the voice, which only creates further tension.

Also, if there has been a history of voice loss or strain, we may lose trust in our throat's ability to operate healthily and so we may unconsciously hold in the throat to protect it and so end up bringing about the very vocal strain we are striving to resolve.

We have to learn to trust the throat, our voice and the content of what we say in order that the tension and holding can release. This building of trust needs to go hand in hand with any physical work; otherwise the physical work will be far less effective.

So, ask yourself *'Do I trust my voice? Do I trust my throat? Do I trust what I might say?'* If the answer to any of these questions is *'No'* or *'I'm not sure'* explore why this might be the case. What has happened in the past to 'wobble' your trust? What negative or fearful thoughts are you feeding yourself? What more positive thoughts could you feed in to help you turn the whole situation around?

If you tell yourself that you have a weak or unreliable or tense voice, then, that is what you will have – however much you work on it. However, if you tell yourself that your voice can be just as strong and reliable and relaxed as anyone else's if you do a small amount of appropriate work daily, then, you allow the physical work to succeed.

The second cause of tension is listening to yourself while you are speaking. This is a form of monitoring, of checking, that stops us being completely free and in the moment. It leads to us being slightly behind or slightly ahead of ourselves and even if it only causes slight tension, it will dampen the spontaneity and freedom and lead us to make more controlled and predictable choices.

I would prefer that you focus on how your voice *feels* from inside rather than on how it *sounds*. However, if you feel you must listen, then record yourself and listen later. Never listen *whilst* you are speaking.

Approaching the work with ease

I have talked a great deal about the link between the physical and the mental. If we want physical release then we need mental release, so, approach the exercises in this chapter with a carefree inquisitiveness rather than a careful apprehension.

Two ways of working on release

Initially, we are going to work through the whole throat and neck area, taking a look at each part in detail, because often we are not aware of exactly what is going on where. There is just a general feeling of the area not being as free as it might be. After that I will give you a set of more 'organic' release exercises, which are very useful for warm-ups and working with text.

We are going to start by taking a look at the larynx and what it needs to work well. This will help you to understand exactly why work on the neck, jaw, soft palate and tongue, as well as the larynx itself, is so crucial in releasing the voice.

THE AMAZING MOVING LARNYX

The larynx is situated above the windpipe at the point where the throat divides into the windpipe and the food pipe. (See diagram 1.) It is suspended and supported in such a way that it is capable of being highly mobile. Place your hand on the front of your neck with your fingers on either side of the bony bulge. This is your larynx. Men's larynxes are larger than women's and so the bony bulge is more prominent. It is what is referred to as the Adam's Apple.

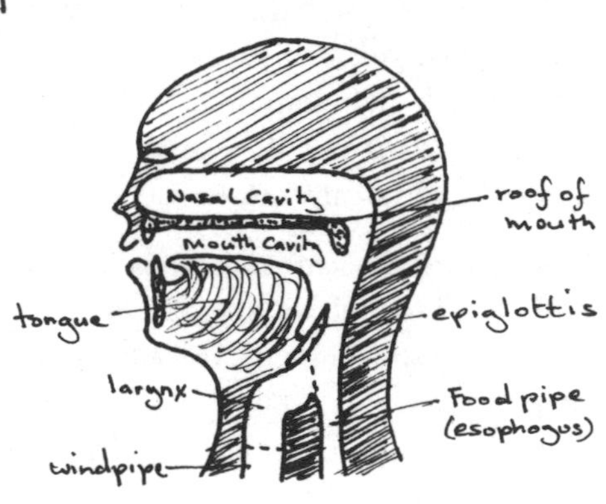

- *With your fingers on the bony bulge swallow and, then, yawn, without opening your mouth too wide. Repeat this sequence a few times.*
- *Can you feel the larynx moving up as you swallow and down as you yawn? If not you might be still opening your mouth too wide on the yawn, so try again, keeping the mouth almost closed as if you were trying to hide the yawn.*
- *Can you feel the upward and downward movement now?*

Ideally the larynx should be able to move freely whatever you are doing, whether it be swallowing, yawning, singing or speaking. If your larynx feels tight don't worry because the exercises in this chapter will take care of that. All you need to know here is that fixing the larynx in any one position is never a good idea.

So what affects the free movement of the larynx?

The head–neck relationship

The position of the head and the neck has a profound effect on the movement of the larynx.

- *Lift your chin up so that the front of your neck lengthens and the back of your neck shortens. Now, swallow and yawn as before. Can you feel that the whole of the front of the neck is tight and that the larynx is far less mobile?*
- *Now, tuck your chin down and in, so that the front of the neck practically disappears. Swallow and yawn again. Can you feel how crushed the front of the neck is and how little room there is for the larynx?*
- *Now, poke your head forward. Can you feel the tautness in the front of the neck and the contraction in the back? Can you feel that the larynx has had to rise and again has less space and mobility? Don't worry if you can't feel everything I suggest or if you feel different things. My questions are just a framework to help you explore.*
- *Whatever you felt, now think of the spine lengthening. Imagine the tailbone dropping towards the floor and the rest of the spine lengthening towards the ceiling. Imagine the shoulder blades dropping gently down the back. As always, don't physically 'do' this, just imagine it happening.*
- *Then, have a sense of the crown of the head floating upwards directly above the spine. Let the jaw and chin and the front of the neck soften.*
- *Then, swallow and yawn again. Can you feel how much freer the larynx is now?*

This doesn't mean that you have to keep your head in one position. If you regularly work with the exercises for lengthening the spine (see page 132) and for freeing the head and neck (see page 135) you will develop a habit of lengthening and releasing that can be taken into any number of positions. What we want to get rid of is any habit of contracting or fixing.

Upper body stability

While you don't want to contract or fix anywhere in the back, neck or head, there is a need for stability in the upper body, neck and head, because the larynx requires a stable framework from which to hang.

If the upper spine collapses and the neck and head poke forward as we speak, the larynx loses its stable framework and so cannot move freely. Also, it is much harder to connect with the breath and almost impossible for the many of the support muscles to work properly.

The lengthening and widening work is, again, of great help here (see page 132). It encourages the postural muscles in the upper back to engage and keep the upper spine and neck aligned, so enabling the head to balance.

Working against the wall (see page 133) is, also, very useful. The more you think of resting back into the wall as you speak, the better: as if the more you rest back the more the sound releases forward.

Imagining the shoulder blades gently dropping down your back as the upper spine lengthens is also very helpful and can have an amazing effect. It is one of my favourites.

If you practise regularly, then, as with all the previous exercises, you can forget about it once you are performing, since you will have built up the habits you want and they will occur naturally.

Opening and releasing, not grabbing and pushing

Too often actors feel the need to grasp and push sound out rather than opening and releasing it. This happens, I suspect, because when they grasp it feels as if they are doing something, whereas with opening and releasing it can feel frighteningly easy and even vulnerable. So, there can be a fear that not enough is being done or that the voice is out of control.

This is why I always work on the support muscles first, as we did in the earlier chapters. Then, you can feel you have somewhere to work from, while leaving the neck and throat area free and open.

Active opening

The only work we are going to explore in relation to the throat area is *active opening.*[16]

This is opening that occurs as a result of muscles *working* as opposed to *passive opening,* which occurs as a result of muscles *relaxing*. We need active opening because this is the best way to counter the tendency of the throat to close or constrict.

16 Jo Estill's work on the larynx has hugely influenced my work in this area. To find out more about her work visit her web site: www.evts.com.

Laughing and crying are examples of *active opening*, whereas yawning is an example of *passive opening*.

We will look later at exercises to actively open the throat. They are great fun and very easy to do and they produce great results. For now explore the following exercise just to get an idea of what I am talking about.

❍ *Silently begin to call out or sing with joy. Can you feel how the base of the neck widens in anticipation of release? There is no sense of strain or tension in the neck just a feeling of the muscles in the base of the neck, just above the collarbone, widening.*

The same happens if we call out in alarm or scream. The larynx may be in a different position but the neck stays wide. These are not grasps they are releases and a free scream, as I mentioned in the last chapter, is the ultimate release.

❍ *Try silently calling out with joy, again and, then, silently scream. Can you feel that the neck movement is similar? Not only the neck but the whole body galvanises itself for release because there is an impulse to express that is not blocked.*

❍ *So keep reminding yourself of this and as often as you like in the day silently call out in joy just to remind yourself what release feels like.*

Note

Working with a feeling of joy is important because when we are happy the body tends to open, so, by using a joyful feeling you can encourage the body to open further and counteract any tendency to close. Then, once you have developed the habit of opening, even if you are working on a very closed character you will be able to retain a degree of openness and so prevent strain.

The jaw position and tension

The *position* of the jaw also affects the freedom of the larynx and the free release of sound.

❍ *Try jutting your lower jaw forward. Can you feel how that tightens the area under the chin and raises the larynx, again decreasing its mobility?*

❍ *Now try opening your mouth as wide as you can, without of course forcing the jaw open! Can you feel how the lower jaw moves down and back making it almost impossible for the larynx to move? This is the jaw position often favoured by pop singers and can be one of the reasons why so many of them suffer vocal fatigue.*

❍ *Now try opening your jaw again, but this time no more than a finger's width. Place your finger between your teeth to check you don't open the front of the jaw much wider than that and then imagine opening more between the back teeth, as if someone has given you a wonderful surprise. Can you feel how much freer your larynx is or how much more space there is in the back of your mouth and throat?*

Again, don't worry about how on earth you are going to act and find this jaw position!

As always it is just a matter of practising the exercises and then forgetting all about it.

Tension in the jaw muscles, even when the jaw is not protruding or over opening, also affects the larynx and the free release of the voice.

The muscles that work the lower jaw are the most powerful in the body.[17]

❍ *Place your hands just below and in front of the ears and clench and unclench your back teeth a few times. Can you feel the muscles bulge out as you clench? Clench and unclench a few more times and see if you can feel a tightening in the temples as well.*

❍ *Tense your jaw muscles again by clenching your teeth and feel what happens under the chin, in the back of the neck and in the shoulders. Can you feel the whole area stiffen up?*

❍ *Try moving the larynx. Can you feel how much less flexible it is?*

❍ *Try opening and shutting the jaw. Can you feel how stiff it is?*

There can be little freedom, flexibility or release when the jaw muscles are tight.

Ideally the jaw needs to hang rather than be held or placed. Using the exercises later in the chapter, you can practise so that such a loose jaw becomes natural and you can forget all about it on stage.

Tension in the back of the neck

The other muscles which affect the free movement of the jaw and, therefore, of the larnyx are those at the top of the back of the neck, either side of the spine, just underneath the back of the skull.

17 See Meribeth Bunch – *Dynamics of The Singing Voice* (page 114).

- ❍ *Try tightening those muscles and then opening and closing your jaw. Can you feel that not only does the back of the neck tighten up but also the front of the neck and the side of the face and under the chin? Can you feel that your jaw does not open and close so freely?*

Loosening the muscles at the top of the back of the neck can lead to a great increase in the freedom of the jaw and this is well worth exploring, which we will do later in this chapter.

A free, comfortable and appropriately open jaw will not only allow the voice to release fully and freely but also enable it to be far more powerful for far less effort.

Note

What to do about clicking jaws

I am always being asked about clicking jaws, why they click and how to stop them. Clenching the back teeth can cause jaw clicking, so the section on Loosening the Jaw (see page 142) will help. In my experience clicking is also often caused by over-opening the jaw. So if your jaw clicks, try the following:

Place your fingers just below your ears behind the jawbone. Then, slide your fingers down the jawbone until you find the corner. Place your fingers just after the turn.

Focusing on the back of the jaw where your fingers are, let that part of your jaw drop open, without force, so that there is no more than a finger's width between the back teeth. Then, lift the jaw back up so that the back teeth lightly touch again.

Drop and lift your jaw in this way several times, keeping your focus on the back rather than the front of the jaw and imagining that your jaw works rather like that of a ventriloquist's dummy.

This should do the trick.

If it doesn't, it may be that the jaw is not moving straight down but rather moving down to one side. This can occur if the muscles on one side are stronger than those on the other side, which might be the case if you tend to chew more on one side than the other.

Try opening and closing your jaw in front of the mirror and see whether or not it is moving straight down.

If it is hard to tell, place your hands firmly on either side of your face, rather like splints, and open and close your jaw slowly, remembering to keep your shoulders and upper back relaxed. This usually picks up any sideways movement.

If you do find some sideways movement, then, continue working with the hands as splints and guides, opening and closing your jaw very slowly so that you can keep the jaw moving straight down.

If none of this does the trick and you are worried about your jaw talk to your doctor or dentist.

The larynx and the tongue – another delicate relationship

The part of the tongue that is visible in the mouth is only two thirds of the whole. The other third extends down into the throat and is attached to a 'horse-shoe-shaped' cartilage called the Hyoid bone.[18] The larynx also attaches to this cartilage, so tension in the tongue affects the larynx. This is especially true of tension in the back of the tongue.

❍ *First, tense the back of the tongue by pushing it up against the roof of the mouth. What effect does this have on the larynx?*

❍ *Then, tense the back of the tongue by pushing it down towards the floor of the mouth. What effect does this have on the larynx?*

❍ *Then, tense the back of the tongue by pulling it back to the rear wall of the mouth. What effect does this have on the larynx?*

❍ *Can you feel how these various tense tongue positions restrict the larynx's mobility? Even if you are not precisely sure what is happening, I am sure you can feel a tightness in the throat area.*

So, keeping the back of the tongue relaxed is important. We'll look at how you do that later in the exercise section. All you need to bear in mind here is that releasing tension in the tongue will allow release in the voice and that flexibility in the tongue will give the voice energy and subtlety, making it more responsive to your thoughts and feelings.

The soft palate

The soft palate is the soft back part of the roof of the mouth (Diagram 2). If you slide the tip of your tongue back across the roof of your mouth you can feel that there is a point where the roof changes from being hard and fixed to being soft and moveable. The soft, moveable part is the soft palate.

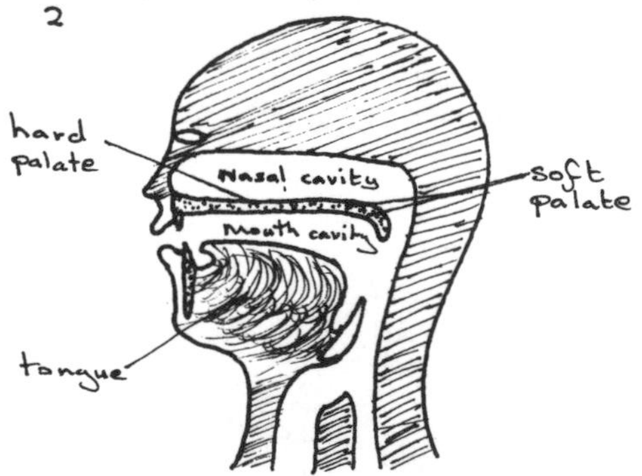

18 This is Meribeth Bunch's description of the hyoid cartilage in *Dynamics of the Singing Voice* (page 63).

The soft palate has the ability to lift or to lower. When you yawn or gasp with surprise it lifts up and back. When you make a 'm, n or ng' sound it drops.

Tension in the soft palate has an effect on the larynx, because there is a muscular connection between the two.

❍ *To locate the soft palate make a 'g' sound a few times.*

❍ *The soft palate lowers to form a closure with the back of the tongue in preparation for the 'g' and, then, lifts up away from the back of the tongue as the 'g' is released.*

❍ *Imagine the area, that has been moving down and up to make the 'g', tensing up and see what effect that has on the throat and larynx.*

❍ *Can you feel how tension in that area tenses up the whole throat? Don't worry too much if you can't feel anything, this can be a difficult area to sense at first.*

Tension in the soft palate also affects the tongue, causing the back of the tongue to be pulled upwards. Equally, tension in the tongue affects the soft palate causing it to be pulled down.[19] So, both need to be released in order for free movement of the larynx and free release of the voice.

INSIDE THE LARYNX

As I described earlier, when we decide to make sound the vocal folds come together to form a light closure across the larynx. Breath flows up from the lungs and is stopped by the light closure of the vocal folds. As a result breath pressure builds up below the folds until the pressure is strong enough to open the folds. As soon as they have been opened breath escapes, so reducing the pressure and, therefore, the folds close again. This all happens incredibly quickly and as a result of this rapid opening and closing the folds are set in vibration. Their vibratory activity in turn causes the breath passing between the folds to also be set in vibration and sound is produced as a result.

What is important here is the *quality of closure of the vocal folds* and the *appropriateness of the breath pressure below the vocal folds*, to the job in hand.

19 See *Dynamics of the Singing Voice* by Meribeth Bunch (page 119).

The *quality of the closure of the folds* is important because it dictates whether the initial sound is firm or breathy or harsh. It also affects our ability to make louder sound.

The *appropriateness of the breath pressure below the vocal folds*, is important because appropriate pressure is the 'fuel' for the voice and without it vocal fatigue and strain can occur. It also affects our ability to make higher sounds.

Quality of closure – firm

Co-ordination is the key to firm closure. This ensures that as the breath begins to flow the folds come together firmly but not tightly. The breath pressure, then, builds up appropriately and is released without force.

Co-ordination is greatly helped by any rhythmical physical activity-swinging, stepping, running or dancing to a regular beat. Rhythmic activity is co-ordinated activity. That is why I have started all the sessions so far with two minutes of marching with arm swinging to free and co-ordinate the body and breath.

Quality of closure – harsh

If the folds come together too tightly, the breath has to build up to a greater pressure before it can open the folds. As a result, the breath bursts the folds apart quite violently, which, in turn, means that they slam together again quite violently. Also, the breath passes through rapidly, because the pressure is so great, and this causes a great deal of friction against the folds. Both the violent opening and closing and the air friction can cause damage to the edges of the folds.

> **Note**
> This type of harsh closure is sometimes referred to as 'harsh glottal attack' and even as 'glottaling'.

This kind of closure is the result of excess tension and effort. It can be caused by an over *effortful* or over *large* in-breath. Over *effortful* in-breaths lead to a great deal of tension in the shoulders and neck. While over *large* in-breaths often result in the vocal folds closing to hold in the large volume of air.

Another cause of harsh closure is over-emphatic speech. This may simply be due to a *physical* habit of over-forceful use but it may also reflect a forceful *attitude*, a *mental* over-compensation. This can be caused by distrust of one's ability to be heard by others, so extra force is added. Obviously, the speaker is not usually aware of how they are closing the vocal folds but the result of their mental push is over-tight vocal closure.

Harsh closure occurs particularly in speech before any vowel that begins a word or syllable, that is why, in the last chapter, we placed an 'H' in front of the vowels because this helps to keep the throat open.

Many of the exercises in the last two chapters on breath and support help to guard against harsh closure. Later in this chapter we will look at some more specific exercises to deal with this issue. (See page 152.)

The point to remember here is that excessive effort when breathing and speaking can lead to harsh closure. For this reason, whenever I am working with people who use excessive effort, I encourage them to work as if they are very, very bored. When we are bored we never try too hard and so this really helps us to ease off the effort without feeling we have to hold back which would not be helpful. So if you suspect that you try too hard, start to practise working with an attitude of confident boredom. It makes a huge difference and really starts to release the voice.

Note

Some accents and languages have hard glottal attack sounds in them that are not the result of excess effort. For example 'water' and 'butter' in cockney. The 't' is not sounded but is replaced by a full but not tense closure of the vocal folds. Because this closure is not tense it does not last so long and so the build-up of pressure is not as strong nor the release as violent. So if hard glottal attack is a natural part of your accent and you have checked that it is not the result of tension, then don't worry about it.

Quality of closure – breathy

If the folds do not come together firmly enough the result is breathy sound because some of the breath is able to escape through the extra space between the folds without being converted into sound. Unless there is an actual problem with the vocal folds, caused by overuse, misuse, illness or external irritants, the cause of insufficient closure is lack of necessary muscle action. The muscles responsible for bringing the vocal folds together fail to work effectively. It could be said they behave rather tentatively and fail to commit.

This may simply be due to a habit of under-energised use but it may also reflect a tentative attitude, a mental holding-back, a wish to not fully commit. This tentativeness may be due to a lack of trust, either in oneself and what one might express, or in the response of the listener or listeners. Breathiness seems to be more common in women than men, at least in the cultures of which I have experience. I have often wondered if this is to do with women being ambivalent about how acceptable their power is – especially to men – or to do with a greater tendency to take on the placating and pleasing role.

Now this is a thorny area to get into and I am not saying breathiness always means this or that. I merely want you to think about the links between how people feel about communicating, what they use communication for and how they actually speak. Often once this link is made and understood, it is easier to change vocal habits. If, of course, that is what the person wishes to do.

Using mental bounce together with the support work, as we did in the last chapter (see page 98) helps breathy attack and we will also look at some more specific exercises later in this chapter. (See page 155.) The main point here is that tentativeness does not help here. Where people have breathy closure I encourage them to work with a sense of easy interest and sureness, since this helps the muscles to more fully and actively engage without the danger of over-effort.

Breath pressure – appropriate

As I mentioned earlier, appropriate breath pressure is the 'fuel' for the voice. Appropriate breath pressure is helped by good posture, easy, unforced breath and engaged and alive support muscles, all of which we have begun to explore.

Breath pressure – too much

If the breath is expelled from the body overforcefully the breath pressure is increased and flows so strongly through the folds that it prevents them from coming together appropriately. Excessive pressure causes friction and can, at the very least, dry the folds.

So what causes excessive breath pressure? Forced expiration of any kind. Taking in a huge amount of breath and, then, dropping the upper chest rapidly and, so, forcing the breath out may be the cause. Also, over working the belly muscles. So, finding an easy in-breath, a long spine and engaged rather than forced belly muscles on the out-breath guard against excessive breath pressure.

Breath pressure – too little

Too little breath pressure affects our ability to make higher or louder sounds.

Under-active *out-breath muscles* (i.e. the abdominal and pelvic floor muscles) will, therefore, prevent us from producing high notes effectively and healthily. While under-active *laryngeal muscles*, responsible for closing the vocal folds appropriately, will prevent us from producing louder sounds effectively and healthily.

We looked in the last two chapters at engaging the out-breath muscles effectively (see page 86 on and 98 on) and later in this chapter we will look at closing the vocal folds appropriately. (See page 156.) The main point here is to remember that if you work with easy interest and sureness and a lot of mental bounce both the muscles in the larynx and the belly will naturally be more engaged.

NOW TO WORK

Hopefully the introduction to this chapter will have given you some idea of the areas we need to work on to release sound. Some of the areas are continuations of work in previous chapters – for example the work on lengthening and widening. Other areas of work are new – for example freeing the jaw, tongue and soft palate and opening the throat.

As in the body work chapter, don't try to force relaxation and release. Just be present with any holding, letting yourself become more aware of what you are up to. In this way, what is actually happening will become clearer and clearer and so it will be easier to apply the exercises and build up new more helpful habits.

Use the session suggested at the end of the previous chapter as preparation and then explore the sections in this chapter one at a time, moving on to next section as and when you feel ready.

Stabilising the Upper Body

All the exercises in this section use *mental focus* to engage and strengthen the muscles that hold the body erect. By feeding in directions to lengthen and widen, the postural muscles are stimulated to engage. By *continuing* to feed in lengthening and widening directions the postural muscles are stimulated to continue to engage and so they are strengthened.

Lengthening

To engage and strengthen the postural muscles

This is a reprise of an exercise from the body chapter, with a few additions.

- *Stand with the feet hipbone width apart and parallel and the ankle, knee and hips joints loose.*
- *Check that the hips are resting directly over the ankles, with the weight evenly distributed between both feet and between the heels and the balls of the feet. Imagine the buttocks dropping gently downwards.*
- *Check that the ribs are resting directly over the hips and that the shoulders are resting directly over the ribs, with the shoulder blades dropping gently down the back.*
- *Check that the neck is resting directly over the shoulders and that the head is resting directly over the neck.*
- *Then, focus on the spine. Imagine the tailbone dropping down towards the floor while the top of the spine moves up towards the ceiling, so that the spine lengthens.*
- *As always simply imagine this rather than consciously 'doing' it. Keep soft and flexible so the muscles lengthen subtly as a result of your mental focus rather than tensing and stiffening because you have pulled your back straight.*
- *Imagine the crown of the head floating towards the ceiling in the same way, so that the head stays soft and flexible.*
- *Once you have gone through the above directions, focus on a project or idea that really interests you. Let that feeling of interest flood into the spine and lengthen it further.*
- *Stay with this sense of an interested, lengthening spine for a minute or two.*

The more you can do the exercise throughout the day the better: try it whenever you are waiting for a bus or train and, also, when in the queue at the post office or supermarket. You can also practise it sitting down, when commuting and even while working at the computer.

Little and often is the best way to build up a new habit and the more you practise the more you won't have to think about your posture in rehearsals and on stage.

Widening

To further engage and strengthen the postural muscles

Having revisited the lengthening we are now going to revisit the widening.

- *Stand as above with a sense of lengthening in place then, focus on the hips and imagine them widening.*
- *Then, focus on the shoulders and, in the same way, visualise them widening.*
- *As always there is no need to consciously 'do' the widening just imagine it and let your imagination direct the muscles.*

> **Note**
> When waiting for an audition, it is very useful to practise lengthening and widening, together with the centring from the bodywork chapter. It stops you from tightening up and closing down.

Again, this can be practised whenever you are standing or sitting and waiting or travelling.

Working against the wall

To avoid spine slumping and head poking

As I mention earlier, this exercise is very useful if you have a tendency to poke your head forward and really allows your voice and your work to be released rather than pushed out.

- *Stand with your feet parallel, hipbone width apart and a couple of inches away from the wall, and your knees very slightly bent.*
- *Rest your back against the wall just as you did in previous chapters (see page 84). Remember the whole back will not be touching the wall since there is a natural arch in the small of the back, but to check you are not over-arching think of the tail bone dropping towards the floor as the rest of the spine lengthens towards the ceiling.*

- *If your head rests easily against the wall without the back of the neck shortening and the chin lifting that is fine. However, if the back of the neck is shortening and the chin lifting, place a cushion behind your head. (See diagram 3.)* 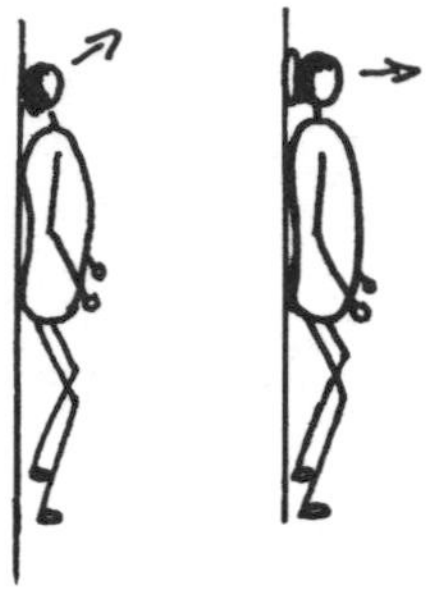
- *Imagine lengthening and widening as before, but also imagine resting back against the wall.*
- *Then, practise any of the sustained breath or sound exercises which focus on the sound coming from the belly (see page 84 and 109) checking that you continue to lengthen, widen and lean back throughout.*
- *Then, try a piece of text allowing yourself to be as animated and committed to the piece as you would like to be in performance, but imagine that the more you want to release the piece forward, the more you lean back.*
- *Feel free to move your arms about as much as you like, as long as your shoulder blades stay touching the wall and gently dropping downwards.*
- *In this way you will break the habit of wanting to poke your head forward to contact the audience or the other actors or to emphasise a point.*

Wide arms

To further avoid spine slumping and head poking and further strengthen the postural muscles

This is a reprise of another exercise from the body work chapter (see page 54). It is excellent for preventing the spine from slumping and the head from poking forward and it will really help you to open up and reconnect with your breath and support.

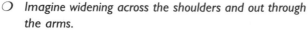

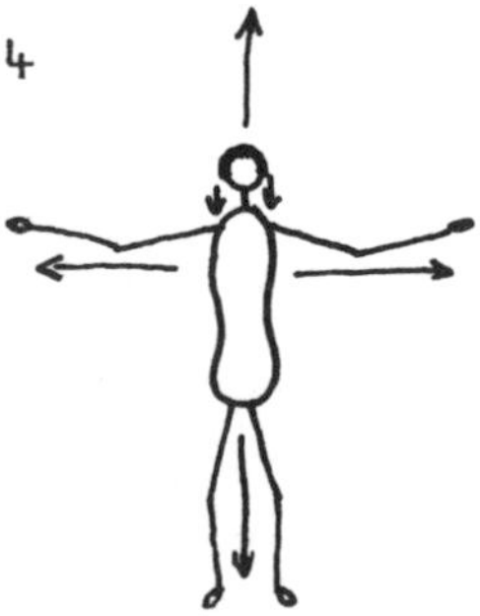

- *Stand away from the wall, lining yourself up as you did in the lengthening exercise.*
- *Let your arms float out and up to shoulder level, with the palms facing forwards. Check that the shoulders stay low and soft, by imagining that your shoulder blades are dropping gently down your back. (See diagram 4.)*
- *Imagine widening across the shoulders and out through the arms.*
- *Then, try any of the sustained breath or voice exercises, which focus on the sound coming from the belly (see pages 84 and 109) thinking of lengthening and*

widening as you do so. Obviously, rest your arms when you need to rather than using tension to keep them in place.

- *Then, try a piece of text, in the same position, thinking of lengthening and widening as you say it. Again, rest your arms as necessary.*

Putting the 'Stabilising the Body' section together

Most of this section can be practised as you go about your daily life. The wall and wide arms exercises can be practised with text to finish the session outlined at the end of the last chapter, which would therefore only add a couple of minutes, making the session twenty-two minutes long.

Releasing the Shoulders and Neck and Balancing the Head

Once you have created stability in the upper body it is much easier to release tension in the shoulders and neck and find a balanced and free position for the head.

Side to side

To release the neck and shoulder muscles. To strengthen and balance the front and back neck muscles. To centre and balance the head

This exercise is based on one that comes from a set of exercises known as 'Brain Gym'.[20] These physical exercises enhance 'whole brain learning' – in other words they get all the parts of the brain working effectively. I use it because I find it excellent for releasing shoulder and neck tension. As before keep the movement flowing and the breath easy.

- *Stand or sit, as before, with the spine lengthening, the hips and shoulders widening, the joints loosening and the shoulder blades and buttocks dropping gently down the back.*
- *Place your right hand on your left shoulder and, with your fingers, gently squeeze just behind the shoulder bone. Check your shoulder blades are still dropping gently down your back, so that your body spine is staying straight rather than slumping due to the weight of the head. (See diagram 5.)*

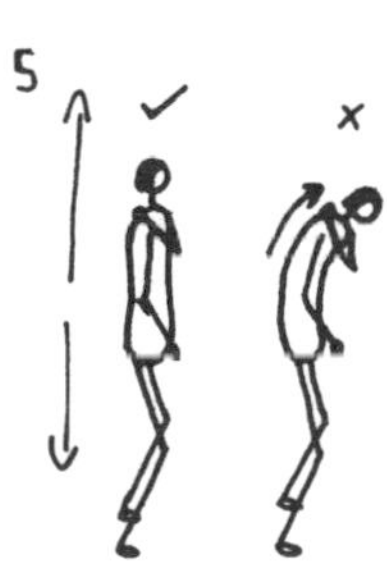

20 *Brain Gym, Teacher's Edition,* can be ordered from Body Balance Books, 12, Golders Rise, Hendon, London, NW4 2HR. Tel: 020 8202 9747 Fax: 020 8202 3890. The teacher's edition is the best one to get because it explains what each exercise is for. It is simple to follow and has pictures, which are always a plus!

- *Turn your head to look over your left shoulder as you breathe out. Then, breathe in while your head rests in this position and, then, on the next out-breath turn your head round to look over the right shoulder. Again, breathe in this position and, then, again on the out-breath turn your head back to look over the left shoulder.*
- *Repeat this whole sequence five times. Then, let your head roll down, so that your chin rests on your chest while the body spine stays long. Rest in this position for a few breaths, then, on an out-breath starting from the base of the back of the neck build up through the neck spine, placing each neck vertebra on top of the one below until you are looking straight ahead.*
- *Then, repeat the exercise with the left hand on the right shoulder.*

Half neck circles

To release the neck

This is a simple exercise but can be very effective. Keep the movement smooth and flowing and make sure you breathe easily. Check that the jaw is as loose as it can be at the moment.

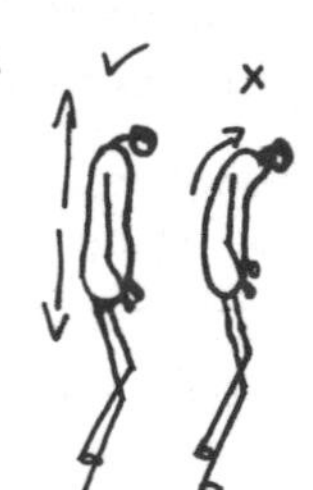

- *Stand or sit, as before, with the spine lengthening, the hips and shoulders widening, the joints loosening and the shoulder blades and buttocks gently dropping down your back.*
- *Drop the head forward so that the chin is on the chest. Check that the body spine stays long and that the shoulder blades are continuing to drop gently down your back, so your upper spine does not slump. (See diagram 6.)*
- *Keeping your chin as close to your chest as possible, roll your head over to the left and, then, up until the left ear is directly over the left shoulder. Breathe in in this position and then, as you breathe out, roll back down to the centre and on up to the right, until the right ear is over the right shoulder. Again, breathe in in this position and on the out-breath roll back down to the middle and up to the left.*
- *Remember to gently drop the shoulder blades down the back throughout.*
- *Repeat this whole sequence five times. Then, let your head roll down so that your chin rests on your chest again. Rest in this position for a few breaths then, on an out-breath, starting from the base of the back of the neck build up through the neck spine, placing each neck vertebra on top of the one below until you are looking straight ahead.*

Nose Circles

To release the back of the neck

This is an excellent exercise for massaging and releasing the back of the neck. Again keep the movement flowing and the breath easy. Let the jaw relax and hang slightly open.

- *Stand or sit, as before, with the spine lengthening, the hips and shoulders widening, the joints loosening and the shoulder blades and buttocks gently dropping down your back.*
- *Imagine that you have a felt-tip pen on the end of your nose and that you are going to draw a circle with it.*
- *Start to circle smoothly and quite slowly round in a clockwise direction, making the circle bigger or smaller as necessary until you can feel the movement massaging the base of your neck.*
- *Once you can feel this, circle three times clockwise and three times anti-clockwise. Imagining that you are easing out the back of the neck as you do so.*
- *Then, make the circle a little smaller so that you feel that you are massaging just above the base of the neck. Again circle three times clockwise and three times anti-clockwise.*
- *Continue slowly in this way with the circles getting smaller and smaller until you have worked your way up to the top of the neck.*

Nose figures of eight

To further release the back of the neck

This exercise is identical to the one above but instead of circles you trace sideways figures of eights with your nose.

- *As before start with large figures of eights so you are massaging the base of the neck and remember to go three times in both directions. Then, gradually let the figures of eights get smaller and smaller, keeping the movement smooth and fairly slow.*

Head nods

To further release the back of the neck

- *Stand or sit, as before, with the spine lengthening, the hips and shoulders widening, the joints loosening and the shoulder blades and buttocks gently dropping down the back.*

- *Keeping the neck long and the jaw loose and, just pivoting from the top of the neck, nod down a little and then relax so you are looking straight ahead again.*
- *Think of the nod downward as a drop and of the movement back up as a release. Make sure you end up looking straight ahead each time rather than looking up.*
- *Repeat this several times thinking 'drop – release, drop – release, drop – release' and keeping your neck spine long and your jaw loose.*
- *As you nod, focus on the idea of the muscles either side of the spine at the top of the neck softening.*

Once you have finished this set of exercises, stand for a moment, imagining the spine lengthening and the crown of the head floating up towards the ceiling.

Putting the 'Releasing the Shoulders and Head and Balancing the Neck' section together

These exercises need take no more than a minute each, which means this section need take no longer than five minutes in total.

You may want to add these exercises to the session you are already doing so that they come after the floor work.

Together with the two minutes from the last section in this chapter that would give you a twenty-seven minute session.

Opening the Throat and Releasing the Sound

Some of the exercises in this section are inspired by the work of Jo Estill, which I have found very valuable. The 'Widening and opening' and 'Giggle and Sob' exercises are my versions of a few aspects of her work that I have found most useful when working with actors.

Widening and Opening

To engage and strengthen the muscles in the side of the neck

- *Sit or stand as before, directing the back to lengthen and the shoulders and hips to widen. Check the feet are parallel and hip width apart, the joints are loose and the shoulder blades and buttocks are dropping gently down the back.*
- *Imagine that someone has done something or given you something that is a wonderful surprise. The kind of surprise that completely opens you up. I call this*

a 'soft surprise' as opposed to the 'hard surprise' that is more shocked and, so, more grabbed and tight.

- *Breathe in almost silently with that feeling of wonderful soft surprise. Can you feel what happens in the base of your neck just above the collarbone? Can you feel the neck widening and opening? If you are not sure try again with a bigger sense of surprise.*
- *Try this a few times until you really get a sense of this opening. Then, as you breathe out imagine the neck widening and opening even more with surprise.*
- *Then, practise breathing in and out silently for about a minute keeping this sense of surprise constant so that the base of the neck just above the collarbone stays constantly wide and open. I find it helps to imagine being a little more surprised with each in-breath and each out-breath.*
- *Once you have got the hang of this you can practise speaking some text with the sense of surprise and the widening, opening neck.*

Eventually you won't need to think of the surprise, you will simply be able to direct your neck to widen and it will do so. The surprise is a 'device' to initially achieve the behaviour you want.

As always, it is your mental direction that engages the muscles and you will notice that, although they are working, the neck never becomes rigid.

Freeing the Larynx – I

To relax the muscles that suspend the larynx

Having widened and opened the neck and thereby created space and stability, we are going to focus on the larynx itself.

- *Sit or stand as before, directing the back to lengthen and the shoulders and hips to widen. Check that the feet are parallel and hip width apart, that the joints are loose and that the shoulder blades and buttocks are gently dropping down your back.*
- *Find your larynx by gently moving the thumb and fingers of one hand up and down the front of your neck until you find the boniest part.*
- *Hold the larynx between your fingers and thumb and very gently move the larynx very slightly from side to side. Check that the neck spine continues to lengthen and that the chin stays level rather than lifting. Let the jaw be loose and slightly dropped so there is a finger's width gap between the teeth.*

- *Continue this gently for thirty seconds to a minute focusing your attention on the area surrounding the larynx and imagining all the muscles there softening.*

Freeing the Larynx – 2

To further relax the muscles that suspend the larynx

We are going to use an image for this exercise. I find this image helpful because it is very mobile and so discourages holding or fixing.

- *Sit or stand as before, directing the back to lengthen and the shoulders and hips to widen. Check that the feet are parallel and hip width apart, that the joints are loose and that the shoulder blades and buttocks are gently dropping down your back. Let the lower jaw fall loosely open.*
- *Focus your attention on the larynx. Imagine that it is like the basket underneath a hot air balloon.*
- *Now, imagine that the head is like the hot air balloon itself and that it is floating upwards.*
- *Now, imagine the muscles that suspend the larynx are like the ropes that run between the balloon and the basket allowing the basket to hang freely.*
- *Keep imagining the balloon (head) floating upwards whilst the basket (larynx) hangs down and the ropes (muscles) in between soften and lengthen, so that the balloon, the basket and the ropes can all move freely.*
- *Now, try speaking some text while keeping your attention on the image of the hot air balloon and its freely hanging basket. Imagine that the more you wish to communicate the more the ropes between the balloon and the basket soften and lengthen.*

If you work with this exercise regularly you will break any habit of contracting and shortening in the muscles that suspend the larynx and then, as usual you won't need to worry about this on stage.

Giggle and sob

To engage the laryngeal muscles which open the throat

Yawning, as I mentioned earlier, opens the throat passively which can be useful to release tension but will not sufficiently help you to counter any tendency to close or constrict in the throat. Laughing and crying, as shown in Jo Estill's work, open the throat *actively* so they are much more useful in countering closure in the throat.

It makes a great deal of sense: when we truly and freely laugh and cry we don't hold back, we commit to how we feel and to fully releasing that feeling. Whereas, when we are ambivalent about our feelings or about the acceptability of those feelings as far as others are concerned, that ambivalence can cause us to close in the throat.

> **Note**
>
> Feeling ambivalent about how we sound can also lead to closing in the throat. For example, where someone has moved locations, especially as a child or young adult, and has felt that they had to change the way they sounded to fit in with their new surroundings, holding often occurs in the throat, usually unconsciously, as they mentally hold back their natural sound and replace it with one that 'fits'.

So, we are going to use laughing and sobbing as 'devices' to learn how to actively open the throat.

- *Sit or stand as before, directing the back to lengthen and the shoulders and hips to widen. Check that the feet are parallel and hip width apart, that the joints are loose and that the shoulder blades and buttocks are gently dropping down your back.*
- *Focus your attention inside your throat just above the collarbone.*
- *Giggle easily on 'hee hee hee hee' or 'hoo hoo hoo hoo' and notice what happens inside your throat just above the collarbone. Can you feel an opening or expansion there? It can be quite a subtle feeling, so if you are not sure try again and trust any sense of opening that you feel there.*
- *Now, count from one to ten, giggling on each number and feeling the opening or expansion on each number. Again, trust what you feel even if it is only slight.*
- *Once you have even the slightest sense of opening or expansion alternate between giggling each number and then speaking each number. As you giggle notice the opening or expansion in the throat just above collarbone level and, then, as you speak imagine the same opening or expansion.*
- *At first you may find that the throat doesn't open as much when you speak as when you giggle. Don't worry about this, simply notice the difference and then keep asking your body to open in the same way when you speak as it does when you giggle.*
- *Now, try exactly the same exercise with a sob. Make sure that it is an enjoyable sob and has no angst in it.*

You may notice that the giggle works better than the sob for you or vice versa. If this is the case you can work with the one which helps you to open most.

If both the giggle and sob seem to work equally then you can alternate between one and the other as you please.

Once you can easily find the opening on the numbers try giggling or sobbing some text and then alternating between giggling or sobbing it and speaking it until, again, you feel the same opening or expansion when you speak as when you giggle or sob.

Putting the 'Opening the Throat and Releasing the Sound' section together

This section need only take four minutes to work through once you are comfortable with the exercises. You can add it to the end of the workout from the previous chapter and the earlier exercises from this chapter to make a thirty-one minute workout.

Loosening the Jaw

The two crucial jaw-loosening points are just in front of and below the ears and at the top of the back of the neck just below the skull bone. We are going to start with the point just in front of and below the ears.

Jaw muscle massage

To locate and loosen the jaw muscles just in front of and below the ears

❍ *Stand or sit, as before, with the spine lengthening, the hips and shoulders widening, the joints loosening and the shoulder blades and buttocks gently dropping down your back.*

❍ *Clench and release the jaw to locate the jaw muscles. Then, place your fingers over the area on either side of your face where you feel the bunching when you clench.*

❍ *Unclench the jaw muscles and massage the area gently but firmly with a circular motion. Check that your spine continues to lengthen and your shoulder blades drop gently down your back as you massage so that your upper spine does not slump.*

❍ *As you massage put your attention deep inside the muscles and imagine them softening and the back of the jaw gently dropping so there is more space between the cheekbone and the jawbone.*

❍ *Continue for about minute checking that your shoulders and hands also stay relaxed.*

Lower jaw drop –1

To encourage the jaw muscles to release further

- *Sit or stand as before, directing the back to lengthen and the shoulders and hips to widen. Check that the feet are parallel and hip width apart, that the joints are loose and that the shoulder blades and buttocks are dropping gently down your back.*
- *Place the heel of your hands on the side of your face just below your cheekbones and just above the jawbone. Press firmly in between the two bones and then let the weight of your hands rest on the jawbone.*
- *Continue to rest in this way for about thirty seconds, keeping the spine long and shoulders relaxed. As you rest imagine the jaw muscles softening and extending so allowing the jaw to drop.*
- *Then, smooth down with your hands letting the lower jaw drop open.*
- *Release your hands and gently shake out the arms and shoulders. Then, gently shake the face from side to side letting the jaw hang loose as you do so.*

Lower Jaw Drop – 2

To practise releasing the jaw while talking

This feels like a very stupid exercise when you are doing it but it is fantastic for releasing the jaw.

- *Sit or stand as before, directing the back to lengthen and the shoulders and hips to widen. Check that the feet are parallel and hip width apart, that the joints are loose and that the shoulder blades and buttocks are dropping gently down your back.*
- *Place your hands under the back of the jaw just in front of the corner of the jaw. (See diagram 7.) Imagine that your lower jaw is like that of a ventriloquist's dummy and that it drops straight down, going neither backward nor forward.*
- *Focusing on the back of the jaw let it drop open and, then, gently close it again. Think ' Drop' as you drop the jaw and 'Lift' as you close it. Repeat this slowly four or five times with your eyes closed just focusing on dropping and lifting the back of the jaw while the spine continues to lengthen and the shoulder blades continue to drop gently down your back.*

7

- *Once you have got used to the idea take a simple piece of text – a nursery rhyme is a good idea – and say it slowly allowing the jaw to drop on every syllable:*

drop – lift drop – lift drop – lift drop – lift
Hump -ty Dump -ty

drop – lift drop – lift drop – lift drop – lift
sat on a wall

drop – lift drop – lift drop – lift drop – lift
Hump -ty Dump -ty

drop – lift drop – lift drop – lift drop – lift
had a great fall

- *It is very important to relax and drop the jaw rather than placing it open. You need to go fairly slowly to do this and give each syllable the same amount of time, which is not, of course, what happens in ordinary speech.*
- *Practise this for no more than a minute because it takes a great deal of attention.*
- *Hopefully you will have some sense of greater looseness in the jaw. If your jaw is usually very tight it may ache a little after this exercise. This is fine as long as you didn't force the exercise.*
- *Now speak the same text normally but with the same sense of looseness as you do so.*
- *Each time you try this exercise take a different piece of text so you get practise at releasing the jaw on many different sounds and words.*

'Upper jaw' release

To release the muscles at the top of the back of the neck which inhibit the free movement of the 'upper jaw'

This exercise looks at the other important jaw loosening point, that is at the top of the back of the neck where the neck and head meet. This area can get very tight and restrict the jaw movement a great deal. The 'Smallest nose circle' and 'Figure of eight' exercises both help to release this area as do the small 'Head nods'. But now we are going to work on the area in a little more detail.

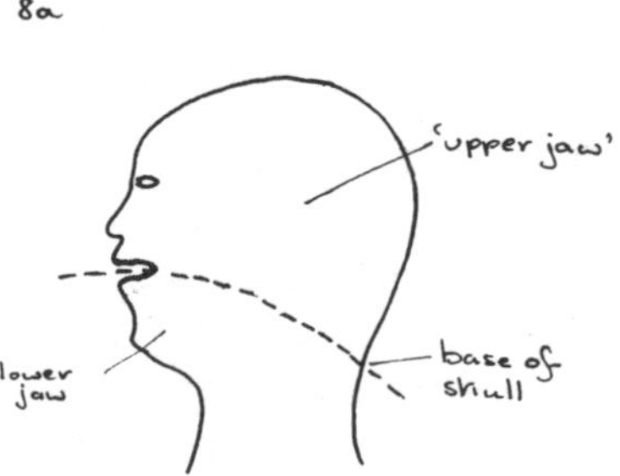

There is no such thing as the upper jaw but for the sake of this exercise we are going to imagine that the whole of the head from the upper teeth upwards and round to the back of the base of the skull is your upper jaw. (See diagram 8a.)

❍ *For this exercise you need to rest your chin on a tabletop or chair back, with your back straight and your head level. (See diagram 8b.)*

❍ *Place your hands either side of your spine just below the skull, this is the pivot point for the 'upper jaw'.*

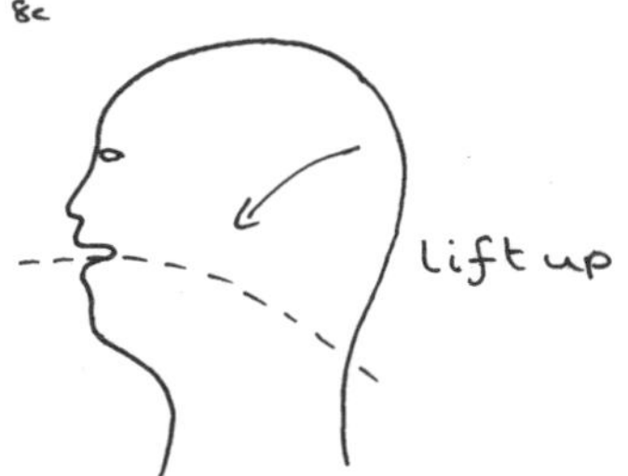

❍ *Leaving your lower jaw resting on the chair and keeping the back of your neck long, let the back of your head drop back so you are looking at the ceiling and your upper teeth lift away from your lower teeth. (See diagram 8d). Then with your hand on the back of your head push gently so your head comes back up until you are looking straight ahead again and your mouth is closed. (See diagram 8c.)*

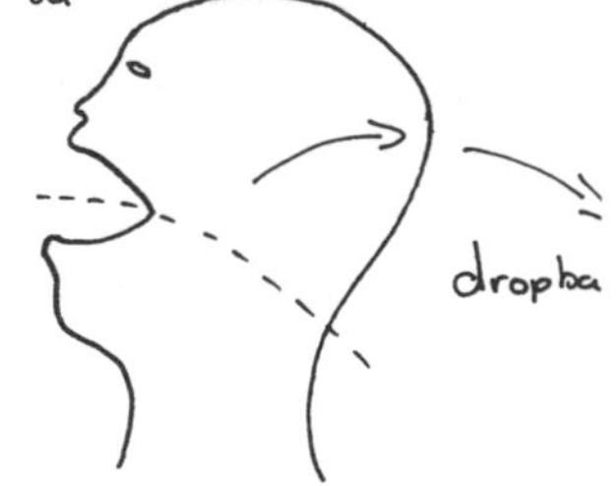

❍ *This can feel very odd at first and, indeed, you may find it hard to do at all since the muscles at the top of the back of the neck, just below the base of the skull, can often be very stiff. Loosening this area can have a tremendous releasing effect on the jaw and also helps the whole head-neck relationship.*

❍ *So, keeping the back of the neck long and the chin resting on the chair-back or table, drop the head back and then lift it up again slowly a few times. Always keep the neck spine long as you drop back and always think of the head lifting back up from the back of the skull.*

❍ *As you drop back and lift up the head, imagine that you are easing out the muscles at the top of the back of the neck either side of the spine.*

❍ *Once you are comfortable with this try speaking some text dropping your upper jaw back on each syllable and then lifting it up again.*

drop back – lift up drop back – lift up drop back – lift up drop back – lift up
Hump -ty Dump -ty

drop back – lift up drop back – lift up drop back – lift up drop back – lift up
sat on a wall

drop back – lift up drop back – lift up drop back – lift up drop back – lift up
Hump -ty Dump -ty

drop back – lift up drop back – lift up drop back – lift up drop back – lift up
had a great fall

❍ *Each time you try this exercise take a different piece of text so you get practise at releasing the jaw on many different sounds and words.*

> **Note**
> We have been dropping the lower or lifting the upper jaw on each syllable to release the jaw muscles. When speaking normally, however, the jaw remains loosely still. We will look at this further in the chapter on articulation.

Putting the 'Loosening the Jaw' section together

Once you have worked through this section and the jaw has begun to loosen, you only need to work on the last two exercises on a regular basis. These need not take any longer than a couple of minutes, so, added to the session you are already doing, the whole session need take no longer than thirty-three minutes.

Loosening the Tongue

In this chapter we are looking at releasing tension in the tongue to allow full vocal release. In a later chapter we will look at toning up the tongue muscles so you can achieve the energy and clarity you need for performance.

Cleaning the teeth with the tongue

To release tongue tension

This exercise is excellent for releasing tongue tension if you do it really slowly. I was amazed when I first did it at just how much tension I became aware of in my tongue. You may really feel it in the back of the tongue, which often stores a great deal of tension. The more you play with this exercise the more tension you will release.

❍ *Sit or stand as before, directing the back to lengthen and the shoulders and hips to widen. Check that the feet are parallel and hip width apart, that the joints are loose and that the shoulder blades and buttocks are dropping gently down your back.*

- *Starting at one end of your upper teeth, slowly move the tongue around the front of each tooth as if you are cleaning it. The slower you go the better.*
- *Then in the same way go back across the back of the upper teeth, as if you are slowly cleaning each one.*
- *Then do exactly the same with the bottom teeth, again really taking your time.*

Flapping tongue

To relax the tongue while making sound

This exercise counters any tendency the tongue may have to tense and pull backward while you are making sound.

- *Sit or stand as before, directing the back to lengthen and the shoulders and hips to widen. Check that the feet are parallel and hip width apart, that the joints are loose and that the shoulder blades and buttocks are dropping gently down your back.*
- *Slide the tongue slightly forward so it is resting on the lips. Keeping the jaw loosely still and open, flap the tongue up and down so it moves between the top and bottom lip making a loose kind of 'l' sound.*
- *Carry this on for about thirty seconds and then yawn a couple of times. Then repeat for about thirty seconds, again finishing by yawning a couple of times.*

Back of tongue stretch

To release tension in the back of the tongue while both silent and making sound

This is an excellent exercise for releasing tension in the back of the tongue that I first encountered in the work of Kristin Linklater. Don't worry if it makes you yawn a lot. This often happens as you begin to release tension in the back of the mouth and the throat.

- *Sit or stand as before, directing the back to lengthen and the shoulders and hips to widen. Check that the feet are parallel and hip width apart, that the joints are loose and that the shoulder blades and buttocks are dropping gently down your back.*
- *Open your jaw so there is a finger's width gap between the back teeth and smile with soft surprise, this will help the upper jaw to lift and the whole jaw to stay still and open in this position without tension.*

- *Place the tip of the tongue behind the lower front teeth. Imagine a piece of cotton thread is attached to the middle of your tongue. Imagine pulling on that thread so that the middle of the tongue is pulled out of the mouth while the tip stays behind the lower front teeth and the jaw stays still and open.*
- *With this image roll the middle of the tongue out of the mouth and relax it back in several times, again keeping the tip of the tongue behind the lower front teeth and the jaw still and open. It is also helpful to imagine the head moving backward slightly to stop the chin moving forward as the tongue rolls out.*
- *It is worth practising this exercise in the mirror to check that your jaw is still. If you find it difficult or even impossible to keep the jaw still, work very, very slowly and if necessary hold your chin to help your jaw stay still. It's worth persevering with this because not only does it help the sound release it also helps with clarity as you will see later.*
- *Once you are happy with this exercise then try adding easy sound:*

  'Hee-yuh-yuh-yuh-yuh-yuh Hee-yuh-yuh-yuh-yuh-yuh' etc.

- *Let the tongue be very loose, as if it is falling forward out of the mouth and then falling back into the mouth and let the sound take care of itself.*

Under chin massage

To loosen the root of the tongue, while silent and speaking

The state of the back of the tongue can also be felt under the chin.

- *Sit or stand as before, directing the back to lengthen and the shoulders and hips to widen. Check that the feet are parallel and hip width apart, that the joints are loose and that the shoulder blades and buttocks are dropping gently down your back.*
- *Place your thumb under the chin, just behind the jawbone and press gently upward. Massage this area gently. How does it feel? Hard or soft? If it feels hard gently massage the area imagining the tongue softening as you do so. Then move onto the next part of the exercise. If it feels soft move straight on to the next part of the exercise.*
- *Now make an 'hee' sound and see what happens in the area under the chin. There will be some movement but does the tongue stay relatively soft or does it go rigid? Repeat the 'hee' sound several times gently but firmly massaging the area under the chin and exploring how you can make a 'Hee' sound and keep the tongue relatively relaxed.*

- *Then, go through the following vowels massaging under the chin and exploring how you can keep the tongue soft:*

'Hey' 'High' 'Hah' 'Hor' 'Hoh' 'Hoo'

- *Then try some text, massaging under the chin and exploring how you can keep the tongue soft as you speak.*
- *Finish this exercise by yawning a couple of times.*

Lazy forward tongue talk

To further loosen the tongue while you talk

This is similar to the 'Flapping tongue' exercise and again counters any tendency of the tongue to tense and pull back in the mouth. I learnt it from another superb singing teacher, Mark Meylan. It is excellent for releasing tension in the tongue and is worth doing regularly if your tongue is tight. Your speech will sound very indistinct, which is fine since we are not focusing on clarity here but rather on relaxation.

- *Stand or sit as before with the spine lengthening, the hips and shoulders widening and the joints loose.*
- *Open the jaw so there is a finger's width gap between the back teeth. Slide the tongue forward so it is resting on your lips. Place one hand under the chin so the jaw can rest on the hand and remain relatively still.*
- *Then try speaking some text while letting the tongue stay forward and loose.*
- *If you find the tongue wanting to pull back into the mouth, try holding the front of your tongue with the fingers of your other hand to help keep the tongue forward.*
- *Play with this exercise for about a minute and then release the tongue and yawn a couple of times to finish off.*

Putting the 'Loosening the Tongue' section together

This section need take no longer than five minutes, which will make your whole session thirty-eight minutes long. Don't worry that the session is going to keep expanding. Once we get to the end of this chapter we will reorganise all the exercises into a shorter session.

Bringing the Soft Palate to Life

Surprise breath – I

To engage and lift the soft palate on the in-breath

Again, we are going to use the soft surprise to help the opening-up process, but, instead of focusing on the neck as we did before, we are going to focus on what happens at the back of the mouth as you breathe in and out on a surprise breath.

The attention needed for this exercise can be enormous, especially if your soft palate doesn't want to move much, so remember only work for a minute or two and then move on, even if you haven't got very far. There is no point just banging away at it, you'll only get disheartened and you won't achieve anything productive. Simply revisit this exercise for a minute or two regularly and you will find that one day you suddenly make the connection and the soft palate starts to move.

- *Sit or stand as before, directing the back to lengthen and the shoulders and hips to widen. Check that the feet are parallel and hip width apart, that the joints are loose and that the shoulder blades and buttocks are dropping gently down your back.*
- *Open the jaw so there is a finger's width gap between the back teeth and place a hand under your chin so that your jaw can rest loosely still in this position.*
- *Breathe in almost silently as if someone has given you a most wonderful surprise that has really touched you.*
- *Repeat this a few times and feel what happens in the back of your mouth. Can you feel a space opening up there? Don't worry if you can't feel anything at first as this is often an area with which we are not particularly in touch.*
- *Try looking in a mirror, you need to get some light shining into the back of your mouth so you can see what is going on. You may also need to open the jaw a little wider so you can see, but try to keep the neck spine long and avoid poking your chin forward.*
- *Do you notice that the back of the tongue lowers and the soft palate lifts up and back as you breathe in with surprise? What we are looking for is a lot of movement in the soft palate and less movement in the tongue, which is really just flattening out.*
- *The stiller you keep the jaw the more likely it will be that the tongue and soft palate will move. Also keep the tip of the tongue forward touching the back of the lower front teeth. If the tongue wants to draw back in the mouth and bunch up, place a finger on the front of the tongue to encourage it to stay forward.*

- *Don't worry if the movement upward of the soft palate and downward of the back of the tongue is small at first as long as you get some space between the two*
- *Try using each of the following images in turn as you breathe in and, then, use whichever you find most helpful:*

  1) Imagine the soft surprise feeling is in the back of your mouth lifting the soft palate up and back.

  2) Imagine that there is a mouth in the back of your neck and that that mouth is opening with surprise.

  3) Imagine a smile across the back of the roof of the mouth, as you open up with surprise.

Then, just keep practising regularly and little by little you will find that you will have more sense of your soft palate and find it easier to raise.

Surprise breath – 2

To engage and lift the soft palate on the out-breath

- *Once you have some sense of the soft palate lifting and space being created between the back of the tongue and the soft palate as you breathe in, focus on the out-breath as well, breathing out as if you are still surprised and are about to say 'Oh you shouldn't have'.*
- *Breathe in and out in this way a few times without the mirror, simply working with the sense of surprise and using one of the images from above. Then check with the mirror to see what is going on. What you are looking for is the space created between the back of the tongue and the soft palate, as you breathed in, to remain as you breathe out.*
- *There is often a tendency to want to close on the out-breath, so imagine opening up even more with surprise as you breathe out.*
- *Practise this exercise regularly both with and without the mirror until the soft palate lifts easily on the in-breath and stays lifted on the out-breath.*

'Ng – Ah'

To increase the flexibility of the soft palate

Now you have some sense of the soft palate we are going work on making it more flexible.

- *Sit or stand as before, directing the back to lengthen and the shoulders and hips to widen. Check that the feet are parallel and hip width apart, that the joints are loose and that the shoulder blades and buttocks are dropping gently down your back.*
- *Open your jaw so there is a finger's width between the back teeth.*
- *Make an easy 'ng' sound. Can you feel how you are making the 'ng'? The soft palate lowers and the back of the tongue raises so that they meet each other.*
- *Now make an easy 'ah' sound. Can you feel what has happened now? The soft palate has raised and the back of the tongue has lowered, just as it did with the surprise breath.*

Moving between the 'ng' and the 'ah' positions exercises the soft palate increasing its flexibility and allowing it to become more responsive to your thoughts and feelings so the voice is more alive and expressive.

- *Remember to keep the jaw loosely still since this helps the soft palate and tongue to move more.*
- *Practise sliding from 'ng' to 'ah' thinking of the soft surprise as you move into the 'ah'. It can also be helpful to imagine the roof of the mouth lifting as you say 'ah' as if you were creating a huge domed ceiling space in the back of your mouth.*
- *Another helpful device is to use your hands to mimic the movement of the soft palate. Place your hands either side of your head at cheek level with the fingers pointing backward. Let the fingers drop down so that they are at right angles to your hands, this mimics the position of the soft palate as you say 'ng'. Leave your fingers in this position while you say 'ng' and, then, lift them as you say 'ah'.*
- *You can also practise sliding from 'ng' to 'igh' and from 'ng to ey' using the same devices of the soft surprise, the lifting ceiling image and the moving fingers.*

Putting the 'Bringing the Soft Palate to Life' section together

This section need take no longer than two minutes, which gives you in total a forty-minute session.

Removing Harsh and Breathy Closure

As I mentioned earlier in the chapter *harsh closure* is the result of the vocal folds *coming together too tightly.* The breath then has to build up to a greater pressure before it can open the folds and so it eventually bursts them apart quite violently, which leads them to slam together again fairly violently. Also, the breath passes through rapidly, because the pressure is so great and this causes a great deal of friction against the folds. Both the violent opening and closing and the air friction can cause damage to the edges of the folds.

Breathy closure occurs when the folds do not come together firmly enough. As a result, the sound is breathy because some of the air is able to escape through the extra space between the folds without being converted into sound. Because less air is being converted into sound the voice will lack power. Breathy closure is not, in itself, usually, damaging to the voice but, because the voice lacks strength and energy, a person with breathy closure might end up tensing and pushing to achieve a stronger voice.

The first two exercises help to remove harsh attack, while the third exercise helps to remove breathy attack.

Bored 'Hoo Hoo Hoo'

To remove excess tension in the throat and stop harsh glottal attack

As I said earlier, it is very good to work with a sense of boredom if you have a tendency to push too hard. It is also good to work with a sense of carelessness, because being over-careful can also lead to holding in the throat. Bored carelessness helps you avoid either pushing or holding back.

This first exercise is very much a releasing one, to build up the habit of opening and releasing rather than grabbing and pushing. Don't worry if you feel you are losing energy, just use this exercise to build up the habit of release and then move onto the next exercise, which is more dynamic.

❍ *Lie in the Alexander position (page 24) as before, with your legs bent and your head resting on some books. Place your hands just below your navel.*

❍ *Sigh out a few times from the belly with a feeling of great boredom. Imagine that your throat is in your belly and that the sound is made there. This helps to keep your attention away from your throat and so will further help the release.*

❍ *Then, sigh out on 'Hoo Hoo Hoo' again with a feeling of great boredom. Have a sensation of carelessly sliding or melting into the sounds.*

❍ *Then repeat the same exercise on the following sounds:*

'Hoh Hoh Hoh'
'Hor Hor Hor'
'Hah Hah Hah',
'High High High'
'Hey Hey Hey'
'Hee Hee Hee'

- *Then, sigh out in the same way on the following phrases:*

  'Hello, how are you?'

  'HI'm fine thanks'

  'Hand how are you?'

- *Then, sigh out some text in the same way, adding 'H' before any phrases that begin with a vowel.*
- *Then, stand up and try some text in the same way, standing against the wall as you did in earlier exercises.*

Top-of-diamond bounce

To help remove harsh glottal attack

When the top of the diamond support moves out it helps to open the throat and so avoid tension and closing there. Keep your attention on the top of the diamond, imagining that your throat is there and the sound is made there. Again, this is a device to keep your attention away from your throat.

- *Stand as before, directing the back to lengthen and the shoulders and hips to widen. Check that the feet are parallel and hip width apart, that the joints are loose and that the shoulder blades and buttocks are dropping gently down your back.*
- *Place your thumb just below the breastbone and say 'psh psh' confidently and easily as if you are shooing away a cat.*
- *Then, focusing on the idea of speaking from the area under your thumb bounce the sound out on 'Hoo Hoo with a sense of great boredom and carelessness. Allow the jaw to be loosely open and still as you do so.*
- *Then, repeat the exercise with the following sequence:*

  'Hoh Hoh', 'Hor Hor', 'Hah Hah', 'High High', 'Hey Hey', 'Hee Hee'

- *Then, repeat the exercise in the same way with the following phrases:*

  'Hello, how are you?'

  'HI'm fine thanks'

  'Hand how are you?'

- *Then, repeat the exercise with some text in the same way, adding 'H' before any phrases that begin with a vowel.*

Black ink sounds

To remove breathy glottal attack

We are going to repeat the last exercise but with a different feeling since here we are trying to get a more energised and committed closure.

Working with certainty and interest, whilst visualising the sounds being clearly and sharply written or typed in black ink, seems to help the muscles involved to work more effectively, which eliminates the breathiness.

- *Stand as before, directing the back to lengthen and the shoulders and hips to widen. Check that the feet are parallel and hip width apart, that the joints are loose and that the shoulder blades and buttocks are dropping gently down your back.*
- *Place your thumb just below the breastbone, as before, and again say 'psh psh' confidently and easily, as if you are shooing away a cat.*
- *Then, again focusing on the idea of speaking from the area under your thumb, bounce the sound out on 'Hoo Hoo this time with a sense of great certainty. As you do so, imagine the sounds written or typed in dark, sharp clear ink so they are very precise. This doesn't mean you actually have to 'see' them, I certainly don't. You just have the 'idea' of them.*
- *Then, repeat the exercise with the following sequence:*

  'Hoh Hoh', 'Hor Hor', 'Hah Hah', 'High High', 'Hey Hey', 'Hee Hee'

- *Then, repeat the exercise in the same way with the following phrases:*

  'Hello, how are you?'

  'HI'm fine thanks'

  'Hand how are you?'

- *Then, repeat the exercise with some text in the same way, adding 'H' before any phrases that begin with a vowel.*

Putting the 'Removing Harsh and Breathy Closure' section together

This section need take no longer than three minutes and so makes your total session time forty-three minutes. Don't worry we are nearly at the end of the chapter so there are only a couple of exercises to add!

Getting the Breath Pressure Right

Allowing the body to heave up as you breathe in and collapse as you breathe out can lead to the breath being forced out of your body faster than is either helpful or healthy, so we are back to the practice of lengthening and widening.

Lengthening and widening while releasing breath and sound

To avoid excessive breath pressure

- *Stand as before, directing the back to lengthen and the shoulders and hips to widen. Check that the feet are parallel and hip width apart, that the joints are loose and that the shoulder blades and buttocks are dropping gently down your back.*
- *Place your hands just below the navel.*
- *Blow the air out on an 'ff' imagining the air coming up from the belly to the lips. As you do so, alternate between imagining the breath flowing from the belly to the lips and thinking of the spine lengthening and the hips and shoulders widening.*
- *Then, repeat this on a sustained 'Hoooooooooo'. Again alternating between the image of the sound pouring up from your belly to your lips and the idea of lengthening and widening.*
- *Then, repeat the exercise on the following sequence:*

  'Hoooooooooh', 'Hoooooooooor', 'Haaaaaaaaah'

  'Hiiiiiiiiiiiigh', 'Heeeeeeeeey', 'Heeeeeeeeee'

- *Then, repeat the exercise chanting the text, by which I mean singing it on one comfortable note allowing each word to run into the next.*

You will probably find you use up a great deal of breath very fast, which is fine. I'll talk more about chanting in the next chapter so don't worry too much about it here. The main focus is on continuing to lengthen and widen so that you work against any tendency to collapse and force the breath out. In time lengthening will become habitual and you won't have to worry about collapsing.

The 'sliding sh' exercise

To ensure sufficient breath pressure

This exercise is based on one I learned from the excellent speech and language therapist and voice teacher, Christina Shewell, when we worked together on a client with nodules. Christina was working in her capacity as a speech therapist and I in my capacity as a voice teacher. We saw the client together every two weeks and I worked with the client daily. Within six months her nodules were gone even though she was performing fairly regularly.

- *Stand against the wall, as before, with the feet no more than a couple of inches from the wall and the knees slightly bent. Again, let your back rest against the wall. Place a cushion behind your head, if necessary, to ensure that the back of the neck stays long.*
- *Place your hands just below the navel.*
- *You are going to let the air out on an easy 'sh', sliding from a quiet 'sh' to a loud 'sh' and back to a quiet 'sh'. At all times imagining that the 'sh' is flowing up from the belly and that the area above the armpits stays relaxed and open.*
- *Keep your focus on your belly and imagine it being pulled in more as the 'sh' gets louder.*
- *Also, reach down mentally for breath in the second half as you always have done.*
- *Play with this exercise for about a minute, remembering to release the belly and pelvic floor muscles at the end of the out-breath.*

Putting the 'Getting the Breath Pressure right' section together

The two exercises in this section can be done in a couple of minutes, so added to the exercises so far that gives you a session of forty-five minutes.

Whole Release Exercises

We have been through each individual part of the throat and mouth and looked at releasing these parts. Having done this it is good to look at more organic exercises for voice release. You could say we have been looking at vocal release from the logical, detailed left brain perspective and now we are going to look at it from the more instinctive, 'big picture' right side of the brain.

We are going to look at activities that involve physical release of the whole body, for as the rest of the body releases so it becomes easier for the neck, throat and mouth area to release.

Drop and release

To release the voice by releasing the body

This is one of my favourite exercises and is great for releasing the body and voice. It can be very useful before a show for grounding and release.

9

- *Stand, as before, with feet parallel and hipbone width apart, the spine lengthening, the hips and shoulders widening, the joints loosening and the shoulder blades and buttocks gently dropping. Blow out the breath easily and then as the new in-breath comes in let your arms float up until they are above your head. (See diagram 9a.)* 
- *Then, as you breathe out, release in the ankle, knee and hip joints so that your legs bend and your upper body drops over from the hips. (See diagram 9b.)* 
- *Having dropped over, allow your upper body and arms to swing loosely back and forth, as your legs bounce up and down. (See diagram 9c.) When you run out of breath gently roll back up and then let your arms float above your head again.*
- *Play with this a few times so the whole body feels released. Check especially that you are not holding in the neck. Also, check that you are dropping, swinging and bouncing gently rather than with any force.*
- *Once you are comfortable try the exercise on a long 'Hah' and then on the following vowels: 'High', 'Hey', 'Hee', 'Hoo', 'Hoh', 'Hor'. Your breath length may change a great deal as you do this exercise, sometimes it may be long, sometimes short. Just let it do what it wants while you focus on releasing.*
- *Then you can try the exercise with text. Keep the articulation very loose and just let the sound fall out. Don't worry about matching the breath to the phrase, just breathe when you need to and pick up the phrase where you broke off.*
- *Once you feel comfortable with the exercise it is a good idea to alternate between doing it and standing still. In this way you 'trick' the body and voice into staying released even when you are still.*

Door handle swing

To release the voice through grounding

This is another great exercise, which I mentioned in the 'Body Work' chapter, but you do need to check the strength of the door you are going to use. The frame, the door hinges and the door handle all need to be really strong, so be warned!

- *Facing the end of the door grab hold of both door knobs and bend your legs so you are half sitting or squatting. There is no need to go too low – just find a comfortable position where you are dropping down a little. Imagine your hips and buttocks dropping down and away from the door while your spine lengthens forwards and up towards the door. (See diagram 10.)*

- *Then allow yourself to swing from side to side, keeping the feet soft and spread, as you breathe easily.*
- *Once you are comfortable try sounding out on a long 'Hah' and then on the following vowels: 'High', 'Hey', 'Hee', 'Hoo', 'Hoh', 'Hor'.*
- *Then, try swinging with some text.*
- *As with the previous exercise, once you are comfortable with it, alternate between swinging and standing still so you can again 'trick' the body and voice into staying released when you are still.*

These are my favourite exercises and the ones I find most useful, but you can also try rolling on the floor, swinging from side to side, easy running and gentle jumping. The swinging march we use as a warm up is also excellent for using with text to increase vocal release.

Putting 'Whole Release Exercises' section together

These exercises are best done at the end of your session since they are about letting go. They allow you to let go of the focused, specific work you have done in the session and allow the voice to just get on by itself. This is vital. Having worked with the left brain, taking the whole vocal process apart and working on each element, we need to work with the right brain, allowing the whole vocal process to come back together and work instinctively.

Putting this Chapter together with the previous Chapters

As previously, the session below is only a suggestion. Working through this chapter you will have discovered which exercises help you to release most, so feel free to leave some out if they feel less helpful and include others that feel more helpful. Trust yourself to make the best decision for your voice and remember to construct a session that is as enjoyable as possible.

Warm-up (2 minutes)

Freeing the breath (68)

Floor work (3 minutes)

Centring the breath (69)
Opening the throat (72)

Engage, release and 'H' breath (this is not described above as such. It is simply the version against the wall – page 84 – done on the floor)

Standing (7 minutes)

Lengthening and widening (132)
Working against the wall or wide arms (133 or 134)
Side to side (135)
Half neck circles (136)
Nose circles or Nose figure of eight or Head nods (137)
Engage, release and 'H' breath (against wall) (84)
Engage, release and 'H' breath (with chair) (84)

Sitting or Standing (10 minutes)

Widening and opening (138)
Freeing the larynx 1 and 2 (139)
Giggle and sob (with text) (140)
Lower jaw drop 2 (with text) (143)
Upper jaw release (with text) (144)
Cleaning the teeth with the tongue (146)
Back of tongue stretch (147)
Under chin massage (with text) (148)
Lazy forward tongue talking (with text) (149)
Ng-Ah (151)

Standing (10 minutes)

Sliding 'sh' (156)
Bouncing sound from the diaphragm (99)
Bouncing sound from the lower belly (102)
Bouncing sound from the 'oomph points' (103)
Calling (with text) (114)
Engaging the lower belly and pelvic floor muscles throughout the sound (109)
Engaging the 'oomph points' throughout the sound (110)
Lengthening and widening while releasing (with text) (132)
Drop and release (158)
Door handle swing (158)

6

Filling out the Sound: Resonance

In the last chapter we looked at removing tension from the throat and mouth area so that the voice could be freely and fully released. In this chapter we are going to explore how that freely released sound is 'filled out', giving it strength, richness and complexity.

What exactly is 'filling out' the sound?

It is the *amplification* of the initial sound made in the larynx.

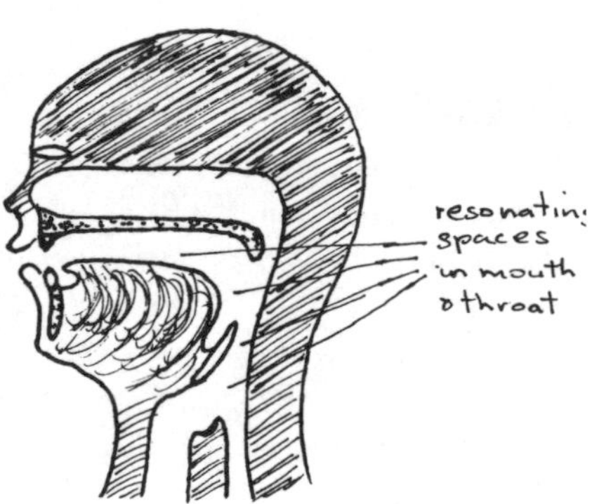

As the initial sound passes through the spaces of the vocal tract – i.e. the throat and mouth spaces (see diagram) – its *own vibrations* set the air within the throat and mouth into *sympathetic vibration*, so adding volume and texture.

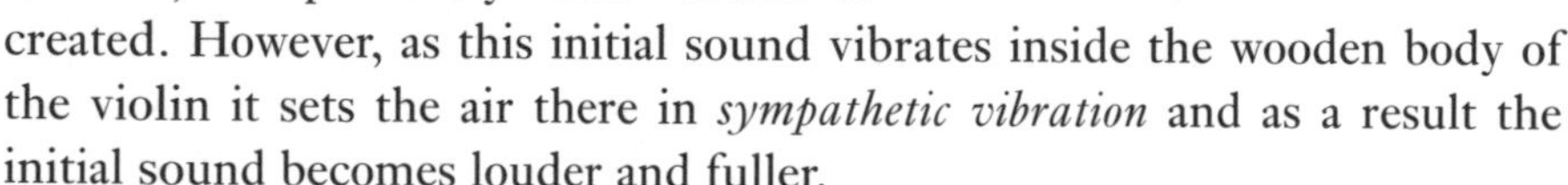

Think of a violin string. When it is plucked a small, comparatively 'thin' sound is created. However, as this initial sound vibrates inside the wooden body of the violin it sets the air there in *sympathetic vibration* and as a result the initial sound becomes louder and fuller.

This *sympathetic vibration* is known as resonance. It gives the voice its specific quality and is determined by the shape of the individual's throat and the mouth spaces.

What interferes with full resonance?

Lack of space If the *space* in the throat and mouth is reduced this will affect the resonance.

The throat and mouth have many moveable parts as we saw in the last chapter. The position of the head and neck and of the larynx, the jaw, the tongue and the soft palate can all radically alter the shape and the size of the throat and mouth spaces and so affect the resonance.

Smaller spaces reinforce higher sounds while larger spaces reinforce lower sounds, so if the areas in the throat and mouth are reduced there may well be an accompanying loss of lower resonance. Very often when a voice sounds high it is due to the lack of lower resonance rather than because the pitch itself is too high.

So creating space in the throat and mouth is vital for full resonance. Fortunately all the work in the last chapter will have opened up the throat and mouth space, so some of this chapter's work is already done.

Tension and sluggishness Tension also affects resonance. Meribeth Bunch has described the throat area as being like a 'mobile muscular sleeve'.[21] If the walls of this sleeve are tense the sound will be harder and may even become shrill. If the walls are sluggish and insufficiently toned the sound will be muffled and dull, lacking energy and vibrancy. Only when the walls are well toned will the sound be full and alive.

Again, the work we did in the last chapter on the head and neck position and upper body stability will have helped to remove tension and sluggishness in the walls of the throat and to develop good tone.

Tension in the chest, shoulders and face will also affect resonance. Again, the postural work we did in the 'Body Work' chapter, and at the end of the last chapter, will have helped to keep the body released and the resonance unrestricted.

Why work on resonance at all?

Resonance brings substance and energy to the voice. When the voice is fully resonant it is fully alive. You can feel the resonance in your body. The voice and body feel fully awake and connected and so they can be more responsive to and expressive of your thoughts and feelings. What is more, all this substance and energy is produced without effort on your part. It is energy for free.

21 *Dynamics of the Singing Voice* by Meribeth Bunch (page 85).

What resonance work isn't about

Working on resonance is not about creating a beautiful sounding voice. The job of the voice is to fully express your thoughts and feelings and neither you nor the listener should be aware of it separately from this. A good voice is one that communicates, that engages the listener, and that honestly reflects your internal world. You work on resonance to bring all the possibilities of your voice to life, not to create a particular type of sound, and, as always once you have worked on it you let go, you trust and get on with the job of communicating. If you are thinking about your voice you can't be connecting with the text or the other actors or the audience – it is as simple as that.

So called 'chest' and 'head' resonance

As I mentioned earlier, it is the vibration of the initial sound in the *throat and mouth spaces* that produces the sympathetic vibrations we call resonance. However, as we make sound or speak we also have a physical *sensation* of vibration in the chest and head. As such, these sensations are not believed to contribute to the resonance as heard by the listener. Nevertheless, focusing on them for yourself *does* help to bring the voice to life.

Nasal resonance

Nasal resonance is the resonance that occurs when the soft palate is lowered and the sound is amplified in the nasal cavity. (See diagram 2.) There are certain sounds in English – m, n and ng – which are nasal sounds and need the soft palate to drop when they are being made. Also, certain languages have a large degree of nasal resonance – for example French.

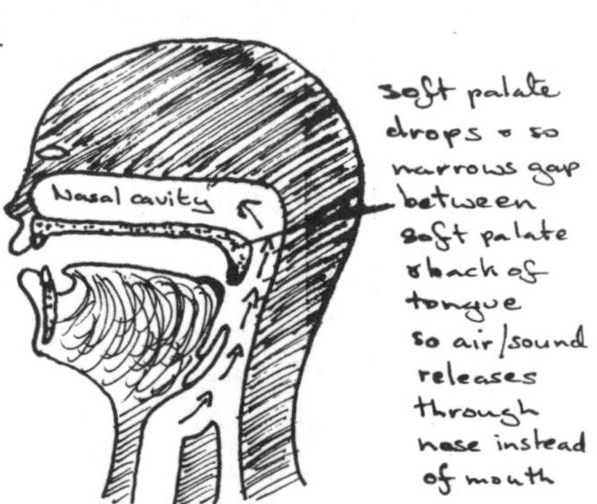
2
Nasal cavity
soft palate
drops & so
narrows gap
between
soft palate
& back of
tongue
so air/sound
releases
through
nose instead
of mouth

Such nasal resonance is appropriate. However, sometimes people sound nasal even when this is not part of their accent. This excessive nasal resonance can be caused by a sluggish soft palate hanging down at the back of the mouth and so blocking off the mouth space. It can also be caused by tension in the back of the tongue, which leads it to bunch up in the back of the mouth, again blocking off the mouth space.

It is, therefore, important to get the soft palate toned and flexible and to release tension in the tongue because doing this enables the free release of the voice and brings energy. The work on the soft palate and tongue in the last chapter (see page 146 on and 150 on) begun this process and we will look at further exercises later in the chapter.

When we have a cold and our head is full of catarrh the voice can sound dull and muffled. This is now believed to be due to the fact that, because we are feeling under the weather, the face and soft palate become sluggish and their lack of energy is reflected in the lack of life in the voice.

Some people sound as if they have a cold even when they do not and this will often be due to sluggishness in the face and soft palate. Waking up the face and soft palate will bring a brightness and energy to the voice without it sounding false or over-animated.

NOW TO WORK

As I have already mentioned effective resonance needs space and toned, rather than tense or sluggish, muscles. The exercises in the last chapter will have helped a great deal, especially in terms of releasing tension, building tone and starting to create space. Now we are going to look at creating more space, focusing the sound and taking the time to let the resonance build.

An important tool when working on resonance is chanting, by which I mean singing on one note, ideally your most comfortable speaking note. When we chant we elongate each vowel and flow from word to word without stopping. This gives the time and space necessary for the sound to bounce back and forth and fill out. It also gives you the time to feel this fuller sound. For this reason, chanting is excellent for building resonance.

> **Note**
>
> Chanting also helps the breath to release rather than holding back. So, you may find yourself running out of breath quite quickly, which is fine. Just make sure you stop as soon as there is no comfortable breath left, even if you are in the middle of a phrase.

Creating more Space in the Mouth and Throat

We are going to start with the soft palate. As I have mentioned previously, waking up the soft palate creates space in the mouth and brings energy to the sound.

'Ng –Ah'

To connect with the soft palate, practise lifting it to bring it to life and to create more space in the mouth

We are going to work with the feeling of surprise or smile to help lift the soft palate, as we did in the soft palate exercises in the last chapter (see page 150).

- ❍ *Sit or stand as before, directing the back to lengthen and the shoulders and hips to widen. Check that the feet are parallel and hip width apart, that the joints are loose and the shoulder blades and buttocks are dropping gently down your back.*

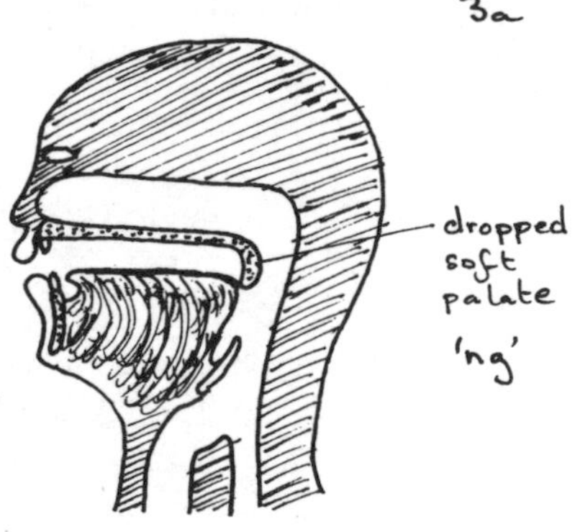

- ❍ *Open your jaw so there is about a finger's width between the back teeth and place one hand under the jaw so that it can rest loosely still.*
- ❍ *Make a gentle but firm 'ng' sound and have a sense of the soft palate dropping to make contact with the back of the tongue, as you make the sound. (See diagram 3a.)*

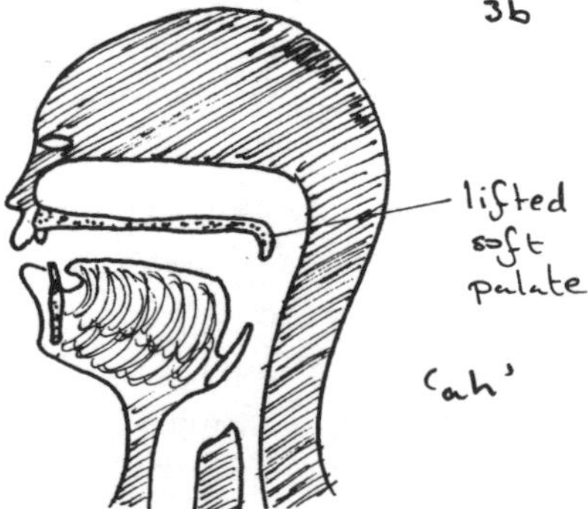

- ❍ *Then, say 'ng – ah' with a sense of soft surprise and focus on the soft palate raising and the back of the tongue dropping as you say the 'ah'. Check in the mirror, as you did in the last chapter, to see that the jaw stays relatively still and the soft palate lifts on the 'ah', while the back of the tongue drops slightly. (See diagram 3b.)*
- ❍ *Once you have checked, continue working with the 'ng – ah' using whichever of the following images works best as you open up on the 'ah':*

1) Imagine the soft surprise in the back of your mouth lifting the soft palate up and back.

2) Imagine there is a mouth in the back of your neck and that that mouth is opening with surprise.

3) Imagine a smile across the back of the roof of the mouth.

❍ *Then, use the same image on 'ng –igh' and 'ng-ay'.*

'Ng-Ah' into talking

To take the feeling of a lifted and alive soft palate into speech

This exercise helps to bring a 'bright', energetic quality to the voice and is useful for lessening excessive nasal resonance because it encourages the soft palate to stay lifted as you talk.

❍ *Choose out of the 'ng-ah', 'ng-igh' and 'ng-ay' whichever sound seems to help the soft palate lift the most.*

❍ *Then, open from 'ng' again and as soon as you have moved onto the vowel you have chosen and can feel the soft palate lifting in the back of the mouth start to speak some text, retaining that lifting feeling as you do so. Here is an example using lines from one of Hamlet's soliloquies.*

ng-ah To be or not to be that is the question
ng-ah Whether tis nobler in the mind to suffer

❍ *When you come to the comfortable end of your breath wait for the in-breath and, let it come in by itself, then, open again from the 'ng' to the chosen vowel and, again, move straight into speaking with the lifted soft palate.*

In this way you will build up the habit of speaking with an engaged and lifted soft palate.

❍ *It is important to keep the palate flexible so that it can drop when necessary so finish this exercise by alternating fairly rapidly between 'ng' and the various vowels to keep the soft palate alive: 'ng-ah ng-igh ng-ay ng-ah ng-igh ng-ay etc.'*

'Hng-Ah'

To create more opening and space in the back of the mouth and the throat

Now we are going to look at co-ordinating the lifting of the soft palate with the opening of the throat. This creates a great deal of space in the throat and the mouth and can feel wonderful. This exercise is again based on the excellent work of Janice Chapman.

- *Sit or stand as before, directing the back to lengthen and the shoulders and hips to widen. Check that the feet are parallel and hip width apart, that the joints are loose and the shoulder blades and buttocks are dropping gently down your back.*
- *Call out freely and bouncily on 'hng' a few times. As you do so imagine a smile at the back of the base of the neck.*
- *Then, call out freely again but this time moving from the 'hng' into the 'ah'. As you move from the 'hng' to the 'ah' imagine a mouth, covering the whole of the back of your neck from the base of the neck to the base of the skull, opening up with easy surprise and the sound escaping freely out of the back of the head.*
- *Call out freely on 'hng-ah' a few more times with this feeling and then call 'hng – igh' and 'hng – ay' a few times in the same way. Have a sense of fluidity and movement as you call, so there is no tendency to fix in one position. Also, as in the last chapter, work with a carefree rather than a careful attitude.*

'Hng–Ah' into talking

To take the opening and space created into speech

- *Choose out of the 'hng-ah', 'hng-igh' and 'hng-ay' whichever sound seems to create the most opening and space. Call as before and as soon as you feel the opening and space move straight into talking, while keeping the image of the surprised mouth opening up the whole of the back of the neck.*
- *Repeat this a few times keeping flexible and loose and carefree.*

Focusing the Sound Forward

Focusing the sound forward is very important in two ways. Firstly, it moves the attention away from the throat, so less strain is likely. Secondly, it makes the sound more present and alive and committed.

Again, it is a question of attention. By focusing on the lips and the front upper teeth and gum ridge and on the *idea* of the sound flowing forward to these points, the sound will actually flow forward instead of being swallowed.

Of course, as always, it is important that you only mentally focus the sound forward and avoid *consciously doing* anything physically. Also, once you have done the exercises, leave the voice alone to place itself freely, since it is a free, rather than a placed voice that we are after.

Focusing the sound forward – 1

To encourage the sound to flow forward into the front of the mouth

- *Sit or stand as before, directing the back to lengthen and the shoulders and hips to widen. Check that the feet are parallel and hip width apart, that the joints are loose and the shoulder blades and buttocks are dropping gently down your back.*
- *Move your lips and face around to ease them out.*
- *Blow through the lips like a horse. If you find this difficult flick your lips with your finger as you blow.*
- *Then, hum gently and easily while moving the lips around. Have a sense of a slight yawn in the back of the mouth to create space between the back teeth.*
- *Focus your attention on the lips as you hum. Imagine that the sound is flowing forward into the lips. As always don't try to do anything to move the sound forward, simply imagine it flowing forward.*
- *If it helps, imagine that the sound is a bright colour and that as it flows forward it turns your lips that colour.*
- *Practise for about a minute and then move on to the next exercise.*

> **Note**
>
> When you hum, you may feel your lips tingling or tickling. This is a good sign that the sound is flowing forward. If there is no tingle, don't worry – it will come in time. Move the lips and face around and blow through the lips regularly to loosen everything up, because effort and tension are the enemies of free sound.

Focusing the sound forward – 2

To keep the sound flowing forward into the front of the mouth on different sounds

This exercise is excellent for helping the sound to flow forward, whatever the position of the lips and tongue. It helps to create a consistency of resonance.

- *Sit or stand as before, directing the back to lengthen and the shoulders and hips to widen. Check that the feet are parallel*

> **Note**
>
> Often you will find that one vowel feels far easier and freer than the others or that another vowel feels far tighter. If this is the case, use the easiest vowel as a model moving back and forth from it to the tightest vowel until the tight vowel frees up.

and hip width apart, that the joints are loose and the shoulder blades and buttocks are dropping gently down your back.

- *Move the face and lips around again to ease them out and blow through the lips again.*

- *Round the lips, keeping the neck and face relaxed, especially the front of the neck under the chin. Again, imagine a slight yawn in the back of the mouth to create space between the back teeth.*

- *Keeping the lips rounded and the slight yawn in the back of the mouth, sound out easily on a long 'hoo' and imagine the sound flowing forward into the lips. Repeat this a few times.*

- *Then, keeping the lips rounded, sound out sliding from 'oo' to 'oh' as follows: 'hoo-oh-oo-oh-oo-oh-oo-oh-oo-oh etc'. There is no pause or break between the vowels. Slide straight from one vowel to the next. As you do so imagine the sound flowing continually forward into the lips as before. Repeat this a few times.*

> **Note**
>
> Always start with an 'H' before the first vowel to keep the throat open and the breath flowing freely.

- *Then, still keeping the lips rounded, sound out sliding from 'oo' to 'oh' to 'or' as follows: 'hoo-oh-or-oo-oh-or-oo-oh-or-oo-oh-or etc'. Again imagining the sound flowing forward into the lips. Repeat this a few times.*

- *Then, sound out sliding from 'oo' to 'oh' to 'or' to 'ah' as follows: 'hoo-oh-or-ah-oo-oh-or-ah-oo-oh-or-ah etc'. Keep the lips rounded on 'oo', 'oh' and 'or' and then, as the lips open on 'ah', imagine the sound flowing forward to the upper teeth and gum ridge and the cheekbone slightly smiling. Repeat a few times.*

> **Note**
>
> On 'oo', 'oh' and 'or' the lips are rounded and it is easy to imagine the sound flowing forward to the lips. On 'ah', 'igh', 'ey' and 'ee', which don't have lip rounding, it is helpful to imagine the sound flowing forward to the front teeth and upper gum ridge and to imagine a gentle smile in the cheekbones. The imagined smile helps to bring life to the face and soft palate. A feeling of soft surprise in the back of the roof of the mouth can also be helpful, on 'oh' and 'or' the lips are rounded and it is easy to imagine the sound flowing forward to the lips. On 'ah', 'igh', 'ey' and 'ee', which don't have lip rounding, it is helpful to imagine the sound flowing forward to the front teeth and upper gum ridge and to imagine a gentle smile in the cheek bones. The imagined smile helps to bring life to the face and soft palate. A feeling of soft surprise in the back of the roof of the mouth can also be helpful.

- *Then, sound out in the same way on 'hoo – oh – or – ah – igh – oo – oh – or – ah – igh etc'.*
- *Then, on 'hoo – oh – or – ah – igh – ey – oo – oh – or – ah – igh – ey etc'.*
- *Then, on 'hoo – oh – or – ah – igh – ay – ee – oo – oh – or – ah – igh – ey – ee etc'.*

Focusing the sound forward with text

To encourage the sound to continue to flow forward to the front of the mouth when speaking text

If you find that your voice is free and forward during exercises but disappears back into your throat when you speak then this exercise will be especially useful.

- *Sit or stand as before, directing the back to lengthen and the shoulders and hips to widen. Check that the feet are parallel and hip width apart, that the joints are loose and the shoulder blades and buttocks are dropping gently down your back.*
- *Round the lips as before and keeping the lips rounded chant some text and imagine the sound flowing forward as it did in the two previous exercises.*
- *Then, alternate between chanting and talking the text imagining the text flowing forward to the front of the mouth when you talk in the same as it does when you chant.*

Building up the Resonance

Now that the sound is flowing forward we can begin to fill out the sound. By focusing the sound into the mouth or chest cavity or certain bones in the face and imagining the sound vibrating there and those vibrations increasing, the body and voice is brought to life and this helps to build the resonance.

'Middle resonance'

We are going to start with what I call 'middle resonance'. By 'middle resonance' I mean the vibration we feel in the mouth. This resonance is important because it gives substance to the voice. It builds a central core and fills the 'gap' between the lower and higher resonance and so stops you from having two separate voices.

The work we have just done on bringing the voice forward will already have started to build up the middle resonance so we are just going to build on it a little more specifically here.

Focusing on the vibrations in the mouth

To build up the middle resonance

We are going to work with the 'hoo – oh – or – ah – igh – ey – ee' sequence from 'Focusing the Sound Forward – 2'. However, now we are going to focus inside the mouth on the vibration there.

- *Sit or stand as before, directing the back to lengthen and the shoulders and hips to widen. Check that the feet are parallel and hip width apart, that the joints are loose and the shoulder blades and buttocks are dropping gently down your back.*
- *Move the face and lips around again to ease them out and, then, blow through the lips.*
- *Open the jaw, as before, so that there is a finger's width between the back teeth and smile a warm, genuine smile. Again, have a sense of soft surprise in the back of the mouth.*
- *Keeping the jaw open, round the lips and sound out on 'hoo – oh – or – ah – igh – ey – ee – oo – oh – or – ah – igh – ey – ee etc' imagining the sound flowing forward to the lips as before.*
- *Then, put your attention inside the front of your mouth and sense the sound bouncing back and forth there.*
- *Once you have a good sense of the sound bouncing back and forth in the front of the mouth, begin to chant some text, taking time with every vowel so that you can feel the sound vibrating on each one. Remember to flow from word to word without pause and to stop as soon as there is no comfortable breath left, even if you are in the middle of a phrase.*
- *Continue until you have the same sense of sound bouncing back and forth in the mouth when you chant the text that you had when you sounded out on 'hoo – oh – or – ah – igh – ey – ee etc'.*
- *Register how it feels physically when you chant the words. Then, alternate between chanting a line of text and speaking a line of text, keeping the same sensation when you speak that you had when you chanted.*
- *Don't worry if this is difficult and there seems to be a big change between the chanting and the speaking. Use this to learn. How does the chanting feel? What*

changes physically when you speak? Does it feel as if there is less space? Do you lose the sensation of the sound flowing out when you speak? Does it feel chopped up?

- *Once you have a sense of what changes between the chanting and speaking, go back and focus on the chanting alone. Feel the space, feel the flow, feel the vibration of the sound on each vowel. Then, alternate again between speaking and chanting until physically the speaking feels the same as the chanting.*
- *Keep working with different texts so that you can begin to build up a habit of resonating in the mouth. Then, as usual let the voice take care of itself.*

'Lower resonance'

'Lower resonance' gives the voice weight, depth and breadth and stops it from sounding shrill or thin. In larger spaces it helps the voice to fill the space in terms of size.

The relaxation, releasing and opening work that we looked at in the previous chapters will have already begun to encourage the 'lower resonance'. However, now we are going to work more specifically on developing this resonance by focusing attention on the chest and the sensation of vibrations there.

Focusing on the vibrations in the chest

To encourage lower resonance

- *Sit or stand as before, directing the back to lengthen and the shoulders and hips to widen. Check that the feet are parallel and hip width apart, that the joints are loose and the shoulder blades and buttocks are dropping gently down your back.*
- *Start by humming on a comfortable note, neither high nor low, just whatever note comes out if you don't think about it.*
- *Move the lips around as you hum, as before and, again, imagine the sound flowing forward into the lips.*
- *Once you have established this easy hum, focus on the bony bump on the upper part of the breastbone and imagine sound coming out through the bump as well as through the lips. You may find it helpful to place your fingers lightly on the bony bump to help you focus there.*
- *Staying on the same note and letting the sound flow forward to the lips as well as out of the bony bump on the breastbone, start to gently but firmly tap down and up your breast bone with your fingers and notice the sensation of vibration you feel there.*

- *Don't worry if it is small at first. The more you pay attention to this area the more the sensation of vibration will grow.*
- *Then, hum again and this time gently but firmly tap out across your chest.*
- *Once you have a good sense of the sound vibrating in the chest, open onto an 'ah' without letting the sound scoop down to a lower pitch.*
- *Keep patting your chest whilst you chant 'mmaaah mmaaah mmaaah etc'.*
- *Check that the sound stays forward by first feeling the hum come forward to the lips before focusing on the chest.*
- *Once you have a strong sense of vibration in the chest start to chant the text, as you did in the previous exercise, taking time with every vowel so that you can feel the sound bouncing back and forth in the chest on every sound. Remember to flow from word to word without pause and to stop as soon as there is no comfortable breath left, even if you are in the middle of a phrase.*
- *Continue until you have the same sense of vibrations in the chest when you chant the words as you had when you chanted 'mmaaah mmaaah mmaaah'.*
- *As before, register how it feels physically when you chant the words. Then, as before, alternate between chanting a line of text and speaking a line of text, keeping the same sensation when you speak as you had when you chanted.*
- *As before, keep working with different texts so that you can begin to build up a habit of resonating in the chest. Then, as usual let the voice take care of itself.*

'Upper resonance'

Upper resonance gives the voice brightness, energy and focus. It helps the voice to carry and prevents it from being dull and muffled. In order to develop good upper resonance the face needs to be alive – particularly the area between the top lip and the eyebrows.

To understand the link between the face and the voice think what happens when someone is very depressed: their face often becomes immobile and expressionless and their voice is correspondingly flat and lifeless. Conversely, when someone is happy and full of life, their face is alive and full of expression and their voice is correspondingly animated and expressive.

Now in the above cases the face is accurately reflecting how the person feels and so the resulting voice is appropriate.

Yet, all too often, the face becomes disconnected – ending up either stiff and immobile or over-animated – so that whatever the person may be feeling does not show through in their face nor in their voice.

So, however inwardly animated a person may feel, if this area of their face is stiff and motionless their voice will be similarly lifeless: lacking energy and flexibility of tone and colour. Equally, however sincere a person may feel, if this area of their face is overly mobile and expressive the voice will be similarly overblown and we may find it difficult to believe them or feel truly touched by them.

So how does this disconnection come about? There are many reasons. Constant catarrh can deaden this area and, even if the catarrh has now passed, the habit of sluggishness may remain. Concern over the appearance of the teeth, especially the top ones can lead to the top lip being held still to hide them and this tends to stiffen up the whole area between the upper lip and the eyes. Also, if a person is physically sluggish throughout their body this, not surprisingly, carries through into the face.

Another reason may be that a person felt they needed to damp down the expression of their feelings or even hide them completely. They wouldn't be aware of having immobilised the face: this simply happens as a result of being less willing to reveal how they feel. The stiff upper lip is a form of hiding one's feelings. If you stiffen the upper lip it stops the lower lip from quivering as it might do if you were on the verge of tears.

Often, a person's decision to hide their feelings was made years ago and is no longer relevant since they no longer feel the need to hide their feelings. However, the face may still be lifeless, because that is the habit that has developed unconsciously. As a result, they may now be very frustrated that their face and voice do not reflect how they feel.

Sometimes people try to compensate for this and the face and voice can become over animated. The problem with this is there is still no connection and so the person can come across as insincere.

Equally, an over-expressive face can be the result of an attempt to hide one's feelings in a different way. For instance, if a person felt that they had to pretend to be happier than they were, to put on a brave face, or even perhaps to hide certain feelings they may have felt less easy about, such as anger, then their facial expression would begin to express the pretended feeling rather than the real ones. If this pretence were repeated for some time the face muscles would eventually set into the patterns of the pretended feelings. As before, the person would not be aware of this and so, even though they may now wish to reveal how they feel, the face would be stuck in its repertoire of pretended feelings rather like a mask.

Now, to some degree we all hide our feelings from time to time. This is quite natural. The problem occurs when the face becomes fixed in a pattern of movements and cannot change to reflect our feelings when we wish it to.

Of course, some actors make their livelihood from their deadpan or over expressive faces and voices. There is no right or wrong. It is simply a matter of choice. If you feel that your face and voice don't reflect what you feel – that they lack energy and expression or that they are inappropriately animated – and if you would like to change this then it is worth working on the exercises for waking up the face.

Waking up the face

To remove tension and bring the face to life, so bringing life to the voice

- *Sit or stand as before, directing the back to lengthen and the shoulders and hips to widen. Check that the feet are parallel and hip width apart, that the joints are loose and the shoulder blades and buttocks are dropping gently down your back.*
- *Move the face around and as you do so focus on the area between the upper lip and the eyebrows.*
- *Then, massage this area, starting with the top lip and moving on to the cheeks. Feel as if you are waking this area up, reconnecting with it, bringing it to life. Remember that where you bring your attention, you bring energy.*
- *Then, hum easily as you move your face around and imagine the sound flowing out of every pore between the upper lip and the eyebrows, including the eyes.*
- *Now chant a piece of text and move your face around while you chant it. Try not to make faces, rather think of loosening the face up, bringing it to life while you speak and, again imagine the sound flowing out of the area between your upper lip and eyebrows, including the eyes.*
- *Then, chant the text again, without moving the face around, but still imagining the sound flowing out through the same area.*
- *Doing this regularly will really bring the face to life and free it from habitual facial expressions and vocal patterns.*

Easing and waking up the eyes

To remove tension from the eyes and bring them to life, so bringing life to the voice

This exercise is excellent for removing eye tension and is certainly worth trying because free, alive eyes bring a real sparkle to the voice and indeed, to our whole being and presence.

- *Sit or stand as before, directing the back to lengthen and the shoulders and hips to widen. Check that the feet are parallel and hip width apart, that the joints are loose and the shoulder blades and buttocks are dropping gently down your back.*
- *Start by looking straight. Then, keeping your head loosely still, look up and then down, four times.*
- *Then, again keeping your head loosely still, look to the left and, then, to the right, four times.*
- *Then, again keeping the head loosely still, circle the eyes round four times clockwise and four times anticlockwise.*
- *Then, close your eyes and rest your fingertips lightly on your eyes for 30 seconds.*

Focusing on the vibrations in the face

To bring brightness, clarity and energy to the voice

We are going to start this exercise by focusing on the brow of the nose. Focusing here helps to bring the sound forward in preparation for focusing it out into the cheeks.

- *Sit or stand as before, directing the back to lengthen and the shoulders and hips to widen. Check that the feet are parallel and hip width apart, that the joints are loose and the shoulder blades and buttocks are dropping gently down your back.*
- *Place two fingers on the brow of the nose between the eyebrows and focus your attention there. Begin to hum – 'mmmmmmmmm etc' – on a slightly higher pitch than you did in the last exercise and imagine the sound flowing out through the brow of the nose.*
- *Once you have even the slightest sense of vibration or tickling in the brow of the nose, slide from the hum into a long 'ee' – 'mmmmeeeeeeee' – imagining the 'ee' sound still flowing out through the brow of the nose. Repeat this a few times.*
- *Then, place the fingers of both hands on the bridge of the nose and hum again. Draw your fingers down and out from the bridge of the nose along the cheekbones and, as you do so, imagine the hum is being drawn down and out*

with your fingers. Repeat this a few times until you have a sense of buzz or vibration in the cheekbones.

- *Then, slide from the hum into a long 'ee' – 'mmmmeeeeeeee' – imagining the 'ee' sound still vibrating in the cheekbones and flowing out through them.*
- *Once you have the same sense of vibration in the cheekbones on the 'eeee' as you had on the hum, start to chant some text taking time with every vowel so that you can imagine each one flowing out through the cheekbones. As always, remember to slide from word to word without pause and to stop as soon as there is no comfortable breath left, even if you are in the middle of a phrase.*
- *Continue until you have the same sense of vibration in the cheekbones when you chant the words as you had when you sounded out on 'mmmmmeeeeeee'.*
- *Then, alternate between chanting a line of text and speaking a line of text, imagining the sound flowing out through the cheekbones when you speak in the same way as you are doing when you chant.*
- *Again, keep working with different texts so that you can begin to build up a habit of focusing the sound into the cheekbones. Then, as usual, let the voice take care of itself.*

Joining up the middle, lower and upper resonance

To sense the vibration of sound throughout the whole upper body and head and beyond

Now we are going to put the work on the middle, lower and upper resonance together and extend the sense of vibrations into the forehead, back of head and upper back.

- *Sit or stand as before, directing the back to lengthen and the shoulders and hips to widen. Check that the feet are parallel and hip width apart, that the joints are loose and the shoulder blades and buttocks are dropping gently down your back.*
- *Hum easily and imagine the sound flowing into the whole area from your chest to your eyebrows. Keep the lips, tongue, jaw and throat relaxed and the sound easy and without any push. Take your time to let the sound fill the whole area.*
- *Once you have a sense of the sound vibrating in the whole area from chest to eyebrows, then focus on your whole back as far down as your waist and imagine the sound also flowing into that area and vibrating there. You may feel very little at first or you may feel a great deal. Just work with what you have. Nothing will be achieved by force.*

- *Then, hum easily again and focus on the back of the neck and imagine the sound flowing into that area and vibrating there.*
- *Work in the same way focusing on the back of the head, then the top of the head and then the forehead. You may find it helps to raise the pitch a little. Have patience and don't force. If you just focus your attention and imagine the sound flowing to the area you are focusing on and vibrating there then, in time, the whole of the upper body and head will come alive.*
- *Once you have a sense of the whole upper body and head vibrating, start to chant easily and imagine the sound still flowing into the whole area and vibrating there.*
- *Once you feel the vibrations throughout on the chanting, then, as before, alternate between chanting and speaking until you feel as much vibration when you speak as you did when you chanted.*

Putting the Chapter together

It is good to work through all the resonance exercises regularly. I have added them into the session below. As always this is no more than a suggestion.

If you are feeling confident about the work feel free to disregard it completely and build your own session around the exercises that feel good for you. Obviously, it is good to start with any relaxation and posture work and then move onto breath and support and then into the exercises for releasing the sound before coming to the resonance work.

If you're less sure use the order of the session as a basis, selecting the specific exercises that you feel helpful.

Never work for more than forty minutes. The session below is about 38 minutes long and at least a third of it is silent work on posture and breath.

Warm-up (1 minute)

Freeing the breath (*68*)

Floor work (3 minutes)

Centring the breath (*69*)
Opening the throat (*72*)
Engage, release and 'H' breath (*this is not described above as such. It is simply the version against the wall – page 84 – done on the floor*)

Standing (7 minutes)

Lengthening and widening (*132*)
Working against the wall or Wide arms (*133 or 134*)
Side to side (*135*)
Half neck circles (*136*)
Nose circles or Nose figure of eight or Head nods (*137*)
Engage, release and 'H' breath (*against wall*) (*84*)
Engage, release and 'H' breath (*with chair*) (*84*)

Sitting or Standing (11 minutes)

Widening and opening (*138*)
Freeing the larynx 1 and 2 (*139*)
Giggle and sob (*with text*) (*140*)
Lower jaw drop 2 (*with text*) (*143*)
Upper jaw release (*with text*) (*144*)
Cleaning the teeth with the tongue (*146*)
Back of tongue stretch (*147*)
Under chin massage (*with text*) (*148*)
Lazy forward tongue talking (*with text*) (*149*)
Ng-Ah and Ng-Ah into talking (*166 and 167*)
Hng – Ah into talking (*168*)

Standing (16 minutes)

Sliding 'sh' (*156*)
Bouncing sound from the diaphragm (*99*)
Bouncing sound from the lower belly (*102*)
Bouncing sound from the 'oomph points' (*103*)
Calling (*with text*) (*114*)
Engaging the lower belly and pelvic floor muscles throughout the sound (*109*)
Engaging the 'oomph points' throughout the sound (*110*)
Focusing the sound forward – 1 and 2 (*169*)
Focusing on the mouth (*172*)
Focusing on the chest (*173*)
Waking up the face and the eyes (*176*)
Focusing on the face (*177*)
Putting the resonance together (*178*)
Lengthening and widening while releasing (*with text*) (*132*)
Drop and release (*158*)
Door handle swing (*158*)

7

Extending the Sound: Range

In the last chapter we looked at filling out the sound to give the voice strength, richness and complexity. Now we are going to look at extending the range. The reason for this work, as for all the other work on the voice, is to allow your thoughts and feelings to be expressed fully and subtly.

Just as we weren't trying to create a beautiful voice in the resonance work, so in the range work we are *not* trying to create an impressive range. Vocal gymnastics distract from the act of communication; they do not enhance it!

The purpose of the work in this chapter is to develop the full range, of which your voice is capable, so it can accurately reflect your internal world.

How changes in pitch occur

Changes in pitch are achieved by changes in the length and thickness of the vocal folds. The higher the pitch, the longer and thinner the folds. The lower the pitch, the shorter and thicker the folds. These changes in length and thickness are brought about by the action of various laryngeal muscles. These muscles need to be toned and flexible so they can make the minute changes necessary to produce the various different pitches easily and rapidly. We will look at the best way of doing this later in the chapter (see page following).

Powering the range work from the support muscles

Increases in pitch require increases in breath pressure. To achieve these increases it is *vital* that the support muscles – the abdominal and pelvic floor muscles – are working effectively (see page 109). As always, this does not mean that you need to pump air, simply that you need to retain a sense of *connection* with the support muscles so that they naturally engage. Despite the fact that the pitch is rising, it is important that your attention does not move up away from the support points in the lower body. Working with the *image* of the mouth or throat being *in* one of the support points and of actually speaking *from* there is very useful (see pages 102–105 and 109–110). It is also useful to work with the sobbing exercise (see page 140) to prevent tightness in the throat.

Freeing and Extending your Range

As I mentioned in the introduction to this chapter, the larnygeal muscles need to be toned and flexible in order to make the minute changes in length and thickness necessary to achieve a free and extensive range. The best way to tone these muscles, and make them more flexible, is to practise gliding slowly through the range. This gives the muscles time to make the necessary changes in length and thickness. With practise you will find that you can move around your range more freely and easily and this will provide a firm basis from which you can extend your range.

'OOEE' glide

To enable free and easy movement around the range, maintaining consistent forward focus and quality

- *Sit or stand as before, directing the back to lengthen and the shoulders and hips to widen. Check that the feet are parallel and hip width apart, that the joints are loose and the shoulder blades and buttocks are dropping gently down your back.*
- *Place your hands just below your navel.*
- *We are going to use a continuous 'ooeeooeeooee' sound, keeping the lips rounded on the 'ee' as well as the 'oo'. The reason for this is that it helps to keep the sound forward.*

Note

Breaks At first you may notice breaks in pitch as you glide through your range. Sometimes these can seem quite dramatic. However, they are nothing to worry about, unless you are experiencing a sore throat or vocal fatigue, in which cases it is best not to do any range work until you are fully recovered. Obviously, if you are in any doubt about the health of your larynx arrange to see an ear, nose and throat specialist to have yourself checked out.

Otherwise, just glide very slowly through the break and in time the laryngeal muscles will learn to make the minute adjustments that are needed in order to move smoothly through the range.

You may also notice changes in vocal quality as you move from one register to another. These can also be helped by gliding slowly and by focusing the sound forward as you do so.

The main point here is never to force or tense to smooth over pitch breaks or changes of quality. Time and appropriate focus will smooth out the breaks – not effort.

Also, we are going to use a slight sob to help keep the throat open. Remember to keep the sob enjoyable, with no angst in it.

- *Before you start to make any sound, blow the air out easily and fully from the belly, keeping the spine long and then release the belly and pelvic floor muscles and allow the new in-breath to come in as and when it wishes. Repeat this a few times to wake up the breathing system. As you do so remember to focus on the breath flowing from the belly to the lips so you remind yourself of the connection with the belly.*

- *Then, blow out again and as the in-breath flows in imagine that in-breath taking you up above the note you are going to glide down from so that you drop onto your highest comfortable note rather than reaching up for it. I find it helpful to imagine this starting note being placed in the bridge of the nose; it helps to keep the sound forward.*

- *If you feel any tension in the throat start on a softly surprised or bored 'hoo'. Think of melting or sliding into the initial sound rather than grasping at it or jumping on it.*

- *Once you have started the sound, let it slide down your pitch range slowly, as if it were like a feather or leaf gently floating downwards. The slower you go the better and don't worry about running out of breath. Allow a new breath in and then slide on downward from more or less where you stopped.*

- *Go especially slowly around any break areas, so the muscles have time to make the necessary smaller changes that they are not used to. With patience and no force the breaks will gradually disappear.*

- *Remember to keep the lips rounded and imagine the sound sliding down your nose and then resting in your lips. As you slide down into the lower part of your range, imagine the sound continuing to come forward to the lips and then dropping forward out of the mouth into the chest. Never let the sound drop back and down.*

By mentally 'pegging' the sound forward you will find, in time, that you can glide down the whole range without changes in quality, so that although you may be moving from register to register you will have one voice rather than several different ones.

Practise this exercise regularly for about a minute and then move on to the next one.

Roller coaster

To develop vocal range

The best way to develop more range is to play and to allow your imagination to extend your voice rather than trying to work at it or force it.

- *Stand as before, directing the back to lengthen and the shoulders and hips to widen. Check that the feet are parallel and hip width apart, that the joints are loose and the shoulder blades and buttocks are dropping gently down your back.*
- *Place your hands just below your navel.*
- *Again we are going to use 'ooeeooeeooee', keeping the lips rounded and the sound flowing from the belly to the lips.*
- *Imagine a roller coaster in front of you and imagine that your voice is a carriage travelling up and down along that roller coaster. If you find it hard to get your voice to move up and down use your hand to trace the journey of the carriage on the roller coaster.*
- *Let your voice take care of itself and really allow yourself to be absorbed by the roller coaster and the journey of the carriage along it. Allow the upward and downward curves of the roller coaster to increase so it is dropping right down and then soaring right up. The more you play and get lost in the image, the more the image will stimulate the voice to move around.*
- *If you do find your voice tiring then focus your attention more on the belly and the idea of the sound releasing from there, but still let the sound take care of itself. Avoid pushing the voice up or down and don't listen to it to check whether or not it is moving up and down, just TRUST that if you really go with the image, the image will move your voice around.*
- *You can also draw your name or a pattern or a picture. Again, forget about your voice and just play, allowing the image's movement to lead your voice's movement.*

As with the previous exercise spend a minute or two regularly with this exercise and then move on to the next one.

Car revs

To check that the range work is well supported and to increase the support

Car revs are excellent for checking that you are supporting the sound with the breath rather than throat tension.

- *Stand as before, directing the back to lengthen and the shoulders and hips to widen. Check that the feet are parallel and hip width apart, that the joints are loose and the shoulder blades and buttocks are dropping gently down your back.*
- *Place your hands just below your navel.*
- *Blow through your lips like a horse; loosen your lips by flicking your finger up and down across your lips if necessary. Then, add sound – 'brrrrrr' (i.e. sound you make when you are cold). Focus on the sound coming from the belly to the front of the mouth.*

> **Note**
> This exercise is excellent for warming up as well as for doing on a regular basis, because it really sparks the support muscles into action and stops you from straining when doing pitch work.

- *Then, do short bouts of this sound as if you are imitating a car revving up, again, focusing on the sound coming from the belly to the front of the mouth.*
- *Then, car rev on different pitches, still focusing on the sound coming from the belly. Really play at the car revs as if you are a child.*
- *You can, also, try this exercise on a rolled 'r' – 'rrrrrrr'.*

Down and up

To free and extend the range

This exercise is based on one that I learned from the singer and voice teacher Helen Chadwick and, like so much of her work, it is both helpful and fun. It is excellent for freeing up the range and I use it a great deal in vocal warm-ups. As always, my description below reflects how I use the exercise and may not be exactly as Helen would use it.

You can do this exercise on 'ooeeooeeooee' or 'bllllllll' or the car rev 'brrrrrrrrs'.

- *Start standing with your right arm in the air. (See diagram 1a.) Let your body and arm drop over from your hips, letting your arm also drop. (See diagram 1b.) Imagine your chosen sound sliding down through your arm as you drop down.*

- *Then, as soon as you have dropped down, allow yourself to bounce back up again letting your left arm go up in the air and your sound slide easily up through your range as you roll up. (See diagram 1c.)*

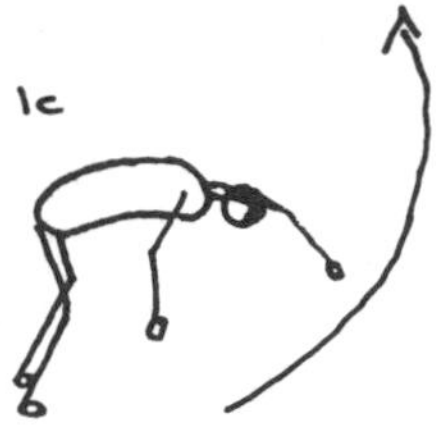

- *As always let the sound take care of itself and simply enjoy dropping and bouncing back up. The freer you are with the movement and the more you let the sound slide down and up of its own accord the better.*
- *As you let the new breath in, lower your left arm and simultaneously raise your right arm.*
- *Repeat three times leading down with the right hand and up with the left. Then, three times leading down with the left hand and up with the right.*

Connecting the Range

Once you have 'oiled' the range, that is, once you have toned the muscles, by doing the various exercises, and can move easily and smoothly around your whole range with consistent strength and quality, then you can start to put that range to use.

As I mentioned earlier, artificially manipulating pitch is a bad idea. So, how do you work on getting more range into your speaking voice? Again, it is a question of *connection.*

Internally, we remain as expressive as when we were children, but, as mentioned in previous chapters, this inner expression can become 'unplugged' from our outer expression. We may shut down out of fear of being too passionate, too revealing or too emotional. Or we may mask feelings of depression or tiredness or sadness or boredom – exaggerating the pitch movement in our voice so we seem happier or more upbeat than we feel. Either way, our movement around our pitch range fails to truthfully reflect our thoughts and feelings.

As I also mentioned earlier, we are often not aware of having made a decision to disconnect in this way. So, now, it can be very frustrating, since we don't understand why the life of our internal voice does not show through in the life of our external voice.

Another cause of flatness or exaggerated movement in the voice can be lack of trust, which I discussed, in the opening chapter. If you remember,

I mentioned that one of two behaviours occurs when we lose trust: either we become tentative or we become over-effortful. If we become tentative, the voice will tend to be flatter because we are not committing to expressing our internal thoughts and feelings. If we become over-effortful, the voice will tend to be over exaggerated in its pitch movement since we will not trust our thoughts and feelings to be expressed by the natural movement of the voice and will therefore 'help' everything along.

A further cause of disconnection can be that we are not connecting with what we are saying or with the person we are saying it to. This can happen both with our own words and with text. We need to *see* the pictures or images behind our words and, then, we need to *want* the person we are addressing to see the same pictures and images. This is not a question of *thinking* about what you are saying or trying to *explain* it to your listener. It is about *being present* with the words and images and with the person you're speaking to.

This may sound horrendously complicated but it isn't and when you make this connection you become utterly simple and yet utterly engaging!

The exercises in this section will help not only if you feel there might be a degree of disconnection, but also if you feel fine about the way you move around your range and would simply like to explore a little further.

Three times through

To allow your connection with the words to fully and authentically colour how you say them

This is an excellent exercise to try with text. I have used it both to help actors connect with a new text and to bring fresh life to a text they may have been working with for some time. At any stage, it allows you to connect more fully and deeply with the words you are saying and this extra connection leads to more movement in the voice, without any danger of over-embellishment.

- *Sit comfortably, somewhere that is quiet and private.*
- *Take a piece of text a small phrase at a time, sometimes you may even take one word at a time. The reason for this is that, if you take more than a few words at once, you will find yourself only connecting with some of the words, usually the 'so called' more important ones. Whereas, if you take a few words at a time you can connect with every word. This does not mean that you will end up stressing every word, but rather that each word will have its own place and colour within the whole, which leads to greater variety and greater subtlety.*

- *Take the first phrase and repeat it quietly, but not whispered, three times. Just let the words register. Don't try to find different ways to say them, simply let the words sink in.*
- *Then, move on to the next phrase and say that three times through, again letting the words sink in and register.*
- *Continue in this way, saying each small phrase three times and then moving onto the next.*
- *Don't string all the phrases together, just say each one three times and then leave it and move onto the next.*
- *There is no need to try and achieve anything in this exercise, just receive the words and let them guide your voice.*

Sharing the pictures with the listener

To use the energy of communication to bring life and authentic colour to your speech

This exercise is based on the excellent work of Cicely Berry. It continues the work on connecting with the words and brings in the work of connecting with your listener. It is these two connections, in the end, which will bring your full range into play in a truthful and exciting way. You need a partner for this exercise.

- *Sit comfortably opposite your partner.*
- *Start to speak a piece of text to your partner. Focus on talking rather than acting the text. Put all your attention on your partner and on wanting to communicate with them.*
- *As you are talking, your partner listens and honestly questions any part of the text where they don't get the picture. Here is an example of how the exercise might work using a speech of Yasmin's from 'Pentecost' by David Edgar.*

  YOU: *When she came back*
  PARTNER: *When she what?*

- *You then need to answer by repeating the particular bit of text questioned, but you can't raise your voice or emphasise the word (or words) more to get the images across to your partner. You need to really connect with what that word (or words) mean for you, what they conjure up and then share that.*

  YOU: *came back*

(If your partner feels they have received the picture, you can move on, otherwise, they may ask again)

YOU: *at first it looked quite normal*
PARTNER: *When did it look quite normal?*
YOU: *at first*

(Again, if your partner feels they have received the picture, you can move on, otherwise, they may ask again)

YOU: *it looked quite normal*
PARTNER: *Looked quite odd?*
YOU: *quite normal*
YOU: *And as it was the morning*
PARTNER: *The evening?*
YOU: *the morning*
YOU: *it was no surprise to find the door open*
PARTNER: *It was a shock?*
PARTNER: *it was no surprise*
YOU: *to find the door open*
PARTNER: *To find the shop closed?*
YOU: *to find the door open*

- *Your partner has a big responsibility here to not just question you arbitrarily but to really pick you up when they feel that they haven't been communicated with.*
- *Your responsibility is not to take the easy way out and simply raise your voice or emphasise the word more, but rather to really connect with the word and share that.*

'Singing' the text

To help to extend the use of range authentically

This next exercise you can do on your own. It really opens up the voice and encourages a greater use of your range without force or artificiality. Again we are going to use your connection with the word to instigate the pitch movement.

This time we are going to 'sing' the text. The reason for this it that it is easier to be aware of pitch movement when singing than it is when you are speaking.

Don't be put off by the fact that the exercise seems to involve singing. I use the term 'singing' in the loosest sense. In fact it is often the non-singers who find this exercise most liberating and useful. Also, since the idea is to allow the tune to come from your connection with the words, there can be no possibility of being out of tune. This is singing for non-singers!

If you are a singer try not to choose any particular style of singing and also don't let yourself slip into the tune of any particular song. The singing here needs to be free and, perhaps, even a little messy.

- *This exercise is best done on your feet, moving around, rather than sitting or standing still. Sometimes it helps to swing your arms or whole upper body loosely to keep physically free and open.*
- *Despite the fact that you are singing, the focus is still on connecting with the words and sharing that connection. Since you don't have a partner in this exercise you can sing the words to objects in the room.*
- *So, begin to sing freely, allowing the changes of pitch to express your sense of or feeling for the words you are singing.*

Putting the Chapter together

The exercises for creating and extending your range in the first half of this chapter need take no longer than four minutes and I have added them into the suggested session below, which, as always, you are free to ignore. I have taken out the floor version of 'Engaging, releasing and the 'H' breath' and given you a choice of doing the standing version either against the wall or with the chair. This is to ensure that the session is no longer than forty minutes. However, you might want to keep all these exercises and remove some others. As always trust yourself and just make sure that your session is not longer than 40 minutes.

The exercises in the second half of the chapter can be used whenever you feel they are appropriate to help you connect with a piece.

Warm-up (1 minute)

Freeing the breath (69)

Floor work (2 minutes)

Centring the breath (69)
Opening the throat (72)

Standing (6 minutes)

Lengthening and widening (132)
Working against the wall or wide arms (133 *and* 134)

Side to side (135)
Half neck circles (136)
Nose circles or Nose figure of eight or Head nods (137)
Engage, release and 'H' breath (against wall or with chair) (84)

Sitting or Standing (11 minutes)

Widening and opening (138)
Freeing the larynx 1 and 2 (139)
Giggle and sob (with text) (140)
Lower jaw drop 2 (with text) (143)
Upper jaw release (with text) (144)
Cleaning the teeth with the tongue (146)
Back of tongue stretch (147)
Under chin massage (with text) (148)
Lazy forward tongue talking (with text) (149)
Ng-Ah and Ng-Ah into talking (166 and 167)
Hng – Ah into talking (168)

Standing (20 minutes)

Sliding 'sh' (156)
Bouncing sound from the diaphragm (99)
Bouncing sound from the lower belly (102)
Bouncing sound from the 'oomph points' (103)
Calling (with text) (114)
Engaging the lower belly and pelvic floor muscles throughout the sound (109)
Engaging the 'oomph points' throughout the sound (110)
Focusing the sound forward – 1 and2 (169)
Focusing on the mouth (172)
Focusing on the chest (173)
Waking up the face and the eyes (176)
Focusing on the face (177)
Putting the resonance together (178)
Ooee glide (183)
Roller coaster (185)
Car revs (185)
Down and up (186)
Lengthening and widening while releasing (with text) (132)
Drop and release (with text) (158)
Door handle swing (with text) (158)

8

Shaping the Sound: Articulation

So far we have explored all aspects of *creating* sound – posture, breath, support, resonance and range. Now we are going to look at *shaping* that sound into speech.

Obviously, you have been working with speech throughout, but always with the focus on the theme of each chapter. Now we are going to look at the forming of speech itself.

Vowels and consonants – two sorts of sound

Speech comprises of two sorts of sounds, which have distinctive qualities and functions.

Vowels are *open, releasing* sounds. They are formed by shifts in position of the lips and tongue, which *change the shape* of the mouth space, but never *close* it. Vowels carry the emotion. They are like a 'river of feelings' running through the centre of our speech. They need space and time, opening and release.

The consonants are *shaping* sounds. Again, they are formed by shifts in position of the lips and tongue, but these shifts *narrow* or *close off* the mouth space in some way. Consonants carry the *sense*. They *contain* and *shape* the river of sound and feeling. They give definition and clarity. They need commitment, precision and muscular energy.

If the consonants are too loosely made, if they lack definition and clarity, we hear sound and feeling but it makes little sense. If the consonants are too tightly made, the voice and emotion are over-controlled, perhaps even strangled out of existence altogether. We understand the sense but are not touched or moved by what is said.

The balance between the vowels and the consonants needs to be found so that the emotion does not drown the sense, nor the sense strangle the emotion.

Checking the balance between the vowels and the consonants

How do you find out whether there is a balance between vowels and consonants, between emotion and sense, in your speech?

Remember that you can't communicate sense with vowels, nor can you communicate emotion with consonants.

So, think about what people have said to you about your work. If you have often been told that you are not clear, that the emotion seems to be drowning out the sense, then the chances are that you are doing most of your communicating through the vowels and that definition is lacking.

If you have often been told that you are very clear and that you always make perfect sense but that your work lacks feeling, that it doesn't touch the audience, then the chances are that you are doing most of your communicating through the consonants.

So how do you find a balance? As always, you cannot think about it on stage or in rehearsals: that would be disastrous. You need to explore the vowels and consonants separately, as suggested in the exercises below, and then trust that this exploration will filter into your work.

Working on the vowels

Where there is clarity but less emotion you need to work with the chanting, singing and vocal release exercises from the previous chapters. These will help to open you up physically and allow the emotion and sound to be released to the audience, rather than being held back. Be assured such emotional release will not lead to emotional 'gush' and outpourings of feeling. Release never leads to excess, because there is no push behind it. Release allows for subtlety and natural restraint.

Once the sound has been released, then you can begin to explore the vowels more specifically: their different shapes and lengths. This is not done in a dry, technical way. Instead, you explore the vowels practically: how the different vowels feel, how do they make you feel as you say them? This will raise your sensitivity to the nuances of sound and the natural music within a piece of text, which is much more subtle, robust and exciting than the false musicality that is often imposed on text.

Each text is different. Each text has its own balance between emotion and sense, its own particular music, which may just as easily be jagged and harsh as flowing and harmonious. The exercise exploring the movement of vowels in a text, later in the chapter, is a great way of finding the music and emotional tone of any text.

Vowel lengths Although, *scientifically,* there is little measurable difference now in English vowel length, there is a difference to our unscientific ears and this difference is very useful. It helps us find the real emotional rhythm of a text and stops us from making it either grandiloquent or mundane.

Vowels fall into three categories: Short, Long and Travelling.

Travelling vowels are more usually called 'Diphthongs' which means they consist of two vowels. The sound is created by movement from the first vowel position to the second vowel position. You can always tell a diphthong because you can't hold onto the sound endlessly. At some point you have to move from the first sound to the second sound, whereas you can hold on to a long sound forever.

Note

Vowels do change between accents and this change may lead to some change in length. However, on the whole it does not lead to vowels moving category.

The lists below use Standard English examples only because it is Standard English that is usually used as a reference accent. However, I've done this work with people not only using a wide variety of accents but also with people using other languages. What is really being explored is the rhythm created by the vowels and their shifting lengths– the emotional ebb and flow if you like – and this exists in every accent and language.

Short Vowels

'i' as in 'pit'
'e' as in 'pet'
'a' as in 'pat'
'u' as in 'cut'
'o' as in 'pot'
'oo' as in 'put'

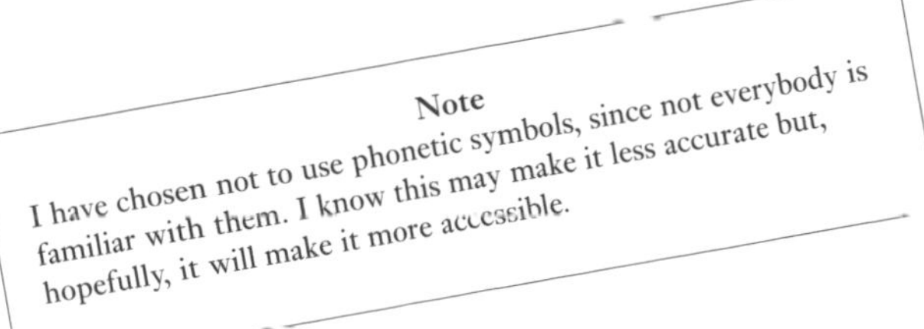
Note

I have chosen not to use phonetic symbols, since not everybody is familiar with them. I know this may make it less accurate but, hopefully, it will make it more accessible.

There is also a neutral sound rather like a grunt. We use it in unstressed parts of many words e.g. mother, sister, immediately, across, around, about, the, and. I have used the spelling 'uh' for this.

Long Vowels

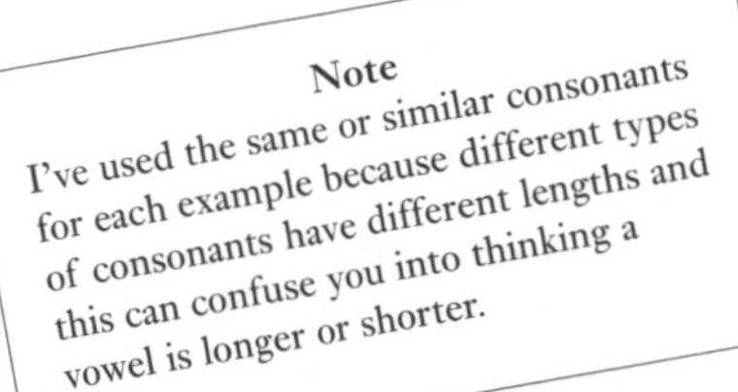
Note
I've used the same or similar consonants for each example because different types of consonants have different lengths and this can confuse you into thinking a vowel is longer or shorter.

'ee' as in 'peat'
'er' as in 'pert'
'ah' as in 'part'
'or' as in 'port'
'ooo' as in 'boot'

Diphthongs or Travelling Vowels

'ay' as in 'bate'
'igh' as in 'bite'
'oy' as in 'buoyed'
'ow' as in 'bout'
'oh' as in 'boat'
'ear' as in 'beard
'air' as in 'paired'
'ooer' as in 'poor' and 'mourning' (nowadays most people would use the long vowel 'or', but it's a lovely sound to play with and sometimes feels right to use in older texts if it suits the emotion. Again it's your choice.)

So to Work on the Vowels

Now you know about the vowels available to you, I would like you to explore them, so you have a sense of their similarities and differences. This is not something you need to 'think' about. Simply do the exercise below and this will raise your level of awareness of the vowels and how they work.

Exploring the vowels

To have a sense of the individuality of each vowel

- *Say the short vowels several times and see how they feel to voice. Do they suggest a certain rhythm? Do they hint at any particular moods? Just see what you notice.*
- *Then, do the same with the long vowels and see how they feel to say. Do they suggest a different rhythm? Do they hint at different moods?*

❍ *Lastly, try the same with the travelling vowels and see how they feel to say.*

❍ *Keep playing with this. There is no right answer. There is just how you feel, your reaction to the different lengths.*

❍ *Try making the short vowels very short, the long vowels very long and the travelling vowels really travel and feel the difference.*

Don't read the next bit until you've tried the sounds out. I want the first impression of the sounds to be yours and not mine.

*

I find the short vowels have a staccato quality, a bounce, they cut through, while the long vowels spread and have more flow and the travelling vowels really seem to open out and release.

❍ *Now try creating a sequence where you move back and forth between the different length vowels. Really commit to the different lengths so that you don't get stuck just doing one length of sounds or allowing one group of sounds to influence the length of the other groups.*

This work is so helpful. If you can really let the vowel lengths shift you will never get stuck in one rhythm in a speech and you will find a variety that comes from the truthful movement within the text and is not something just plastered on.

Also, the emotion will be rooted in the words and will not drown them. It will flow through the heart of the text, giving it a power that will feed you and reach out to the audience.

The grandiloquent and the mundane

When you hear text being delivered that sounds grandiose and pompous and over-theatrical, it is often the case that *all* the vowels are being lengthened. When you hear text being delivered where all the emotion seems small and perhaps too mundane for the scene, it is often the case that *all* the vowels are being shortened.

Neither of these works because they impose a rhythm on a text and they rob it of its variety, its ebb and flow, its shifts of pace.

The next exercise will help you avoid such impositions. Taking your experience of the different vowel lengths we are going to start working with text.

Working with vowels in text

To connect with the inherent music and emotional flow and mood of a text

Choose a piece of text to work on. Perhaps one with which you are finding it difficult to connect or in which you are frightened of being over-emotional. I've used one of Hamlet's soliloquies.

- *Take the text a short phrase at a time. Say the first phrase aloud three or four times so you begin to get a sense of the vowels within the pattern of the whole.*

  E.g. Oh what a rogue ... Oh what a rogue ... Oh what a rogue ...

- *Then, just as if you were playing a game with a child, say the phrase again but this time saying only the vowels.*

  E.g. 'Oh' – 'o' – 'uh' – 'oh' ... 'Oh' – 'o' – 'uh' – 'oh' ... 'Oh' – 'o' – 'uh' – 'oh'

> **Note**
>
> It can be interesting to make a copy of the text and mark the vowels using '/ ' for a short vowel, '_ ' for a long vowel and 'O' for a diphthong.
>
> E.g. 'Oh what a rogue and peasant slave am I.' (marked: o / / o / / / o o /)

- *Repeat the vowels in the phrase several times, allowing the different vowels to have their lengths. Try not to think about what you are doing but rather to trust your instinctive response.*

  E.g. 'Oh' – 'o' – 'uh' – 'oh' ... 'Oh' – 'o' – 'uh' – 'oh' ... 'Oh' – 'o' – 'uh' – 'oh'

- *If you want to check, simply ask: 'Are all the sounds coming out staccato? Or are they all coming out elongated?' If they are all coming out staccato, then, you need to focus on the long and travelling vowels and on letting them have more time and space. If they are all coming out elongated then you need to focus on the shorter vowels and on letting them be very short.*

Don't worry if this exercise feels hard and you have no idea what is going on. Simply by focusing on the vowels and attempting to honour their different lengths you will wake up your instinctive response to the inherent music in a text.

- *Once you have worked through several phrases, and if you are feeling fairly comfortable with the exercise, then, return to the beginning and work through the same phrases again committing strongly to the different vowel lengths you have found. Explore what happens when you do this. Do you begin to get even a slight hint of the emotional movement? Often it is very delicate and can't be described so don't worry about that, simply experience it.*

The more you play with this exercise, without worrying about getting it right or about finding anything at all, the more the text will begin to work its magic on you. Also, working in this way will encourage you to be more adventurous, to go further, without risk of excess!

Working on the consonants

So, what do you do with the consonants? How do you work with them?

Be aware of how the consonants work physically Firstly, you need to explore the consonants, so that you are aware of the movements of the lips and the tongue as you make the various sounds, so you can feel the similarities and differences between various consonants. Then, there is some chance that, when you start to put them together with the vowels in connected speech, you will be able to find definition speedily and easily and without strangling the vowels.

Teach the mind/attention to stay present even when working fast It is quite possible to speak quickly and be completely clear. All that is required is that you are *with* each sound and word as you say it. This means that the brain needs to learn to work fast, but at the same time stay with each moment.

When we gabble the brain runs ahead of itself, so that it is no longer present with each moment and so sounds and words, phrases and thoughts fall over each other and become muddled.

Have you ever seen the words of a song on a karaoke machine? There is a little dot that moves from syllable to syllable, word to word as the music plays. It helps the person singing to stay in time with the music. You need to work with your attention in the same way, allowing it to alight on each sound, very briefly and very quickly. This does not lead to over-emphasis, quite the reverse. Over-emphasis is the result of over-effort, of replacing light mental accuracy with plodding physical stress.

Committing to the sounds The more you commit to the act of speaking, with sureness but no effort, the more energy and definition your speech will have.

We all know how to commit, just as we all know how to be tentative or over effortful. When we are unsure about what we are saying or about the response we will get to what we are saying or to the way we are saying it, we tend to mumble or to become over-emphatic, defending ourselves before we are attacked. Equally, when we really want something or are very sure about the way we feel, and truly want to communicate that; we find no difficulty in speaking clearly, with commitment and energy.

This can work in reverse. If you start to commit to what you are saying and more precisely to commit to the individual sounds within a text you will begin to feel more confident about the text and you may find it helps you find out more about the character and the scene.

Speech is the only tangible physical behaviour of the character that we have; yet we so often ignore it and instead pile a whole load of assumed character behaviour onto the text. If you begin to commit fully but lightly to each sound you will find you get a tremendous amount of feedback as to how the character might be feeling and thinking. What is more this feedback gives a taste of something far more original than you are intellectually likely to come up with. Also, by committing to each sound you will find that a word is not a static 'splat' but rather that there is a sense of movement, of journey within every word.

Now I quite understand that at the moment you might well be thinking: '*This is all well and good but HOW do I do it?!*' The exercises below will take you through the process very simply and clearly.

Lack of mental clarity leads to lack of physical clarity So often, when I've been working on productions and have given a note on clarity, the actor concerned has said: *'I don't like that line'* or *'I don't understand that line'* or *'I don't know what I am meant to be doing at that point'*. In other words, their *external lack of clarity* was the result of *internal uncertainty*, which made them draw back from the line in some way rather than committing to it. So, it is vital to be as clear as possible mentally and then, as I have suggested in the previous paragraph, consciously commit where you are unsure to see if that brings more understanding and clarity.

Other reasons for lack of clarity Of course, different people do naturally have different levels of clarity depending on their own personalities and the particular characteristics of their family's, peer group's and region's speech. These different levels of clarity are neither right nor wrong. As long as they serve the speaker in everyday life, there is no need for any change there. However, if the level of clarity does not serve the person on stage or screen they will need to explore and experiment to find a better balance.

Some people may need to get used to greater movement of the lips and tongue. Some people may need to ease off, since their articulation may be very tight and rigid and over-effortful. Whatever is necessary, it is important not to think of shaping the consonants as some attempt to speak well but rather as part of a commitment to truly communicating. Neither mumbling, nor gabbling nor over-emphatic speech take the listener into account.

So to Work on the Consonants

We are going to start by looking at the individual consonants, exploring how they are made. Moving from the most open consonants, which are most vowel like, through to the most closed consonants. The point of this exercise is to make you aware of the uniqueness of each sound, of its particular dynamic. Having done this you will find it much easier to commit to and define the consonants in connected speech without becoming over pedantic.

Exploring the consonants

To raise awareness of how each consonant is made, of its individual dynamics

The examples I describe below do refer to Standard English. I'm sorry I can't cover all the other accents of English, but there isn't space and, since I'm not an expert on accents, neither could I give an exhaustive list. So if you feel you do something different from what I describe go with your own experience. You're trying to be more aware of the variety of sounds you make and the individuality of each sound, rather than trying to find a so-called 'correct' version.

Note

Here we are looking at the consonants as they are pronounced in words not as they are said when saying the alphabet. Also, we are not concerned with all the letters that occur in the spelling of a word, only the sounds that are actually said. For example, in the word 'comb' the 'b' is silent.

Again, I have chosen not to use phonetic symbols because I don't want to blind everyone with science. Where I think there might be confusion as to the sound intended I have given an example of a word containing that sound.

w, y, r, l – The approximants

The first group is the most liquid. These sounds are made differently from each other but share a quality of openness and fluidity, that makes them closer to vowels, indeed w and y have been called 'semi-vowels'.

W

The 'w' is made with the lips. The lip muscles, responsible for rounding and spreading the lips, gather the lips into a round shape and then the 'w' sound is made by the lips releasing from this rounded shape.

- *Round your lips as much as you can and make an 'oo' sound. Feel the lips gathered together in the round shape. Then, move from the 'oo' into a 'w' sound (i.e. 'oowuh oowuh oowuh') feeling the lips spring open out of the 'oo' shape as you do so.*
- *Feel the energy in the lips as they release from the 'oo' shape. Try moving from 'oo' to 'w' several times, focusing all your attention on the movement of the lips, so that the rest of the vocal mechanism is easy and relaxed.*
- *Then, play with words that begin with 'w', feeling the energy in the lips as they spring apart to make the sound.*

Y

The 'y' is made with the tongue. The tongue muscles lift the middle of the tongue up to the roof of the mouth and, then, the 'y' sound is made by the tongue flicking down from that position.

- *Let the jaw be open about a finger's width for this exercise and allow it to stay fairly still so that it is the tongue that moves rather than the jaw. If it helps, gently rest one hand under your jaw to help it to stay still while the tongue moves.*
- *Make an easy, but committed 'ee' sound. Feel the middle of the tongue rising up to touch the roof of the mouth. Then, move from the 'ee' into the 'y' sound (i.e. 'eeyuh eeyuh eeyuh') feeling the tongue flick down as you do so. There is no need to push or tense, just focus on the tongue and be aware of it flicking down.*
- *Feel the easy energy in the tongue as it flicks down. Try moving from the 'ee' to the 'y' several times, focusing all your attention on the movement of the middle of the tongue, so that the rest of the vocal mechanism stays easy and relaxed.*
- *Then, play with words that begin with 'y', feeling the energy in the middle of the tongue as it flicks down.*

R

This can be a very hard sound to have a sense of, which is why some people find it so difficult to say. If you look at someone when they are making an 'r' you would assume that the 'r' is made with the lips, since there is obvious rounding and releasing there. This is why some people end up saying 'w' for 'r'.

What actually needs to happen, as well as the lip rounding, is that the tongue needs to flick down and forward. So this is what we are going to explore.

- *Again, let the jaw be open about a finger's width and allow it to stay relatively still while the tongue moves. Again, if it helps, gently rest one hand under your jaw to help it stay still while the tongue moves.*
- *Start by drawing the front of the tongue up and back across the roof of the mouth, until the sides of the tongue are touching the sides of the roof of the mouth. Then make a kind of 'er' sound, keeping the sides of the tongue touching the sides of the back of the roof of the mouth.*
- *Then, keeping your jaw still, let the tongue release down and forward away from the roof of the mouth as you say the 'r'.*
- *Once you have a good sense of the tongue flicking downward, play with words that begin with 'r', again feeling the energy in the tongue as it flicks down away from the roof of the mouth.*

L

The 'l' sound is also made with the tongue. There are, actually, two sorts of 'l' the one that comes at the beginning of words or syllables, which is known as a clear 'l' and the one that comes at the end of words or syllables, which is known as a dark 'l'

Clear L

The clear 'l' is made with the tip and sides of the tongue.

- *Again, let the jaw be open about a finger's width and allow it to stay relatively still while the tongue moves. Again, rest your jaw gently on your hand, if it helps.*
- *Prepare to say a 'l'. Feel where the tongue is. You will probably feel the tip of the tongue touching the gum ridge, just behind the upper front teeth, while the sides of the tongue are touching the side teeth.*
- *From this position, feel the tongue flick down as you say the 'l' sound. Repeat this a few times to get a good sense of the tongue flicking down, while the rest of the vocal mechanism stays relaxed.*

❍ *Once you have a good sense of the tongue's movement, play with words that begin with 'l', feeling the energy in the tongue as it flicks down.*

Dark L

The dark 'l' is made with the back of the tongue as well as with the tip and the sides.

In some accents, only the back of the tongue is used and the final 'l' almost becomes a vowel. This is the case in some London accents.

❍ *Again, let the jaw be open about a finger's width and allow it to stay relatively still while the tongue moves. Again, rest your jaw gently on your hand, if it helps.*

❍ *We are going to start with some simple words that end in 'l' – eel, ill, ale, all. Try each word a few times and see what your tongue does at the end of each word as you say the 'l'.*

❍ *Can you feel the tip of the tongue touching the gum ridge just above the upper front teeth and the sides of the tongue touching the side teeth? If not try the words again and as you move from the vowel into the 'l' consciously place the tip of the tongue so it is touching the upper gum ridge. It is also helpful to hold on to the 'l' for a little longer than you really would in speech, so you have time to register the tongue tip resting against the upper gum ridge.*

❍ *Once you have a good sense of the tip of the tongue taking part in the making of this sound, then play with some other words that end in 'l', including those that end in 'ble', 'tle', or 'dle' such as 'table', bottle' and 'meddle'. With each word feel the tip of the tongue rise up to take part in the making of the 'l'.*

m, n, ng – The nasal consonants

The second group of sounds is less open but they still have a flowing quality. These sounds are released through the nose rather than the mouth. To prove this, try the following. Make a continuous 'm' sound, in other words hum. You'll notice that your lips are together, you might feel them buzzing. Keep making the sound, and then pinch your nostrils closed with your finger and thumb. You'll notice that the sound stops.

Sustained M

❍ *Again, make a continuous 'm'. Imagine that you are hiding a slight yawn behind your lips as you make the sound. This will open up a little more space in your mouth and you may feel more resonance in your lips as a result.*

- *If your lips feel very tight or you can't feel any resonance at all, try blowing through your lips to loosen them. Then don't worry about them. It was ages before I felt any resonance – I was such a tense student! – but the less I worried about it the better it got.*
- *Make a long 'm' again and this time focus on the idea of the sound releasing through the nose. Again you might feel a slight tingle but don't worry if you don't. As always the energy and sound will follow your attention, so just trust that.*
- *Once you have a sense of the sound releasing through the nose, play with words that have 'm' in them. Explore words that start with 'm', that have 'm' in the middle and that have 'm' at the end. Can you feel the sound releasing through the nose on each 'm'? Can you feel even a slight sense of vibration in the lips on each 'm'? Say the words a few more times and enjoy the sense of sound in the lips and nose.*

Firm release M

The 'm' has two parts. We have explored how the 'm' feels when the lips are together. I would now like to explore how the 'm' feels as it ends with the lips springing apart.

- *Say a short 'm' several times; first feeling the vibration, when the lips are together and, then, feeling the lips spring apart. Keep the throat completely relaxed so there is no force and focus all your attention on the lips and on them springing open.*
- *Then, try some words that have 'm' at the beginning and in the middle. Feel both the vibration when the lips are together and the spring apart when they release.*

Sustained N

The 'n' is made by the tip of the tongue forming a closure with the gum ridge just behind the upper front teeth, so that, again, the sound is released through the nose rather than the mouth. Try the same test as before. Make a continuous 'n' sound and then pinch your nostrils closed as before. Again you will find that the sound is stopped completely.

- *Make a long 'n' and focus on the front of the tongue where it is touching the gum ridge. You may feel a sense of vibration there. The more relaxed the tongue is, even though it is making a firm connection with the gum ridge, the more likely you will be to feel some resonance, but as always don't worry if you don't, it will come in time.*
- *Make a long 'n' again and this time focus on the idea of the sound releasing through the nose. Again, you might feel a tingling in the nose.*

❍ *Once you have a sense of the sound releasing through the nose, play with words that have 'n' in them. Explore words that start with 'n', that have 'n' in the middle and that have 'n' at the end. Can you feel the sound releasing through the nose on each 'n'? Can you feel even a slight sense of vibration in the tip of the tongue on each 'n'? Say the words a few more times and enjoy the sense of sound in the lips and nose.*

Firm release N

Like the 'm', the 'n' has two parts: the part when the tip of the tongue forms a closure with the gum ridge and the part when the tongue flicks away from the gum ridge.

Say a short 'n' several times; first feeling the tongue against the gum ridge and then feeling it flick away. Keep the throat completely relaxed so there is no force and focus all you attention on the tip of the tongue and on it flicking away.

Then, try some words that have 'n' at the beginning and in the middle. Again, feel the vibration, when the tip of the tongue is against the gum ridge, and the flicking away of the tongue as the 'n' ends.

Sustained NG

The 'ng' is made by forming a closure between the back of the tongue and the back of the soft palate, so that, again, the sound is released through the nose rather than the mouth. Try the same test as before. Make a continuous 'ng' sound and then pinch your nostrils closed as before. Again you will find the sound is stopped completely.

❍ *Make a long 'ng' and focus on the back of the tongue where it is touching the soft palate. You may feel a sense of vibration there. The more relaxed the tongue and*

> **Note**
>
> *Soft Palate Flexibility* We looked at the need for the soft palate to be flexible in the chapters on Releasing and Filling out the Voice. This flexibility is especially important for nasal consonants. The soft palate needs to drop, while they are made, so the sound can come out of the nose and, then, rise again, after they have been made, so the sound can again come out of the mouth.
>
> This is particularly important when the nasal consonants are preceded or followed by a vowel.
>
> *To check that your soft palate is dropping and lifting appropriately practise the following sequences feeling the soft palate raised for the first vowel and, then, dropping for the nasal consonant and, then, lifting again for the following vowel:*
>
> *ahmmmah-ighmmmigh-aymmmay-eemmmee-oommmoo-ohmmmoh-ormmmor*
>
> Use the image of surprise or smile in the back of the mouth to help lift the soft palate on the vowel.

soft palate are, even though they are making a firm connection, the more likely you will be to feel some resonance, but as always don't worry if you don't, it will come in time.

- *Make a long 'ng' again and this time focus on the idea of the sound releasing through the nose. Again, you might feel a tingling in the nose.*
- *Once you have a sense of the sound releasing through the nose, play with words that have 'ng' in them. In English we don't use 'ng' to start words or syllables but try the following words: bang, hang, sing, fling, gong, wrong, rung, tongue, backing, swimming, sighing, rotting, roving, running, hanging, singing, wringing, wronging.*
- *Can you feel the sound releasing through the nose on each 'ng'? Can you feel even a slight sense of vibration in the back of the tongue and the soft palate on each 'ng'? Say the words a few more times and enjoy the sense of sound in the lips and nose.*

Voiced and voiceless consonants

Whereas the consonants in the previous two groups were all voiced, that is *sounded* rather than just made with *breath*, all the following groups of consonants, have *pairs* of voiced and voiceless consonants. Each pair of sounds is made by the same parts of the lips or tongue but one of the pair is sounded and the other only breathed.

Make a long 'f', without releasing into a vowel at the end. Can you hear that there is no voice just breath? Now make a 'v' sound. Can you hear that there is sound? Both these sounds are made in exactly the same way. The only difference is that the first isn't made with sound and the second is. It is a tiny difference and yet in English, especially at the ends of words, this tiny difference can denote a completely different word.

Voiceless	*Voiced*
Tap	Tab
Hat	Had
Back	Bag
Leaf	Leave
Course	Cause

We usually find voiceless consonants no problem, but voiced consonants can be so weakly sounded at the ends of words that, especially over distance, we can confuse them with their voiceless partners and so lose the sense. So, I would like you to be aware of the difference as you explore the voiceless and voiced pairs and make sure that the voiced consonants are, indeed, fully voiced.

f, v, th, the, s, z, sh, je and h – the fricative consonants

The next group of sounds is made by two parts of the mouth coming close together so that a narrow gap is formed and friction is caused as the air or sound passes through.

Try making an 'f' and 'v' sound. What do these feel like? To make them your top teeth rest on your bottom lip and the breath, in the case of the 'f', or the sound, in the case of the 'v', pass through the narrow gap between the top teeth and bottom lip. Say them again, can you feel the light friction? This is why they are known as the fricative consonants. They are very sensuous sounds and this is reflected in the words in which they occur.

F and V

As already mentioned the 'f' and 'v' are made with the top teeth resting on the bottom lip.

- *Start by exploring the 'f'. Make a long 'f' as before and feel the play of the breath between the top teeth and the lower lip.*
- *Then, explore words that have 'f' in, whether at the beginning, in the middle or at the end, and feel the play of breath every time you say the 'f'.*
- *Then, explore the 'v'. Make a long 'v' and feel the buzz or vibration of sound between the top teeth and the lower lip.*
- *Then, explore words that have 'v' in, whether at the beginning, in the middle or at the end, and feel the voiced buzz every time you say the 'v' and especially on final 'v's.*

TH and THE

The 'th' and 'the' are made with the tongue slightly forward so the front rests between the teeth.[22]

22 This is not so in the case of cockney, where there is not a separate sound for 'th' or 'the' – 'f' is used instead.

- *Start by exploring the voiceless 'th', which occurs in words such as 'thin', 'thick', 'bath' and 'mouth'. Make a long 'th' and feel the play of the breath between the tongue and the top teeth.*
- *Then, explore the following words that have 'th' in, whether at the beginning or at the end, and feel the play of breath every time you say the 'th':*

  Thought, through, throw, think, thistle, thimble
  Breath, mouth, death, cloth, teeth, width, breadth

- *Then, explore the 'the', which occurs in words such as 'this', 'that', 'with' and 'bathe'. Make a long 'the' and feel the buzz or vibration of sound between the tongue and the top teeth.*
- *Then, explore the following words that have 'the' in them, whether at the beginning, in the middle or at the end, and feel the voiced buzz every time you say the 'the' and especially on final 'th':*

  Though, them, these, their, than, those
  Bother, dither, mother, father, brother
  With, seethe, breathe, loathe, clothe, teethe

S and Z

The 's' and 'z' are made with the sides of the tongue touching the roof of the mouth and so creating a narrow groove down the centre of the tongue. The tip of the tongue may rest either against the upper or lower gum ridge.

- *Start by exploring the 's'. Make a long 's' and imagine the breath releasing lightly down the central groove.*
- *Then, explore words that have 's' in, whether at the beginning, in the middle or at the end, and imagine the breath releasing lightly down the central groove every time you say the 's'.*
- *Then, explore the 'z'. Make a long 'z' and imagine the buzz or vibration of sound releasing down the central groove.*
- *Then, explore words that have 'z' in, whether at the beginning, in the middle or at the end, and imagine the buzz or vibration of sound releasing down the central groove every time you say the 'z' and especially on final 'z's.*

> **Note**
>
> It can be hard to feel the breath or sound very specifically on 's' and 'z', so simply imagine the breath releasing down the central groove.

Sibilant S

It is very important with the 's' to keep it light rather than forced otherwise it can get very sibilant (full of hiss or sometimes even whistle). If you do find your 's' does get sibilant keep it very light and very short: this will help a great deal.

It can also be helpful to use a 't' sound as a 'guide' to help the 's'.

- *The 't' is made by placing the very tip of the tongue, lightly but firmly, against the upper gum ridge, just behind the upper front teeth, and then flicking it away from the gum ridge as the sound is made. Start by saying 't' very lightly and crisply so there is no hiss.*
- *Then, starting again from the 't' slide briefly and cleanly onto the 's' and let it go the moment you have sounded it, so that the 's' is very short.*
- *Then, try with words as follows:*

tsoo	*sue*
tsoh	*sew*
tsor	*saw*
tsigh	*sigh*
tsay	*say*
tsee	*see*

Once you are able to make the 's' without hiss or whistle you then need to practise with text, making sure that you really do stop on every 's' sound and consciously make the 's' in the new way rather than the old. In this way a new habit will be built up and eventually the new way of saying the 's' will become automatic.

Lisping S

When a person has a lisp the front and sides of the tongue protrude between the teeth to make the 's' so that the sound produced is more like a 'th': e.g. 'thixty thix' instead of 'sixty six'. To remedy the lisp practise the following:

- *Alternate between saying 'th' and 't' and be aware of the tongue drawing back into the mouth on the 't'.*
- *Then, starting by saying 't' and after the 't' raise the sides of your tongue to the roof of your mouth and letting the air out on a very light hiss. This will give you the 's' sound.*
- *Then practise words with 's' in, consciously drawing the sides of the tongue back and up on every 's'. It is helpful to imagine that your tongue cannot bear to touch your teeth and, instead, draws back and up away from them, almost in disgust.*

As with the hissing or whistling 's', you then need to practise with text, making sure that you really do stop on every 's' sound and consciously make the 's' in the new way rather than the old. If you do this regularly, with good attention, a new habit will be built up and eventually the new way of saying the 's' will become automatic.

❍ *So, read some text, stopping on every 's' and practising drawing the tongue up and back into the new position.*

SH and JE

The 'sh' (as in cash) and 'je' (as in measure) are made by the middle of the tongue lifting up and a little back to the roof of the mouth.

❍ *Start by exploring the 'sh'. Make a long 'sh' and feel the play of the breath between the middle of the tongue and the roof of the mouth.*

❍ *Then, explore words that have 'sh' in, whether at the beginning, in the middle or at the end, and feel the play of breath every time you say the 'sh'.*

❍ *Then, explore the 'je', which occurs in the middle of such words as 'treasure', 'leisure' and 'measure'. Make a long 'je' and feel the buzz or vibration of sound between the middle of the tongue and the roof of the mouth.*

❍ *Then, explore words that have 'je' in, feeling the buzz every time you say the 'je'. In English the 'je sound only occurs in the middle of words:*

Measure, treasure, leisure, pleasure, occasion, usual, vision, decision, confusion

H

The 'h' is made by breath passing through the vocal tract. The actual shape of the tract is affected by the vowel that follows the 'h'. In English the 'h' is mostly spoken only at the beginning of words. There are a few exceptions, e.g. 'bohemian'. Also, there is no voiced version of the 'h.

❍ *Start by exploring the 'h'. Make a long light 'h' – rather like a light sigh – and feel the gentle play of the breath in the vocal tract. It is important to keep 'h' very light rather than allowing it to get raspy. If it gets raspy that suggests the vocal tract is narrowing too much or that a great deal of air is being forced out at great pressure.*

❍ *Then, explore words that begin with 'h' and feel the light play of breath every time you say the 'h'.*

p, b, t, d, k, g – The plosives

The next group of consonants is the most closed group. Two parts of the mouth come together to form a complete closure and the sound here is produced when the two parts that have made the closure spring apart.

Start to make a 'p' or a 'b' but don't actually release the sound. What happens? Can you feel that your lips are pressed together and the pressure is building up inside your mouth?

When you release your lips the pressure is released, as breath in the case of 'p' and as sound in the case of 'b'.

The plosive consonants are the ones that stop the flow most completely. The pressure builds up and, then, is explosively released. This gives these sounds a lot of energy and strength.

P and B

As I mentioned, the 'p' and 'b' are made with the lips.

- *Say a whispered 'p' a few times. Can you feel the lips press lightly but firmly together and then spring apart? Put all your attention in the lips, so that the rest of the vocal mechanism stays relaxed and feel the lips spring apart on each 'p'.*

Can you feel the puff of air that releases when you say 'p'? This happens even if you put a vowel after the 'p'. Try the following and see: 'pah', 'pigh', 'pay'. It is this puff of air that can cause such trouble if you are working with a microphone. To avoid any problem it is important not to allow too much air pressure to build up behind the lips. This happens either because the lips are held together for a long time or because too much air is expelled from the lungs. Both are usually the result of excess effort. That is why it is important to focus on short contact, which is firm but light, and on the lips springing apart, finding the energy that way rather than by forcing a lot of breath out.

Try this experiment to feel the difference:

Put one of your hands about an inch in front of your lips.

- *First, make a 'p' with a great deal of force and feel how much air is released. Can you also hear how noisy it is?*
- *Then, make a 'p' very lightly, with no force at all, feeling the spring apart of the lips. Can you feel that there is less air and that it is certainly quieter?*
- *So, explore words that have 'p' in, whether at the beginning, in the middle or at the end, and feel the firm but light coming together and springing apart of the lips on every 'p'.*

- *Say a fully voiced 'b' a few times. Again, can you feel the lips press lightly but firmly together and then spring apart? As before, put all your attention in the lips, so that the rest of the vocal mechanism stays relaxed and feel the lips spring apart on each 'b'.*
- *Then, explore words that have 'b' in, whether at the beginning, in the middle or at the end, and feel the firm but light coming together and springing apart of the lips on every 'b'. Also, check that final 'b's are fully voiced and not half-voiced half-whispered.*

T and D

The 't' and 'd' are made by the tip of the tongue making a firm but light closure with the gum ridge just behind the upper front teet, and then flicking away from there.[23]

- *Say a whispered 't' a few times. Can you feel the tip of the tongue press lightly but firmly against the gum ridge behind the upper front teeth and then flick away? Put all your attention in the tip of the tongue, so that the rest of the vocal mechanism stays relaxed and feel the tongue tip flick away on each 't'.*
- *Then, explore words that have 't' in, whether at the beginning, in the middle or at the end, and feel the tongue tip pressing lightly but firmly against the gum ridge and then flicking away on every 't'.*
- *Say a fully voiced 'd' a few times. Again, can you feel the tongue tip press lightly but firmly against the gum ridge and then flick away? As before, put all your attention in the tip of the tongue, so that the rest of the vocal mechanism stays relaxed, and feel the tongue tip flick away on each 'd'.*
- *Then, explore words that have 'd' in, whether at the beginning, in the middle or at the end, and feel the tongue tip pressing lightly but firmly against the gum ridge and then flicking away on every 'd'. Also, check that final 'd's are fully voiced and not half-voiced half-whispered.*

K and G

The 'k' and 'g' are made by the back of the tongue and the tip of the soft palate coming together to form a firm but light closure.[24]

23 The placing of the tongue does change for differing accents, but the sound remains a plosive – it is just that the closure occurs in a slightly different place.

24 Again the exact placing may vary from accent to accent, but the sound remains a plosive.

- *Say a whispered 'k' a few times. Can you feel the back of the tongue and the tip of the soft palate press lightly but firmly together and then spring apart? Check that the back of the mouth stays free and open and that there is no sense of squeezing. Feel the back of the tongue and the tip of the soft palate spring apart on each 'k'.*
- *Then, explore words that have 'k' in, whether at the beginning, in the middle or at the end, and feel the firm but light coming together and springing apart of the back of the tongue and the tip of the soft palate on every 'k'.*
- *Say a fully voiced 'g' a few times. Again, can you feel the back of the tongue and the tip of the soft palate press lightly but firmly together and then spring apart? As before, check that the back of the mouth stays free and open and that there is no sense of squeezing. Feel the back of the tongue and the tip of the soft palate spring apart on each 'g'.*
- *Then, explore words that have 'g' in, whether at the beginning, in the middle or at the end, and feel the firm but light coming together and springing apart of the back of the tongue and the tip of the soft palate on every 'g'. Also, check that final 'g's are fully voiced and not half-voiced half-whispered.*

ch and j, tr and dr – the affricates

These sounds are actually made up from two sounds, the first sound being a plosive and the second a fricative. So 'ch' comprises of 't and sh' and 'j' (as in jam, jar, jest and joke) comprises of 'd and je', whilst 'tr', more obviously, comprises of 't' and 'r' and 'dr' of 'd' and 'r'.

Ch and J

In the case of 'ch' and 'j' the tip of the tongue starts by forming a closure with the upper front gum ridge, as for the 't' and the 'd'. As the tip of the tongue flicks away from the gum ridge the middle of the tongue moves up to the roof of the mouth, as for the 'sh' and 'je'.

- *Say a whispered 'ch' a few times. Can you feel the tongue tip spring away from the gum ridge and then the play of breath between the middle of the tongue and the roof of the mouth?*
- *Try some words with 'ch' in and feel the spring away by the tip of the tongue and then the play of air between the middle of the tongue and the roof of the mouth on each 'ch':*

  Chin, chapter, choice, charge, change, charm
  Richer, butcher, catcher, nature
  Teach, catch, watch, coach, lunch, branch

- *Say fully voiced 'j' as in 'jam' a few times. Can you feel the tongue tip spring away from the gum ridge and then the buzz of sound between the middle of the tongue and the roof of the mouth?*
- *Then, try some words with 'j' in and feel the spring away by the tip of the tongue and then the buzz of sound between the middle of the tongue and the roof of the mouth on each 'j':*

> *Jury, joke, jewel, jam, jar, gin*
> *Margin, fragile, urgent, major, danger, soldier*
> *Edge, large, huge, age, dodge, sponge, hinge*

Tr and Dr

In the case of 'tr' and 'dr' the tip of the tongue again starts by forming a closure with the upper front gum ridge, as for the 't' and the 'd'. But as the tip of the tongue is flicking away from the gum ridge it is drawn back and up into the 'r' position and then released from there.

- *Say 'tr' a few times and feel the tip of the tongue flicking away from the gum ridge and immediately being drawn up and back into the 'r' position and then released from there on each 'tr'.*
- *Then, try some words with 'tr' in and, again, feel the tip of the tongue flicking away from the gum ridge and immediately being drawn up and back into the 'r' position and then released from there on each 'tr'.*
- *Say 'dr' a few times and feel the tip of the tongue flicking away from the gum ridge and immediately being drawn up and back into the 'r' position and then released from there on each 'dr'.*
- *Then, try some words with 'dr' in and feel the tip of the tongue flicking away from the gum ridge and immediately being drawn up and back into the 'r' position and then released from there on each 'dr'.*

Consonant clusters – ts, dz, tth, tths, lz, lvz, pr, br, kr and gr

These are groups of consonants that come together and they often trip us up. The reason they do so is because we see the sounds as a block rather than a journey, and we muddle the order of the sounds in the block. So, now that you have got to know all the consonants individually, explore these clusters, on their own and in words, until you have a good sense of the movement of the tongue and lips from one consonant to the next. Work slowly so that you learn each pattern of movement and then you will find you won't be tripped up.

ts – pets, bits, hoots,

dz – heads, adds, broods

tth – width, breadth (the 'd' is sounded as a 't')

tths – widths, breadths

lz – tells, walls, bowls, feels

lvz – wolves, valves, solves

pr – proud, praise, pride, precious

br – breed, break, bright, brink

kr – cry, crown, crazy, crow, cream

gr – grab, grip, grow, growl

There are other clusters I have not mentioned, so feel free to add any you find and practise in the same way.

Limbering up the Lips and the Tongue

Once you have explored all the consonants and have a sense of how they are made, you need to tone up the lip and tongue muscles, so they can work with energy, definition and ease. It is rather like taking the lip and tongue muscles to the gym!

As with gym work, you need to start by releasing any tension and warming up the muscles.

Loosening up the face

To release facial tension and so free up the upper lip

If the face is stiff the lips will be stiff, so it is good to start by loosening up the face.

- *Sit or stand as before, directing the back to lengthen and the shoulders and hips to widen. Check that the feet are parallel and hip width apart, that the joints are loose and that the shoulder blades and buttocks are dropping gently down your back.*
- *Move the face around as much as possible, while keeping the neck completely relaxed.*
- *Make as many different expressions as you can so that you are not just moving the face in habitual patterns. Allow the face muscles to explore all their possibilities of movement.*

- ❍ *Check in the mirror to see that the whole face is moving.*
- ❍ *Then, lean forward, resting your hands on your thighs, and looking down towards the floor, and loosely shake your head from side to side as if you are shaking all the skin off your face.*
- ❍ *Repeat the whole exercise once more, humming as you move the face around and sounding out on a loose 'er' as you shake your head.*

Loosening up the lips

To release tension in the lips and wake them up

There can be a great deal of tension in the lips without us necessarily being aware of it. As I mentioned earlier, concern about the state of our teeth can cause us to tense the lips to try and hide the teeth. Also, in an attempt to hide feelings of upset or to prevent tears we may stiffen the upper lip. Or, through tentativeness, we may mumble, hardly moving the lips at all. Or, the lips may be very tight because we over-enunciate, through anxiety as to whether or not we will be heard. So there can be much work to do to loosen and awaken the lips.

As you do the lip loosening exercise, pay attention to your lips. Do they feel stiff? Do they ache when you move them? Do they feel lifeless or hard to contact? Even the act of asking and answering these questions will begin to bring changes since it will focus your attention on the lips and that will bring energy and awareness.

- ❍ *Sit or stand as before, directing the back to lengthen and the shoulders and hips to widen. Check that the feet are parallel and hip width apart, that the joints are loose and that the shoulder blades and buttocks are dropping gently down your back.*
- ❍ *Move both lips around as much as possible, exploring all the possible movements of the lips.*
- ❍ *Then, blow loosely through the lips, as in previous chapters. Remember, if you find this difficult, flick the lips with your finger as you blow.*
- ❍ *Then, repeat the exercise, humming while you move your lips around and then blowing out with sound – brrrrrr* (ie, *the sound we make when we're cold*).

Loosening the tongue

To release the middle and the back of the tongue

The tongue is very sensitive to our state of mind and, like the lips, can carry a great deal of tension without us being aware of it. So, as with the lip loosening, pay attention as you do the tongue loosening exercise. Does any part of the tongue feel stiff? Does any part ache? Does any part of the tongue feel lifeless or disconnected? Again, simply focusing on the tongue will begin to bring energy and awareness.

- *Sit or stand as before, directing the back to lengthen and the shoulders and hips to widen. Check that the feet are parallel and hip width apart, that the joints are loose and that the shoulder blades and buttocks are dropping gently down your back.*
- *Smile a warm smile and open the jaw so there is a finger's width between the back teeth. Again, rest your jaw on your hand if it helps.*
- *With the tip of the tongue behind the lower front teeth, roll the middle of the tongue out of the mouth as you have in previous chapters, while keeping the jaw still and open.*
- *Let the tongue relax back in and roll forward and out several times.*
- *Then, release the tongue tip and flap the tongue loosely up and down between the lips.*
- *Then, repeat this sequence with sound. Sounding out on 'hee yuh ee yuh ee yuh ee yuh ee yuh' while you move the tongue back and forth and 'lllllll' when you flap the tongue up and down.*

Strengthening the Lip and Tongue Muscles

Once you have loosened up the lips and tongue, it is time to start strengthening the muscles. This is done, firstly, by paying attention to the movements of the lips and tongue and feeling the muscles working and then, secondly, by working with a sense of 'bounce' just as you did in the support chapter (see page 88).

Some of the exercises may seem similar to the exploration work you have just done on the consonants and in some ways they are. The difference is that the above work is for occasional exploration whereas the work below can be used regularly, as any exercise might be, to build up muscle tone.

Working with a bone prop

We are going to use a device called a bone prop for some of the exercises in this chapter. It should really be called a jaw prop because what it does is 'prop' the jaw open so the lips and tongue can move while the jaw stays still. It is excellent for encouraging the lips and tongue to be more active.

You can buy actual bone props from chemists such as 'Bell and Croydon' but they are expensive and easy to lose. Andrew Wade, the Head of Voice at the RSC, had the brilliant idea of using the small plastic tubes you can buy in DIY shops, to cut up and use as rawl plugs. A whole length costs 50 to 70 pence and will provide 15 or 16 props!

The length of your prop needs to be about the width of your thumb knuckle and you place the prop between your front teeth. Occasionally, the bone prop will make a person want to gag. If this happens to you, start with one half the length and only increase the size when it is tolerable to do so.

Try to hold the prop very lightly in your mouth. This is especially important if there is a tendency to clench your teeth. In time the jaw muscles will relax. You may feel some stretch and ache in the jaw muscles – this is fine.

Lips – rounding and spreading

To strengthen the muscles which round and spread the lips

Stage one – rounding and spreading silently

- ❍ *Sit or stand as before, directing the back to lengthen and the shoulders and hips to widen. Check that the feet are parallel and hip width apart, that the joints are loose and that the shoulder blades and buttocks are dropping gently down your back.*
- ❍ *Place the bone prop between your teeth and, keeping the neck completely relaxed round and spread the lips as much as you can several times. (See diagram 1.) If it helps imagine that you are silently saying 'oo ee oo ee' etc.*

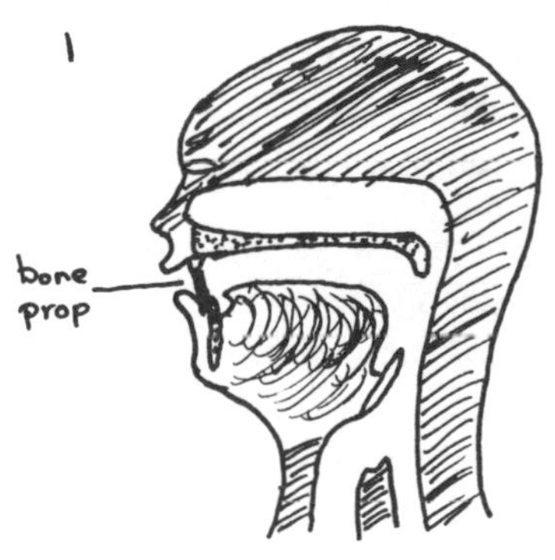

- ❍ *As you round and spread the lips feel the muscles around the lips shaping the lips. Don't worry if they ache, this is often the case, as long as you are not forcing but are simply committing to the most rounding and spreading you can do while keeping the neck completely relaxed.*

Stage two – rounding and spreading with sound

- ❍ *Take the bone prop out but keep the focus on the muscles around the lips. Round the lips again and say 'oowee oowee oowee' feeling the lip muscles flick out from the rounded shape on the 'w', just as you did when we explored the 'w' in the earlier section. Then repeat this on 'oowey oowey oowey' and then on 'oowah oowah oowah' and each time be aware of the lip muscles working.*

- *Then, try the following sequence starting with the lips in the 'oo' position and feeling them spring open on each 'w':*

  'wah wey wee wey wah wor woo wor wah'

- *Repeat the sequence four times with the same focus.*

Lips – closing and opening

To strengthen the muscles which close and open the lips

Stage one – closing and opening silently

- *Sit or stand as before, directing the back to lengthen and the shoulders and hips to widen. Check that the feet are parallel and hip width apart, that the joints are loose and that the shoulder blades and buttocks are dropping gently down your back.*
- *Place the bone prop between your teeth and, keeping the neck completely relaxed, close and open the lips several times.*
- *As you do so, focus on the area above the top lip and feel the muscles either side of the central groove working as the top lip moves down and up.*
- *Then, focus on the area below the bottom lip and feel the muscles just out from the centre working as the lower lip moves up and down.*
- *Then, focus on the area above the top lip and the area below the bottom lip at the same time. Imagine both sets of muscles working equally to bring the lips together and apart.*

Stage two – closing and opening on 'p' and 'b'

- *With the bone prop still in the mouth, say 'ppbb ppbb ppbb' and feel the lip muscles working, springing the lips apart on each sound.*
- *Then, try the following sequence feeling the lips spring apart on each 'p':*

  'pahp peyp peep peyp pahp porp poop porp pahp'

- *Repeat the sequence four times with the same focus.*
- *Then, try the same sequence with 'b' feeling the lips spring apart on each 'b':*

  'bahb beyb beeb beyb bahb borb boob borb bahb'

- *Repeat the sequence four times with the same focus.*

Stage three – closing and opening on 'm'

- *Then, try the same sequence with 'm' feeling the vibration on the lips first and then the lips springing apart as the 'm' is released:*

  'mahm meym meem meym mahm morm moom morm mahm'

- *Repeat the sequence four times with the same focus.*

Lips – bottom lip working with top teeth

To strengthen the making of the 'f' and 'v'

Two sounds, 'f' and 'v', as we looked at earlier, are made not with both lips but rather with one lip, the bottom one, brushing against the top teeth.

- *Sit or stand as before, directing the back to lengthen and the shoulders and hips to widen. Check that the feet are parallel and hip width apart, that the joints are loose and that the shoulder blades and buttocks are dropping gently down your back.*
- *Make a 'f' sound and feel the muscles below the lower lip bringing the lower lip up to meet the upper teeth. Feel the breath passing between the lower lip and upper teeth as you did earlier.*
- *Then try the following sequence feeling the play of breath between the lower lip and upper teeth on every 'f':*

  'fahf feyf feef feyf fahf forf foof forf fahf'

- *Repeat the sequence four times with the same focus.*
- *Then, make a 'v' and again feel the muscles below the lower lip bringing the lower lip up to meet the upper teeth. Feel the vibration where the lower lip meets the upper teeth.*
- *Then try the following sequence feeling the vibration on each 'v':*

  'vahv veyv veev veyv vahv vorv voov vorv vahv'

- *Repeat the sequence four times with the same focus.*

Rounded lip talk

To ensure the lips stay active throughout speech

Having worked on individual sounds, this exercise is a good way of waking up the lips, especially the top lip, throughout speech.

- *Sit or stand as before, directing the back to lengthen and the shoulders and hips to widen. Check that the feet are parallel and hip width apart, that the joints are loose and that the shoulder blades and buttocks are dropping gently down your back.*
- *Round the lips as much as possible while keeping the neck completely relaxed.*
- *Keeping the lips in this rounded position, say some text, particularly feeling the muscles above the upper lip being actively involved as you speak.*
- *Then, repeat the text with the lips in a more normal position but with the sense that the muscles above the upper lip are still active and involved, even though they may not be moving a great deal.*

Tongue tip circle

To increase the flexibility and precision of the tongue tip

- *Sit or stand as before, directing the back to lengthen and the shoulders and hips to widen. Check that the feet are parallel and hip width apart, that the joints are loose and that the shoulder blades and buttocks are dropping gently down your back.*
- *Smile a warm smile and open the jaw so there is a finger's width between the back teeth. Again, rest your jaw on your hand if it helps.*
- *Point the tongue out of the mouth and then curl the tip upwards so that it touches the area above the top lip. Then, slide the tongue tip across the area above the upper lip to the left lip corner. Then, curl the tip down so it is touching the area below the lower lip and slide it across from the left lip corner to the right lip corner. Then curl the tongue tip up so it is touching the area above the upper lip and slide it across to the centre where you started.*
- *Circle round in the same way three more times and then circle the other way four times.*

Tongue tip 'up, down, side, side'

To further increase the flexibility and precision of the tongue

- *Sit or stand as before, directing the back to lengthen and the shoulders and hips to widen. Check that the feet are parallel and hip width apart, that the joints are loose and that the shoulder blades and buttocks are dropping gently down your back.*
- *Smile a warm smile and open the jaw so there is a finger's width between the back teeth. Again, rest your jaw on your hand if it helps.*

- *Again, point the tongue out of the mouth and then curl the tongue tip up to touch the centre of the top lip.*
- *Then, from that position, curl the tongue tip down to touch the centre of the lower lip. Then, bring the tongue back to horizontal and take it across to touch the left lip corner and then back across to touch the right lip corner and then back to horizontal in the middle.*
- *Repeat this sequence four times. Then, repeat it again going to the right corner and, then, the left. Each time feel that you are placing the tongue tip in each position rather than it flailing about. Also, check that the neck stays relaxed and the spine long.*

Tongue tip flick

To further increase the flexibility and precision of the tongue

Stage one – flicking silently

- Sit or stand as before, directing the back to lengthen and the shoulders and hips to widen. Check that the feet are parallel and hip width apart, that the joints are loose and that the shoulder blades and buttocks are dropping gently down your back.
- Place the bone prop between your teeth and place the tip of the tongue on the gum ridge behind the upper front teeth. Flick the tip down to the gum ridge just behind the lower front teeth.
- Repeat this flicking down from the upper gum ridge to the lower gum ridge several times, keeping the back of the neck relaxed and the spine long.

Stage two – flicking on 't' and 'd'

- With the bone prop still in the mouth, say 'ttdd ttdd ttdd' and feel the tongue tip flicking down on each sound.
- Then, try the following sequence feeling the tongue tip flick down on each 't':

  'taht teyt teet teyt taht tort toot tort taht'

- Repeat this sequence four times with the same focus.
- Then, try the following sequence feeling the tongue tip flick down on each 'd':

  'dahd deyd deed deyd dahd dord dood dord dahd'

- Repeat this sequence four times with the same focus.

Stage three – flicking on 'l' and 'r'

- *With the bone prop still in the mouth, say 't-d-l-r t-d-l-r t-d-l-r' and feel the tongue tip flicking down on each of the first three sounds and, then, draw back and flick down on the 'r'.*
- *Then, try the following sequence feeling the tongue tip flick down on each initial 'l' and make good contact with the upper gum ridge on every final 'l':*

  'lahl leyl leel leyl lahl lorl lool lorl lahl'
- *Repeat this sequence four times with the same focus.*
- *Then, try the following sequence feeling the tongue tip draw back and then flick down on every 'r'*

  'rah rey ree rey rah ror roo ror rah'
- *Repeat this sequence four times with the same focus.*

Stage four – flicking on 'n'

- *With the bone prop still in the mouth, say 'nnnn nnnn nnnn' and feel the vibration where the tongue tip meets the upper gum ridge and then feel the tongue tip flicking down on each 'n'.*
- *Then, try the following sequence feeling the vibration and then the tongue tip flicking down on every 'n':*

  'nahn neyn neen neyn nahn norn noon norn nahn'
- *Repeat this sequence four times with the same focus.*

Stage five – tongue forward and back on 'th' and 'the'

- *Make a 'th' sound and feel the breath passing between the tongue and the teeth as you did earlier.*
- *Then, try the following sequence feeling the play of breath between the tongue and the teeth on every 'th':*

  'thahth theyth theeth theyth thahth thorth thooth thorth thahth'
- *Repeat the sequence four times with the same focus.*
- *Make a 'the' sound and feel the vibration between the tongue and the teeth as you did earlier.*
- *Then, try the following sequence feeling the vibration between the tongue and the teeth on every 'the':*

  'the-ahth the-eyth the-eeth the-eyth the-ahth the-orth the-ooth the-orth the-ahth'
- *Repeat this sequence four times with the same focus.*

Stage six – flicking on 's' and 'z'

- *Make a brief 's' sound and feel the breath passing lightly between the tongue and the roof of the mouth as you did earlier.*
- *Then, try the following sequence feeling the play of breath between the tongue and the roof of the mouth on every 's'.*

  'sahs seys sees seys sahs sors soos sors sahs'
- *Repeat this sequence four times with the same focus.*
- *Make a 'z' sound and feel the vibration between the tongue and the roof of the mouth as you did earlier.*
- *Then, try the following sequence feeling the vibration between the tongue and the roof of the mouth on every 'z'.*

  'zahz zeyz zeez zeyz zahz zorz zooz zorz zahz'
- *Repeat this sequence four times with the same focus.*

Middle of tongue flex

To increase the flexibility and precision of the middle of the tongue

Stage one – middle of tongue flex on 'y'

- *Sit or stand as before, directing the back to lengthen and the shoulders and hips to widen. Check that the feet are parallel and hip width apart, that the joints are loose and that the shoulder blades and buttocks are dropping gently down your back.*
- *Place the bone prop between your teeth. Say a silent 'ee' and feel the middle of the tongue rise up to the roof of the mouth. Then, say a silent 'yuh' and feel the tongue drop down. Repeat this several times feeling the middle of the tongue moving up and then flicking down. Without tensing, have a sense of the muscles that move the middle of the tongue working.*
- *Then, again starting from the 'ee' position say 'yuh' several times aloud and again feel the middle of the tongue flicking down.*
- *Then, try the following sequence feeling the middle of the tongue flick down on every 'yuh':*

  'yah yey yee yey yah yor yoo yor yah'

Stage two – middle of tongue flex on 'sh' and 'je'

- *Make a 'sh' sound and feel the breath passing between the middle of the tongue and the roof of the mouth as you did earlier.*
- *Then, try the following sequence feeling the play of breath between the tongue and the roof of the mouth on every 'sh'.*

  'shahsh sheysh sheesh sheysh shahsh shorsh shoosh shorsh shahsh'

- *Repeat this sequence four times with the same focus.*
- *Make a 'je' sound and feel the vibration between the middle of the tongue and the roof of the mouth as you did earlier.*
- *Then, try the following sequence feeling the vibration between the tongue and the roof of the mouth on every 'je'.*

  'ahje eyje eeje eyje ahje orje ooje orje ahje'

- *Repeat this sequence four times with the same focus.*

Back of tongue flex

To increase the flexibility and precision of the back of the tongue

- *Sit or stand as before, directing the back to lengthen and the shoulders and hips to widen. Check that the feet are parallel and hip width apart, that the joints are loose and that the shoulder blades and buttocks are dropping gently down your back.*
- *Place the bone prop between your teeth and say 'kkgg kkgg kkgg' and feel the back of the tongue raising up to make a closure with the soft palate and then flicking down on each sound. Without tensing, feel the muscles that move the back of the tongue working as the tongue flicks down.*
- *Then, try the following sequence feeling the back of the tongue flick down on each 'k':*

  'kahk keyk keek keyk kahk kork kook kork kahk'

- *Repeat this sequence four times with the same focus.*
- *Then, try the following sequence feeling the back of the tongue flick down on each 'g':*

  'gahg geyg geeg geyg gahg gorg goog gorg gahg'

- *Repeat this sequence four times with the same focus.*

Working with Text

Now that you have limbered up and toned the lip and tongue muscles it is time to carry the work over into connected speech.

Bone prop text

To build precision into connected speech

- *Sit or stand as before, directing the back to lengthen and the shoulders and hips to widen. Check that the feet are parallel and hip width apart, that the joints are loose and that the shoulder blades and buttocks are dropping gently down your back.*
- *Place the bone prop between your teeth and speak some text slowly but without over-emphasis.*
- *Be aware of the movements of the lips and tongue on each consonant and give every consonant a chance to be fully made, so that the tongue and lips aren't missing out any sound.*
- *Do this slowly until you are sure that every consonant is being visited. Then you can begin to speed up but keep the precision. The best way to do this is to keep your attention on your lips and tongue as they move about your mouth. It is the precision of your attention that will enable you to find clarity without over-emphasis in your speech.*
- *Work with one piece of text for a couple of days and, then, move on to the next.*

A word about elision Sounds in words are affected by the sounds next to them and a certain amount of sliding from one sound to the next is natural. This is known as elision. Once you have practised the exercises in this section, it is best, as always, to trust the work to take care of itself.

It is rather like letting rip with a dance and letting the separate steps flow together once you are absolutely sure of each step. If you have a good sense of each step of the precise physical journey the lips and tongue make through a word, you can then allow their movements to flow into one another and you will keep the precision and yet at the same time allow the natural elision to take place.

Being present with each sound

To connect with the sounds

- *Sit or stand as before, directing the back to lengthen and the shoulders and hips to widen. Check that the feet are parallel and hip width apart, that the joints are loose and that the shoulder blades and buttocks are dropping gently down your back.*
- *Without the bone prop speak a text and, without stressing or over-emphasising any sounds, stay present with the sounds in each word as you make them.*
- *Have a sense of very lightly, but firmly and with commitment, using the sounds to communicate what you want to say.*
- *Physically be 'with' the act of speaking, so you are mentally in sync with the movements of your lips and tongue rather than ahead of them or behind them.*
- *In this way, not only will you have a better connection with the text, but also there will be no room for self-consciousness because all your attention will be on the words and the need to communicate.*

Connecting – the final energy giver

To further energise your speech

When we really focus on the person or persons we want to communicate with – be they the other actors or the audience – we lose self-consciousness and we gain energy.

So once you have done all the work on connecting with the sounds and words, then you need to turn your attention to connecting with the person or persons to whom you wish to talk.

As always, this involves firm but easy commitment and attention rather than effort. Too often we force in order to communicate with others: we lean forward, we exaggerate, we over-emphasise. None of this is either necessary or useful. Rather you need to really put your attention on the person or persons with whom you are trying to communicate and become totally preoccupied with *sharing* your words with them so that they see or feel or understand what you are seeing or feeling or thinking. This is not about demonstrating or explaining: the first can become indulgent and insincere and the second very heavy and laborious. It is about really sharing, becoming totally involved in your listener and taking them on a journey.

So often actors think they need to feel before they can communicate anything. But in my experience when performing, just as in real life, if you really start to communicate with someone, the feelings and thoughts come naturally.

Obviously, you do need to have made a connection with the text and the images behind the text and, also, to have explored character and scene, but this, hopefully, is what rehearsals are about.

So, how do you practise? It is very useful to start by communicating with inanimate objects because you can practise this on your own and really commit in a way you might not yet be ready to with other people.

- *Take a piece of text and kneel on the floor in front of a chair. Hold onto the chair back or the chair seat and really talk to the chair as if you want to communicate with it.*
- *Check that you aren't forcing or pushing, but rather that you are putting your attention on the chair and talking to it with committed ease.*

There is a very easy way to check whether or not the exercise is working. If all your attention is on the chair and none is on yourself, then, it is working. If you still have a lot of attention on yourself, then, it isn't.

- *Once you feel you can put all or nearly all your attention on the chair, then you can get up and start to move around your room, talking to all the different objects that are there. Again, make sure that all your attention is on the object you are talking to and that none is on yourself.*
- *Once you feel comfortable with this then you can try it out with people, really focusing your attention on them as you talk to them.*

If you allow yourself to commit to this exercise and take the attention off yourself, it can be wonderfully liberating. Your self-consciousness will disappear; the holding back or pushing forward will start to dissolve; and then your work can really take wing and you are likely to surprise and delight yourself as well as the audience!

Putting the Whole Chapter together

The first half of the chapter is exploratory and does not need to be repeated. The exercises in the section on limbering up and toning the lip and tongue muscles are worth doing regularly, but, obviously, they can be condensed once you know them well so that they take no more than about five minutes. The reason I suggest that you keep the work as brief as possible is that, then, you have to pay attention or you get nothing done in the time.

Below I have put the exercises from this chapter together with those from the earlier chapters to form a complete session. As always it is only a guideline to follow if you wish to. Please don't feel you have to do all the exercises I have suggested. The session should be fun rather than a chore.

You'll notice that there are more exercises in the last two sections without there being a corresponding increase in time. This is because some of the earlier exercises will take less time now and so you can fit a greater number of exercises into the same time. The length of time you spend on each exercise will depend on your own needs, but a good attentive 30 seconds to a minute on each exercise will focus you and lead to a better quality of work.

Warm-up (1 minute)

Freeing the breath (69)

Floor work (2 minutes)

Centring the breath (69)
Opening the throat (72)

Standing (6 minutes)

Lengthening and widening (132)
Working against the wall or wide arms (133 or 134)
Side to side (135)
Half neck circles (136)
Nose circles or Nose figure of eight or Head nods (137)
Engage, release and 'H' breath (against wall or with chair) (84)

Sitting or Standing (10 minutes)

Widening and opening (138)
Freeing the larynx 1 and 2 (139)
Giggle and sob (with text) (140)
Lower jaw drop 2 (with text) (143)
Upper jaw release (with text) (144)
Cleaning the teeth with the tongue (146)
Back of tongue stretch (147)

Under chin massage (with text) (**148**)
Lazy forward tongue talking (with text) (**149**)
Ng-Ah and Ng-Ah into talking (**166** *and* **167**)
Hng – Ah into talking (**168**)

Standing (21 minutes)

Sliding 'sh' (**156**)
Bouncing sound from the diaphragm (**99**)
Bouncing sound from the lower belly (**102**)
Bouncing sound from the 'oomph points' (**103**)
Calling (with text) (**114**)
Engaging the lower belly and pelvic floor muscles throughout the sound (**109**)
Engaging the 'diamond points' throughout the sound (**110**)
Focusing the sound forward – 1 and 2 (**169**)
Focusing on the mouth (**172**)
Focusing on the chest (**173**)
Waking up the face and the eyes (**176**)
Focusing on the face (**177**)
Putting the resonance together (**178**)
Ooee glide (**183**)
Roller coaster (**185**)
Car revs (**185**)
Down and up (**186**)
Loosening the face, lips and tongue (**216**)
Lips – rounding and spreading (**219**)
closing and opening (**220**)
bottom teeth working with top lip (**221**)
rounded lip talk (**221**)
Tongue-tip – circle (**222**)
flick (**223**)
Middle of tongue flex (**225**)
Back of tongue flex (**226**)
Lengthening and widening while releasing (with text) (**132**)
Drop and release (with text) (**158**)
Door handle swing (with text) (**158**)

Drawing the Work Together

Once you have worked through the book, in whatever way feels most appropriate for you, then, *trust* yourself to choose the relevant exercises for your personal tool kit.

Work with a sense of confidence and ease, assuming that you *can do the work*. After all, your body and voice were designed to function well. All you need to do is pay them a little attention and they'll flourish.

Don't ever compare your voice with anyone else's or try to imitate them. Each one of us is individual and if we release our habitual tensions and work with commitment our voice will reflect our uniqueness.

Be carefree and creative in putting the work together. Don't think too much – it never helps! Above all, approach the exercises with a sense of play; have fun – it's the best way to learn.

In the Quick Reference section you will find a suggested 20-minute warm up, which can be used before rehearsals and performances. You will also find advice about texts and vocal health and a trouble-shooter list to help with specific problems. I hope you find these helpful and supportive in your journey to finding your own voice.

QUICK REFERENCE SECTION

Warm-Up

This warm-up can be used before rehearsals or performance and need take no longer than twenty minutes including some text work. I have explained the exercises in shorthand here, so if you haven't read the rest of the book you will need to refer to the original exercise.

ALEXANDER POSITION

Releasing the body and waking up the breath

Centring the breath *(see page 69)*

- *Lie on the floor with your legs bent and your head on a book.*
- *Place your hands just below your navel and rest your attention there.*
- *Imagine the central nostrils and mouth deep inside the body just above navel level.*
- *Sigh out gently and then rest and wait for the in-breath to come in of its own accord.*

Note

In the original exercise the hands were placed just above the navel since that was the most helpful point to focus on initially. However, long term, placing your hands below the navel and focusing there will help to centre the breath further.

- *Imagine the breath flowing in freely and easily through the 'central nostrils' and, then, melting into the out-breath and that out-breath flowing out easily and freely through the 'central mouth'.*
- *Continue this for one minute.*

Opening the throat *(see page 72)*

- *Leave your hands resting just below your navel.*
- *As you breathe in through the nose, smile a warm smile and slide your lower teeth forward until they are level with your upper teeth.*

- *Keep smiling and open your mouth until there is a finger's width between the back teeth.*
- *Keep smiling and breathe out almost silently in this position.*
- *Repeat four or five times.*

Engaging, releasing and the 'H' breath (see pages 73-85)

Stage one – with breath

- *Move your hands so they are resting just below your navel.*
- *Imagine that there is a three dimensional 'H' inside your body. The middle of the 'H' stretches across the body just above navel level and the legs of the 'H' reach down to the base of the buttocks and up to just beneath the shoulders.*
- *Then, focus on the area where your hands are and blow out from there, mentally reaching down into the lower belly for more breath in the second half of the out-breath.*
- *At the end of the out-breath release the lower belly and pelvic floor muscles and let the in-breath come in when it likes, imagining it filling into the centre of the 'H' first and, then, into the rest of the 'H'.*
- *Blow out, release and fill 2 or 3 times more in the same way.*

Stage two – with sound

- *Then, release and fill and sound out on a long 'vvvvvv', imagining the sound coming from just below your navel, where your hands are, in the same way that the breath did and mentally reaching down into the lower belly for breath/sound in the second half of the breath.*
- *Sound out, release and fill 2 or 3 times more in the same way, imagining the sound travelling from the belly to the lips the whole time.*
- *Then, release and fill as before and sound out on a long 'hoo', again imagining the sound travelling from the belly to the lips.*
- *Then, repeat the sounding out, release and fill sequence on the following sounds, continuing to make each sound until the end of your breath:*

  'hoh' 'hor' 'hah' 'high' 'hey' 'hee'

  Each time imagine the sound coming from the navel to the lips and mentally reaching down for the breath/sound in the second half of the out-breath.

STANDING I

Waking up the support muscles

Diaphragm bounce (see page 86)

- *Stand with your feet hipbone width apart, with your ankle, knee and hip joints loose, your spine lengthening, your hips and shoulders widening and your buttocks and shoulder blades dropping. Let your arms hang easily by your sides.*
- *Pant silently, checking that the spine continues to lengthen and the hips and shoulders to widen as you pant.*
- *Add in more and more mental bounce by thinking of flirting or teasing or being cheeky or coolly confident. Continue this for 30 seconds.*
- *Now stop panting and, imagine that your mouth is in your diaphragm and that you speak from there. Bounce out the 'Hoo Hoo' sequence with great sureness:*

  'Hoo Hoo – Hoh Hoh – Hor Hor – Hah Hah – High High – Hey Hey – Hee Hee'

- *Repeat the sequence 2 or 3 times increasing the mental bounce each time.*

Lower belly bounce (see page 89)

- *Standing as in the previous exercise, place your hands just below the navel. Now imagine that your mouth is where your hands are and that you speak from there.*
- *Say 'sh' a few times as if you were firmly telling someone to be quiet and feel the area under your hands being pulled in and slightly up.*
- *Then, again with great sureness, bounce out the 'Hoo Hoo' sequence from the belly:*

  'Hoo Hoo – Hoh Hoh – Hor Hor – Hah Hah – High High – Hey Hey – Hee Hee'

- *Repeat the sequence 2 or 3 times increasing the mental bounce each time.*

'Oomph points' bounce (see page 90)

Top-of-the-diamond

- *Again, stand as in the previous exercise, but this time place your thumb just below the breastbone and imagine that this is where your mouth is and where you speak from.*

- *Say 'psh psh' a few times as if shooing away and feel the area under your thumb move out.*
- *Then, again, with great sureness, bounce out the 'Hoo Hoo' sequence from the area just below the breast bone:*

  'Hoo Hoo – Hoh Hoh – Hor Hor – Hah Hah – High High – Hey Hey – Hee Hee'

- *Repeat the sequence 2 or 3 times increasing the mental bounce each time.*
- *Then, do the 'car revs' (see page 185) either on a lip roll or a tongue roll working both with bounce and ease and feeling the area under your thumb bouncing out as you rev.*

Bottom-of-the-diamond

- *Repeat the above sequence with your fingers on the area just above the pubic bone, feeling that area move out as you make the sounds.*

Sides-of-the-waist

- *Repeat the above sequence with your hands on the sides of the waist, feeling these move out as you make the sounds.*

Back-of-the-waist

- *Repeat the above sequence with your hands on the sides of the waist, feeling these move out as you make the sounds.*

STANDING 2

Waking up the resonance, range and articulation

Waking up the face (see page 176)

- *Again, stand with your feet hipbone width apart, with your ankle, knee and hip joints loose, your spine lengthening, your hips and shoulders widening and your buttocks and shoulder blades dropping. Let your arms hang easily by your sides.*
- *Move your face and lips around and hum easily. If any areas of the face feel particularly stiff massage them gently as you hum.*

Waking up the lips (see page 217)

- *Stand as in the last exercise.*
- *Move the lips around to release any stiffness and to wake them up.*

- *Blow through the lips, making a sound like a horse.*
- *Then, blow through the lips again but this time adding voice – brrrrr (like the sound you make when you are cold).*

Waking up the 'lower resonance' (see page 173)

- *Stand as in the previous exercises.*
- *Hum easily, with a sense of yawn behind the closed lips and pat the chest as you do so.*
- *Then, still patting your chest, open from a hum into 'mah mah mah mah mah' etc.*
- *Continue until you have a sense of vibration in your chest.*

Waking up the 'middle resonance' (see page 172)

- *Stand as in the previous exercises.*
- *Keeping the lips rounded, sound out on 'ooeeooeeooeeooee' etc., imagining that the sound is bouncing back and forth inside the mouth.*
- *Continue until you have a sense of vibration in your mouth.*

Waking up the 'upper resonance' (see page 177)

- *Stand as in the previous exercises.*
- *Hum and imagine the sound going into the brow of the nose.*
- *Continue humming, this time moving the whole face about, and now imagine the sound flowing out from the brow of the nose into the cheekbones.*

Drop and release with text (see page 158)

- *Stand as in the previous exercises.*
- *Take your arms up above your head as you breathe in easily. Keep the shoulders and shoulder blades dropped and relaxed.*
- *Then, as you breathe out drop over from the hips and swing back and forth, allowing the ankle, knee and hip joints to be loose so you can bounce down and up.*
- *At the end of the breath gently swing up again, until you are standing with your arms above your head again. You will find that the new breath comes in easily as you do so.*

- *Then, drop and swing and bounce again, sounding out on a hum.*
- *At the end of the breath gently swing up as before, again feeling the new breath come in easily.*
- *Then, drop and swing and bounce sounding out on a long 'mah'.*
- *At the end of the breath swing up again and feel the new breath enter easily.*
- *Then, drop and swing and bounce whilst loosely chanting or speaking some text.*
- *Repeat this last stage a few times.*

Down and up – freeing the range (see page 186)

- *Do this exercise on 'bllllI' or rolled 'r'.*
- *Start standing with your right hand in the air. Drop your body and arm down from your hips, letting your arm also drop. Imagine your chosen sound sliding down through your arm and down your body to your feet and then on down into the ground.*
- *Then, as soon as you have dropped down, allow yourself to bounce back up again letting your left hand go up in the air and letting your sound release up through your body and your left arm and on up into space.*
- *As always let the sound take care of itself and simply enjoy dropping down and bouncing back up. The freer you are with the movement and the more you let the sound slide down and up of its own accord, the better.*

Strengthening the lip and tongue muscles – 1 (see pages 218-226)

- *Stand as in the earlier exercises.*
- *Bounce out this sequence lightly and slowly: p-t-k-t-p p-t-k-t-p p-t-k-t-p p-t-k-t-p*
- *Feel the lips flick apart on the 'p', the tip of the tongue flick away from the gum ridge on 't' and the back of the tongue and the end of the soft palate flick apart on the 'k'. No force or tension is necessary.*
- *Once you are comfortable with the sequence you can speed it up a little, but keep each sound precise, so that they don't run into each other.*
- *Then repeat the exercise on: b-d-g-d-b b-d-g-d-b b-d-g-d-b b-d-g-d-b, again feeling the same flicking apart without tension or force.*

Strengthening the lip and tongue muscles – 2 (see page 218-226)

- *Stand as in the earlier exercises.*

- *Try the following sequence, feeling the lips spring apart on each 'b' and making sure that the final 'b' is fully sounded:*

  'barb-bayb-beeb-bayb-barb-borb-boob-borb-barb'

- *Then, try the same sequence with 'd' instead of 'b', feeling the tip of the tongue flick away from the upper gum ridge on each 'd' and making sure that the final 'd' is fully sounded:*

  'dard-dayd-deed-dayd-dard-dord-dood-dord-dard'

- *Then, try the same sequence with 'g', feeling the back of the tongue and the end of the soft palate flick apart on each 'g' and making sure that the final 'g' is fully sounded:*

  'garg-gayg-geeg-gayg-garg-gorg-goog-gorg-garg'

- *Then, try the same vowel sequence with 'l', feeling the tongue tip flick down on the initial 'l' and feeling it against the upper gum ridge on the final 'l':*

  'larl-layl-leel-layl-larl-lorl-lool-lorl-larl'

Text work

- *Take a piece of text and either sing or speak it while making large, free, easy movements.*
- *Then mouth the text silently and be aware of the lips and tongue shaping the words firmly but without tension.*
- *Then, speak the text and, as you do so, move across the room towards an object, really wanting to release the text to the object. As soon as you get to the object, turn and find another object to communicate with and move towards that object.*
- *Keep going in this way for several sentences.*
- *Then, stand still and speak the text whilst doing a backward circle with your arms. Still speak to the objects in the room. Imagine that the more you stay in your own space the more the text releases out across the room to the various objects.*

Working with Texts

It is good to work with a variety of texts since the different 'voices' – the particular rhythms, sounds and images – of the playwrights will extend your own voice.

Shakespeare's text is excellent to work on for many reasons. Firstly, because the language is less 'every day', we pay more attention to it – its structures and rhythms, sounds and images. This creates a habit of being more precise with text, which can then be usefully taken back into our work on modern plays.

The heightened nature of Shakespeare's text also challenges us. Simply by speaking it we extend ourselves vocally. So, don't worry about whether you understand it or not. Start to speak the words out loud, moving around with freedom and commitment, forgetting about the sense and simply allowing the language itself to open you up.

The depth of Shakespeare's understanding of human beings and the breadth of emotions he explores in his plays also make his work a fantastic training ground for an actor. So dip in, find different speeches, never mind about the age or the sex of the character, just enjoy getting inside the skin of different people and emotions. The more you speak the text aloud, and let it take you on a journey rather than imposing on it, the better.

Other pre-twentieth-century playwrights, whose texts are worth working on, include Christopher Marlow, John Ford, Ben Jonson, the Restoration playwrights and Oscar Wilde. I have not mentioned playwrights whose work is translated, such as Aeschylus, Aristophanes, Sophocles, Euripides, Racine, Chekhov, Ibsen, Strindberg, Calderon or Lorca, because so much depends on the quality of the translation.

Poetry is also excellent to work with, again because its heightened language and compacted imagery really stretches us. Ted Hughes's poems are wonderful to work with and have great physicality – I often use them for warm-ups.

But don't be shy, get a poetry book from the library and just keep dipping until you find what you like. Below is a list of poetry anthologies to give you a start:

Poems on the Underground – there are now at least two volumes

Poems for the Day – edited by Nicholas Albery

The Rattle Bag – edited by Seamus Heaney and Ted Hughes

Of course, there are plenty of wonderful twentieth-century writers you can work with. Among them are Samuel Beckett, Edward Bond, Howard Brenton, Caryl Churchill, David Edgar, Pam Gems, David Hare, Arthur Miller, Sean O'Casey, Harold Pinter, Timberlake Wertenbaker and Tennessee Williams. Then, of course, there is a whole host of younger writers who are producing exciting work. The best way to encounter their work is to go and see as many new plays as possible and find out which playwrights interest you.

It is important to work with both classical and modern texts, shifting back and forth between them. In this way both your voice and acting will be stimulated and stretched.

As with all the voice work, approach text work with a sense of curiosity and playfulness. You don't need to be an academic to decode the text. Plays are about human beings, human experience and all you need to engage with them is commitment and imagination.

Vocal Health

Water

If you are dehydrated all the lubrication systems in your body will be affected. So dehydration will quickly lead to a dry throat. By the time you feel thirsty you are already over 50 per cent dehydrated and it takes a while to re-hydrate, so drinking just before you go on stage isn't going to give you the lubrication you need. Tea, coffee, alcohol and many soft drinks are more dehydrating than they are hydrating, since they encourage the body to release fluid more rapidly. So, if you want to keep well hydrated you need to drink water. Eight glasses a day is the generally agreed amount to aim for, with an extra glass for every cup of tea or coffee, soft drink or serving of alcohol. Now, this can be difficult to achieve if you're not in the habit of drinking much water, so start by drinking two glasses as soon as you get up and two glasses before each meal and then build up from there. Also, try cutting down on tea and coffee so you don't have more than six cups a day.

Obviously, if you are sweating more either because of working in the heat, in a warm costume or because there's physical effort involved then you will lose more fluid and so need to drink more water to compensate.

It is possible to drink too much water, so, unless you are sweating buckets, don't drink more than 4 litres a day without advice from a doctor, sports fitness or nutritional specialist. Also, it needs to be still rather than sparkling water, since the gas in sparkling water is not particularly good for the stomach.

Note

Quick remedy: if you have a dry throat before you go on stage swallowing can help, so take a tiny amount of water, hold it in your mouth for a second and, then, swallow.

If you are feeling dry once on stage, try biting the side of your tongue fairly hard for a moment. When you release you will find that you have more saliva. According to the late Van Lawrence, an American laryngologist, it will give you enough lubrication for one-and-a-half arias!

Steamers

No liquid ever touches the vocal folds. The epiglottis – a tongue-like flap at the top of the larynx – closes to prevent food and drink passing through the larynx into the lungs. So, no amount of hot or cold drinks will soothe your throat – even if they feel as if they do.

Steam, however, can pass over the vocal folds, so steaming can help to moisten the throat area and to temporarily shift the mucus when you have a cold. Rather than using a bowl of boiling water, which can be messy, and dangerous in a busy dressing room, consider buying a steamer. You can get excellent ones for less than £40 at the Welbeck Pharmacy, 38/39, Marylebone High Street, London, W1N 3AB. Tel: 020 7935 4050. They are also happy to send one to you if you live outside London.

Steaming does also relax the throat area so it is necessary to leave a short gap between steaming and speaking on stage so that the folds have time to firm up rather than being over-relaxed. Think about what you would do after a hot bath. You wouldn't go straight out into the cold, nor would you go straight into exercise. So, leave about five minutes and then do a little gentle humming and then some gliding up and down your range on 'ooeeooeeooee etc'. (See page 183.)

Humidifiers

Sometimes rehearsal rooms and dressing rooms can be very dry and dusty and, where it is not practicable to have bowls of water around, a humidifier might be a better bet. These are more expensive than steamers and more finicky to maintain, but in very dry atmospheres they can help enormously. At home, of course, you can put bowls of water out to help keep the air moist and in your dressing room you could hang up a damp towel.

Rest

If the body is over-tired it will not be able to support the voice appropriately. Also, it is likely that the voice itself will be tired as well. So, you do need sufficient rest and sleep to keep the voice healthy. The difference between talking in everyday life and using your voice in performance is like the difference between running for the bus and running a race. As a performer you are a vocal athlete. No runner would tire themselves out before a race, they might train, but they would also rest. As a performer you need to learn how to conserve your energy. You can't spend the morning on the phone, the afternoon at a football match or talking in a noisy restaurant and, then go and perform in the evening. It won't work. You might get away with it for a while but not forever.

Periods

In the same way that many other parts of the body change during the monthly period, so do the vocal folds. They swell slightly and are a little more fragile.Therefore, the voice is not at its strongest. There is no need to worry about this. Simply be aware that it is best to ease up on the vocal demands you are making during this time and to rest as much as possible. The effect will vary from woman to woman.

Relaxation

Stress is a killer for the voice, so if you are going through a period of stress make time to physically relax. Go to yoga or tai chi or swim or walk or have a massage – whatever works for you, but don't leave it until vocal fatigue and strain start to show. After all a troublesome voice is only going to stress you more.

Don't worry

While it is important to take care of your voice it is vital not to worry about it. Worry causes tension and it never helps. If you are concerned about your voice go and get some help immediately. If you can't find a voice teacher or speech and language therapist or laryngologist in your area contact the British Voice Association – 020 7831 1060 – or look on their web site – www.british-voice-association.com.

Watch out when talking on the phone, in the car and in the pub, club, or restaurant

These situations can be very hard on voice. We often don't support the voice properly when we are on the phone, so make sure that you are not all crunched up or slumped over, instead check you are in a position where you can breathe freely and easily. Never hold the phone between your shoulder and chin – that is terrible for the voice.

Talking in the car over the noise of the other traffic, perhaps with the CD or radio on and the car heater drying the air, is another killer for the voice. If you want to talk in the car make sure you can breathe freely and that you are supporting your voice and if there is too much noise, don't battle to be heard over it, just keep quiet. If the heater's on make sure you drink lots of water, even if it means more loo stops.

Pubs, clubs and restaurants with the noise, smoke and dehydrating effects of alcohol, are another cause for concern. In a way they are best avoided if you want to talk and don't want to tire your voice. Obviously the odd night won't hurt, but putting the voice through this night after night, especially while you are rehearsing and performing isn't going to be helpful.

Warming up – warming down

For years dancers have understood the need to warm up before a rehearsal or show and to warm down afterwards. Muscles can't be expected to suddenly leap into action nor can they be expected to suddenly stop. The same is true for the muscles connected with voice production. The warm-up and down do not need to be long but they do need to happen. The minimum is five minutes before and after a rehearsal or show, although, obviously, I would suggest longer – 15 to 20 minutes – before a rehearsal or performance.

Warming up (minimum!)

- *Lie on the floor in the Alexander position. (See page 24.) Place your hands just below your navel and blow out from there. At the end of the out-breath release the belly and let the in-breath come in by itself. Repeat three times.*
- *Then, sound out on 'vvvvvvvvvv' imagining the sound is flowing from the belly to the lips. Repeat twice.*
- *Then, sound out on 'Hoooooooooo' again imagining the sound is flowing from the belly to the lips. Repeat four times. (See page 109.)*
- *Then, stand up and repeat the work you have just done on the floor.*
- *Then, pant easily with a sense of cheekiness or cockiness or flirting. (See page 88.)*
- *Then, bounce out the 'Hoo Hoo' to 'Hee Hee' sequence from the diaphragm. (See page 99.)*

- *Then bounce out the 'Hoo Hoo' to 'Hee Hee' sequence again from the belly and then from the diamond points. (See pages 103 and 104.)*
- *Then, hum gently while rolling the shoulders round and, then, rolling the head from side to side.*
- *Then, blow through the lips like a horse a few times.*
- *Then, move the face and lips around in a chewing movement while continuing to hum.*
- *Then, blow through the lips again but this time add sound and pretend you are revving a car or motorbike.*
- *Then, on a light 'ng' sound slide up and down your range easily and freely, being sure to stop and breathe regularly.*

Warming down

- *Start by sliding up and down your range easily on a light 'ng', first gliding a long way up and down and gradually making the glides smaller.*
- *Then, hum very lightly, perhaps with the chewing movements of the lips and face and gently let the hum get smaller and smaller until it dies away.*

You can do the warm down while you are getting changed or getting your things together to leave, you don't have to stand still and just focus on your voice.

Take care during technical rehearsals and previews

These periods, with their long working days, perhaps constant repetition of scenes and possibly stressful atmosphere, can be very tiring even for very experienced actors. It is important to warm up, however briefly, before the technical. Make sure you drink plenty of water, avoid too many teas and coffees and get as much rest as possible. Also, make sure you eat well rather than filling up with junk food and don't smoke extra cigarettes just because you're sitting around a lot!

Working on raked stages

You need to watch that your back and legs don't tighten up. Lie in the Alexander Position (see page 24) daily for 15 to 20 minutes to allow the body to regain its balance and also do some simple stretches (see pages 20-23) between scenes.

Working in extreme character positions

If you are adopting an extreme physical position as part of your characterisation, as you might for Richard III, then, you need to do physical releasing and balancing work to counteract any tensions that might develop.

Rest in the Alexander Position (see page 24) daily for 15 to 20 minutes to allow the body to return to balance. Follow this with Spine peels, Pelvic rounds, Ankle rotations and Shoulder drops (see pages 28-32). Also, before each show, go through the stretches detailed in the Body Work chapter (see pages 20-23).

Acid Reflux

If you lie down too soon after eating, the acid, produced in your stomach to break down the food, can come back up into the throat and cause irritation and damage. So always make sure you leave a reasonable time – a couple of hours – after a meal before you lie down. It is also advisable to leave an hour's gap between eating and performing because strong movement of the abdominal muscles can cause reflux.

Cigarettes

Of course it is better if you don't smoke – you know that. Cigarettes dry the throat and affect the mucous lining. However, giving up isn't always easy, so just cut down if you can.

If you are going to give up, be aware that it can take two to three months for the mucous lining in the throat to settle down after you have stopped smoking, so you need to choose a time when you are not asking too much of your voice.

Pollutants

Fumes from paint and varnish can also affect the throat, so it's a bad idea to spend the day painting or varnishing if you have a demanding show to do in the evening.

Troubleshooting

Below is a list of common problems, with brief explanations and indications of where in the book you can find further explanation and exercises to solve the problem.

BREATH

Inability to breathe deeply

Tension is a major cause of shallow breath. So, you need to work on physical release (see pages 19-36) before you move onto the specific exercises that help to deepen the breath. Particularly look at releasing the knee joints, the buttocks and the belly.

Posture also affects the breath. Over-erect or collapsed posture will inhibit the movement of the ribs and the diaphragm. So, you need to work on postural alignment (see pages 49-55) to avoid a stiff or slumped stance.

After this preparatory physical work you can, then, move on to specific breathing exercises (see pages 67-73, 77-84).

Further explanation – 59-63

Running out of breath

This is often due to the spine collapsing and to narrowing in the shoulders. Start with work on physical release and postural alignment (see pages 19-36, 49-55). Then, move on to specific breathing exercises (see pages 73-76, 84-86). I find working with the arms out wide to the side or holding a chair above the head (see pages 85 and 134) the most effective ways of avoiding collapse and narrowing and so help the breath to be sustained.

Further explanation – 63-65

Little or no rib movement

This is often caused by slumping in the upper body. Tension in the back and sides, due to other unhelpful postural habits, will also inhibit rib movement. Again, physical work is the key, lengthening the spine, especially the upper spine through work lying on the floor and standing (see pages 19-36, 132-135). Then, using the wide arm exercise and holding a chair above your head (see pages 134 and 85) as you do the breathing exercises will help enormously. It is also important to work on fully releasing the out-breath as this will stimulate rib movement on the in-breath. (See page 72.)

Further explanation – 59-63, Relevant exercises – 78-86

Noisy in-breath

This is usually due to tension and effort on the in-breath, with the breath being sucked in rather than being allowed to flow in freely. Postural tension, in particular the belly being held in tightly rather than being allowed to relax at the end of the out-breath is the root cause of this problem. So, work on physical release and postural alignment (see pages 19-36, 49-55), before moving on to specific exercises to release the belly at the end of the out-breath (see page 77) and to open the throat (see page 72). Throughout, check that you are fully releasing the out-breath since this enables the in-breath to flow in far more easily.

Further explanation – 59-63

VOCAL SUPPORT

Lack of vocal support

This occurs when there is disconnection from the abdominal muscles and they no longer work to ensure that the breath releases at a sufficient and consistent pressure to support the workings of the larynx.

The first areas to look at are physical release and postural alignment (see pages 19-36, 49-55) since these are both necessary if the abdominal muscles are to work effectively.

Once this has been done, you can move on to specific work that reconnects and strengthens the abdominal muscles so enabling them to provide appropriate support (see pages 74-77, 89-116).

It may also then be necessary to look at releasing habitual tension and holding in the throat, jaw, lips and tongue (see pages 138-149).

Further explanation – 65-66

Throat tension/strangled voice

This can have many causes. Whatever may have initiated the problem, it is very important to get the attention away from the throat area and move it down to the abdominal muscles in the lower body, so that these can start to work effectively and appropriately to support the voice. Once this support is established *then* you can work on releasing tension in the neck, throat and jaw area and in the lips and tongue and learn how to actively keep the throat open (see pages 138-149).

It is a good idea to begin by working on the whole body to release tension and to build good postural habits – lengthening, widening and releasing the joints (see pages 19, 36, 49-55) – before you embark on the support work (see pages 86-116).

Further explanation – 10-11, 118-131

Tired/strained voice

This is the result of excessive or inappropriate effort. Excessive effort is the result of mental push, which leads to physical push. Inappropriate effort occurs when the support muscles do not work and the throat is left to struggle by itself.

To counter excessive effort you need to work with a sense of ease (see page xiv), to remove tension and pushing; and with a sense of cheekiness, teasing or flirting (see page 9), to bring relaxed energy. Working with these attitudes brings mental 'bounce' which, in turn, leads to physical 'bounce' and stimulates the muscles to engage and work effectively rather than tensely. Working with the backward circle exercise (see pages 44-45) is also helpful since it grounds and centres the energy preventing push and strain and encouraging freer and stronger release.

To counter inappropriate effort you need to remove the attention from the throat area and put it on the abdominal muscles so that they can engage and start to support the voice. The exercises on support (see pages 74-77, 89-116) will show you how to do this.

Once you have are happy with the support work, you can move on to the exercises for releasing tension in the neck, throat, jaw, lips and tongue (see pages 135-149).

Further explanation – 6-13

Strain when screaming and shouting

This occurs when there is insufficient support from the abdominal muscles for these highly demanding activities. As a result, insufficient breath is released at insufficient pressure and the throat attempts to compensate so leading to strain. Also, there is often a great deal of tension accompanying screaming and shouting which tightens up the breath, the throat and everything in between, so that the whole vocal system is unable to work with any ease or efficiency.

First you need to check that the abdominal muscles are supporting your ordinary speech (see pages 74-77, 89-116) and, then, use the calling work (see pages 105-108) to build the energy, strength and release necessary for screaming and shouting.

Difficulty with dynamic/high-energy scenes

This occurs when the abdominal muscles are sluggish. There is a lack of support and energy, rather like a trampoline with no bounce.

First, you need to work on postural alignment (see pages 49-55) since this will bring energy to the body as a whole and enable the abdominal muscles to work more effectively. Then, you need to generate more mental energy by working with the idea of 'mental bounce' (see page 9). This will give more physical bounce to the abdominal muscles and encourage them to naturally work in a more effective manner.

Then, you need to work specifically on connecting with and strengthening the abdominal muscles to ensure that they always engage appropriately (see pages 76-77, 89-116).

Further explanation – 7-8, 86-88

BEING HEARD

Voice too quiet

This is caused by insufficient breath pressure, which, in turn, is the result of the body working tentatively rather than with commitment. Working with easy sureness, even light cockiness, is a huge help here. This enables the abdominal and laryngeal muscles to work appropriately to ensure that the breath pressure is sufficient to produce the volume required. It sounds complicated but the actual exercises (see pages 74-77, 89-116) are quite straightforward and the sure or cocky attitude will get you off to a really good start.

Further explanation – xiii, 88

Voice too loud

This is the result of excessive effort, of mental and physical 'pushing'. Work on grounding and centring (see pages 36-45) will bring greater ease and appropriateness of effort. In particular, working with the backward circle (see pages 44-45) will remove excess effort without suppressing energy.

Further explanation – xiv, 6-12

Difficulty being truthful when working in large spaces/ having to project

This occurs when the voice is mentally and physically 'pushed out' into the space. It is as if the voice 'unhooks' so that it no longer feels connected. One of the main reasons for this is that usually little or no time is spent in the performance space before the technical rehearsal, all the earlier rehearsals having taken place elsewhere, often in a smaller space. Once in the technical the lights are usually in the scene state so it is not possible to fully sense the full size of the space and so the voice cannot organically grow to fill it. Instead, the volume is raised artificially and disconnection occurs.

To avoid this it is necessary to go into the space when the lights are on and stand in various places on the stage and imagine your attention travelling out to the back walls of the space, as if mentally embracing it. By energetically filling the space in this way you will lead your performance both physically and vocally to fill the space but there will be no sense of strain or disconnection.

Obviously, it is also important to check that you are using your abdominal muscles appropriately to support the voice (see pages 76–77, 89-116) and that you aren't disconnecting from the breath and powering the voice from the throat.

It is also important to check that however large the space you are working in, you always talk and never declaim. When we talk we stay in contact with the person we are communicating with and this is what makes the voice sound real, however loud. However, when we declaim we lose all sense of the person spoken to and address the air in an unfocused way. It is this lack of focus that makes the voice sound false and, indeed, feel false. So, even if you are not facing the person you are talking to or if you are talking to someone who is not present, always keep mentally focused on your listener.

Difficulty being heard when doing intimate scenes

Because the focus is on the intimate space between the actors, it is as if the rest of the performance space does not exist and the voice, therefore, only fills the small intimate space.

To counter this it is necessary to have a sense of mentally reaching out from your small personal space to the further reaches of the audience and drawing them into your intimacy. In this way the voice will reach out, but it will reach out to come back and it will not lose connection with the scene. A good way to work on this is to keep your eyes on your scene partner, so you don't lose contact with them, and, then, as you play the scene, to reach out and back with your arms, as if you are beckoning or inviting the audience to join you. This allows you to build a habit of sustaining the connection with your scene partner and your audience simultaneously. Once the habit of double connection has been built, then, you can physically play the scene how you like.

Working outside

The problem with working outside is that there are no walls to contain your sound or bounce it back to you, so either the voice gets lost or there is a tendency to keep pumping it out until the voice tires or strains.

So, practise with your scene partner/s, taking it in turns for one/some of you to be on stage and one/other of you to be out in the audience. Speak the scene between you with the person/people in the audience moving further and further back. Then, repeat the scene with the same person/people walking around behind the back row. In this way your brain will have a sense of how far your voice has to carry and once you have a sense of the level at which you can be heard you will be less likely to push.

It is important to include this 'speaking across the space' in your warm-up before every performance since your voice will need a constant reminder of how far it has to carry and you will benefit from the repeated reassurance.

Obviously, you may also need to do some support work to check that the abdominal muscles are engaging appropriately to provide the breath to 'fuel' the voice so that the throat is not struggling on its own. (See pages 76-77, 89-116.)

Speaking over noise

Never try to top noise because you will always end up straining. You need to stay very centred (see pages 36-45) and think of cutting through the middle of it.

Check that your abdominal muscles are working well to support your voice so that you have plenty of power without any effort around the neck and throat area. (See pages 76-77, 89-116.) Also, you may need to shape the speech a little more firmly, but be careful not to tense up.

Never wreck your voice trying to be heard over noise. If loud music or sound effects are the cause of the problem the director will simply have to decide whether he/she wants it loud and doesn't mind not hearing you or whether he/she wants to hear you, in which case the music or sound effects need to be turned down. You can't achieve miracles and you shouldn't try.

If the source of the noise is from the audience, or the heating or cooling system or other extraneous noise, again, there are limits to what you can do. Once you have worked on support and clarity (see page 199-229) if you still can't be heard then the problem has to be solved another way.

Working in acoustically dead spaces

Acoustically dead spaces soak up the sound and can be a nightmare to work in. You can tell whether a space is acoustically dead or alive by clapping your hands. If it is dead there will be no echo at all, whereas if it is alive the clap will resound a little.

The tendency in dead spaces is to push and push to try and get some feedback, some sense that your voice is alive and vibrant. Of course, the space just goes on soaking up the sound so you can never get the feedback you want.

What you can do is include a lot of resonance and release exercises in your warm-up (see pages 238-240) so the voice is as alive as possible. Then, work with your scene partner/s, one/some of you on stage and the other/s in the auditorium. Speak the scene back and forth to each other across the space so your brain has a good sense of how far the sound has to reach and you are reassured that you can be heard.

Working in spaces with a lot of echo

When there is a lot of echo clarity goes because the space reinforces the vowels and the delicate balance between the vowels and the consonants is lost.

So in your warm-up, after your support and release work, leave out any work on resonance and focus on exercises for shaping the sound. (See pages 199-201, 218-229.) Also, work with your scene partner/s in the space – one/some of you on stage and the other/s in the auditorium – speaking the scene between you as you move about. Cut down on the volume and instead shape the words firmly, but without exaggeration.

Touring – working in different spaces

It's best if you can do a quick warm-up in the space to get a measure of it. If that is not possible at least go into the space with your scene partner/s and play the scene out with one or more of you moving around the stage and the other/s moving around the auditorium. In this way your brain receives a sense of the size of the space and can adjust the size of your performance accordingly.

HEAD, NECK, SHOULDERS AND JAW

Head pokes forward

This can be the result of the spine between the shoulder blades slumping, rather than engaging and lengthening to support the upper back, neck and head. It can also be the result of straining forward to communicate. Often, there is a sense of disconnection from the lower body and all the energy rises into the shoulders and chin.

Start by doing some centring and grounding work (see pages 36-45), to re-connect with the lower body and anchor the energy there. Then, move on to some alignment work (see pages 49-55) to get a sense of the whole spine coming into line and the part between the shoulder blades really engaging and lengthening to support the back, neck and head. It is also very helpful to lean against the wall whilst speaking text (see pages 133-135), working with the idea that the more you wish to communicate and release your words forward, the more you lean back.

Further explanation – 121-122

Neck tension

This can have many causes. One main cause is a slump in the spine between the shoulder blades so that that part of the spine does not engage and lengthen to support the upper back, neck and head. As a result, the neck muscles have to over-work to keep the head in place, and, since the head weighs over 11lbs you can imagine the amount of strain that would put on the neck muscles. So, work on postural alignment (see pages 49-55) is important here to connect and lengthen the spine so that the head can balance efficiently.

Neck tension can also be caused by tensions lower down the body so it is worth working with the exercises that free the ankles and the small of the back (see page 28). Jaw problems can also cause neck tension, so the jaw is worth releasing (see pages 142-146) as well.

Obviously the specific neck loosening exercises (see pages 135-138) are also useful but only after the posture and related tensions have been worked on.

Further explanation – 121-122

Shoulder tension

This can have many causes. It is good to work on grounding and centring (see pages 36-45). If the legs are tense and the knees locked, if the hips are pulled back and/or the belly and buttocks are tight, then, it is impossible to ground oneself. So, instead of the lower body resting into the floor and being supported by it, the lower body lifts up off the floor. This means that the lower body cannot, then, support the upper body, which also holds itself up off the floor, with much of the tension going into the shoulders.

As well as the work on centring and grounding, it is also good to work on lengthening the spine and opening and widening across the hips and shoulders (see pages 133-135). The backward circle (see pages 44-45) is also particularly good for easing shoulder tension since it encourages the shoulders to drop down and slightly back rather than hunching up and forwards.

Once this work has been done, then, specific exercises for shoulder release (see pages 135-136) can be looked at.

Jaw tension

As with shoulder tension, it is important to look at what is going on lower down in the body. Tension in the hips can lead to tension in the jaw, odd as this might seem. Tension in the thumbs can also lead to jaw tension. Try tensing your thumbs and notice how the tension travels up your arms, across your shoulders and up the neck into the jaw.

So, again, work on physical release (see pages 19-36) is useful, along with work on centring and grounding (see pages 36-45), before going on to specific jaw release exercises (see pages 142-146).

LIPS, TONGUE AND FACE

Stiff lips

If the lips, especially the top lip, are stiff they freeze the whole face and dampen vocal expression. The archetypal 'stiff upper lip' stops the lower jaw from quivering and, therefore, holds back emotion. But the top lip can become stiff for other reasons. If the person is self conscious about their teeth they may try to cover them by keeping the top lip pulled down. A moustache will, also, cause the top lip to become immobile.

If a person has worn a fixed expression for some while, such as a false smile, the lips may become set in a stiff spread position that allows little mobility. Any fixed facial expression will tend to lead to a fixed lip position and restrict the voice's expression. So, work needs to be done to free the lips and then to bring them to life (see page 217).

Lips lack energy and precision

Lack of energy may be due to tentativeness. We tend to mumble when we are unsure, either of what we are saying or of how we are saying it. We also mumble when we are unsure of another person's reaction to what we are saying.

Of course, lack of energy in the lips may also be due to a general lack of physical energy that may reflect a lack of mental energy. Working with a sense of cheekiness, teasing, flirting or cocky sureness (see page 9) brings mental energy and commitment which in turn brings physical energy and commitment. Then, it is simply a question of exercising the lip muscles (see pages 218-222) to tone them, just as you would any other set of muscles.

Imprecision can occur because we are confused about what we want to say or because we are racing ahead of ourselves and end up thinking faster than we can speak. Working with the backward circle (see pages 44-45) helps to anchor the attention and energy and so bring clarity and presence of mind. Then, it is a question of paying attention as you exercise the lip muscles (see pages 227-229) so that you build a habit of *connecting* the mind with the physical act of speaking.

Tongue tension

The tongue is a very sensitive part of the body. It reacts to any tension we might feel in the same way that the stomach muscles might and yet we are often unaware of just how tense it is. The back of the tongue is particularly prone to tension and this tension can in turn affect the freedom of the larynx.

Before working specifically on the tongue (see pages 146-149) it is a good idea to work on physical release (see pages 19-36) and on centring and grounding (see pages 36-45), since, if the body is not aligned, at ease and grounded, tongue tension is more likely to occur.

Further explanation – 126-127

Tongue lacks energy and precision

As with the lips this may be due tentativeness. When we are unsure we do not articulate firmly. Also, like the lips, lack of mental clarity can lead to lack of tongue precision. So, as with the lips, mental commitment and clarity (see pages 199-201) are vital if the tongue is to find energy and precision.

Jaw position and tension also effects the tongue's ability to work with energy and precision. If the jaw is tight and the teeth are held close together there is little room for the tongue to move. If the jaw moves too much, taking over much of the responsibility of shaping the sound, the tongue will not have the chance to work independently and neither muscle tone nor precision can be developed.

There is also a purely anatomical cause of less precision in the tongue. The frenum, a fold of membrane on the underside of the tongue, which attaches the tongue to the floor of the mouth, varies in length from person to person. (See diagram.) Where this frenum is very short the tongue will be more restricted. In my experience clarity is still possible. It is simply that the tongue tip feels far less free to move and, therefore, often remains more static in the mouth and definition is then lost.

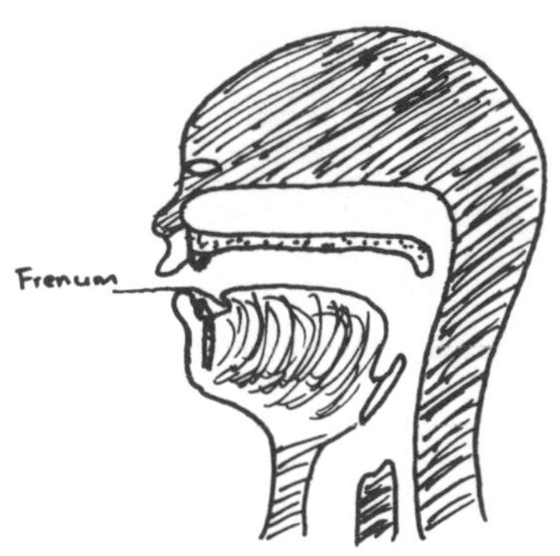

If you find you have a short frenum, simply work with the teeth a little closer together, still with a sense of space between the back teeth, and, without forcing, move the tongue tip up to touch the top gum ridge and, then, down to touch the lower gum ridge until you have a greater sense of flexibility and precision.

Relevant exercises – 222-229

Face stiff/tense/fixed expression

There are a vast number of facial muscles and these can easily become set in habitual patterns which not only limit facial but also vocal expression. The best way to release facial tension and stiffness is to regularly massage the face and move it into as many different expressions as possible to prevent it from fixing in any one.

Further explanation – 175-176, Relevant exercises – 176-177

Face under-energised/sluggish

Lack of physical energy throughout the body may be the cause of facial sluggishness. Another cause may be chronic catarrh. Also, when a person feels depressed or exhausted the face tends to reflect this lack of energy.

To revitalise the face massage it regularly and move it around into as many different expressions as possible, making sure the top lip is fully included in the movement. Then, hum while you move the face around and imagine the sound flowing out through all the pores in the face. Then, move on to the exercises suggested below.

Further explanation – 175-176, Relevant exercises – 176-177

Face over-expressive

Where the face is over-expressive there is a need to work on grounding and centring (see pages 36-45) so that the expressive energy flows into the whole body not just the face. Working with the backward circle (see pages 44-45) is a good way to ground and centre as well as working with the exercises suggested below.

Further explanation – 175-176, Relevant exercises – 176-177

RESONANCE AND RANGE

Lack of resonance

Tension restricts resonance, making the voice sound higher and harder. It is best to begin with work on physical release (see pages 19-36) to remove postural tension, then, look at the vocal release exercises (see pages 158-159). This work may be sufficient. If not you can then move on to the specific resonance exercises (see pages 166-179).

Sluggishness will also affect the resonance, leading the voice to sound muffled and dull. Work on physical alignment (see pages 49-55) and mental bounce (see page 9) is necessary to bring energy both to the body and mind. Then, the specific exercises on resonance (see pages 166-179) need to be worked on.

Further explanation – 162-165

Voice too high

Often a seemingly high-pitched voice is the result of a lack of lower resonance. This lack of lower resonance may be caused by tension, but also by habitual focusing of the sound into the head without balancing that by focusing into the chest.

Postural work (see pages 19-55) helps to release tension generally. Then, you can focus on more specifically releasing tension in the neck, throat, jaw and tongue (see pages 135-149). This work may be sufficient, but it may also be necessary to work on the exercises to balance the resonance more equally between the head and the chest (see page 171-174).

Of course, a high voice may also be caused by a person speaking at a pitch higher than their optimum. The optimum pitch is the one at which our voice is most strongly and easily produced. This does not mean that we speak only on this note, but rather that it acts as our keynote and the pitch travels up and down from there.

There are many reasons why people end up speaking above their most comfortable pitch but, whatever the cause, tension usually plays a part in the result. So, it is important to work on posture and breath (see pages 19-86), support (see pages 86-116) and resonance (see pages 165-179) and let the voice settle in that way.

If, however, the voice is still pitched too high you need to work with vowel glides (see page 183), sliding gently up and down your range for a few minutes daily until an easy, consistent glide is achieved. Then, as you slide look for the note which *feels* the strongest and easiest and play, sliding a little way up and down from this note. Once you feel comfortable doing this, chant text on this keynote and then speak, letting the voice take off from the keynote. If you practise gently and patiently in this way, in time the voice will settle back to its optimum pitch, but please be careful not to push and never start with this work – always look at the posture, breath, support and resonance first.

Voice too low

This can be the result of having consciously chosen to lower the pitch at some point in the past. Boys may do so at puberty if their voices are slow in breaking and women may do so to appear less 'girlie' – either in order to seem more authoritative or more 'sexy'. The trouble is that it leads to the voice being less expressive since it is not operating in the strongest part of its range.

As well as general work on posture and relaxation (see pages 19–55), to remove any tension that may have accompanied the lowering of pitch, it is also necessary to work specifically on the range, sliding up and down in pitch regularly until an easy and consistent glide is achieved. Then, finding the note which *feels* the strongest and easiest, slide up and down a little around that note. Once you feel comfortable doing this, chant text on that strong note and, then speak, letting the voice take off from that same note. If you practise gently and patiently in this way, in time, the voice will naturally return to its natural higher pitch. Then, if you want to add depth to the voice, you can work on the lower resonance (see pages 173–174).

Another cause of an over-low voice is lack of head or upper resonance. Work needs to be done on focusing the sound forward into the area of the face between the upper lip and the eyebrows (see pages 177–178.) In this way the higher resonance will be brought to life and the voice will appear to be higher and brighter.

Voice shrill

This is usually the result of tension. Work needs to be done initially on physical release and postural alignment (see pages 19–36, 49–55). Then, more detailed work is necessary to release tension in the neck, throat, jaw, lips, tongue and soft palate (see pages 135–152).

Voice lacks energy

This occurs when there is a lack of both physical and mental energy. Firstly, mental 'bounce' needs to be cultivated by working with a sense of cheekiness, teasing or flirting (see page 9). Then, using this mental 'bounce', the abdominal muscles, which support the voice, and the muscles of articulation, which shape the voice, need to be connected with and exercised (see pages 86–116, 222–229). For it is the *physical* energy of connected, toned voice muscles which leads to *vocal* energy.

Voice lacks expression/is monotonous

There may be many reasons for this. Whatever the cause it is usually accompanied by tension or sluggishness, possibly in the whole body and particularly in the face. Where there is *tension* the voice will tend to be trapped in a narrow band of expression. Where there is *sluggishness* the voice will lack the energy to move around.

First, it is necessary to look at releasing tension in the body (see pages 19-36) and at energising it using the alignment work (see pages 49-55.) Then, specific work on the face (see page 176), massaging it and moving it around into as many different expressions as possible will help to release the tension there and bring the face to life.

Once this work has been done, then, exercises to access and extend the range (see pages 183-187) are important. Finally, once the range is accessible, it is crucial to work on *connecting* with what you are saying (see pages 187-191) – with the images behind the words – for it is this connection which moves the voice around and gives it colour.

Further explanation – 175-176

Voice over colourful/insincere/false

Here there is usually excessive facial and vocal movement, which is disconnected from the interior feeling. This is usually the result of not trusting that thoughts and feelings will be communicated and, so, working too hard.

The first work to be done is on centring and grounding (see pages 36-45), working particularly with the backward circle (see pages 44-45) to ground the energy and bring ease and trust.

Further explanation – 175-176

CLARITY/ARTICULATION

Lack of clarity – mumbling and rushing

This can be the result of tentativeness, of holding back and mumbling through lack of trust of *what* is being said or of *how* it's being said. This will particularly occur when an actor is unhappy about a scene or character. Physically committing to shaping the sound (see page 228) helps to counteract tentativeness and to prevent mumbling.

Lack of clarity can also be the result of gabbling, where the mind races ahead and the speech, in struggling to keep up, falls over itself and becomes jumbled. Working with the backward circle (see pages 44-45) to anchor the mind and energy in the present is the best way to stop gabbling and rushing.

Further explanation – 199-201, Relevant exercises – 201-229

Over-emphatic/over-articulated speech

This is due to excess effort, which is usually the result of not trusting your performance to reach the audience or to be understood by them. Working with the backward circle (see pages 44–45) helps to bring ease and remove the push. It also helps to connect the voice so that the whole body is involved rather than all the energy moving upwards so that you end up as a talking head.

Further explanation – 199-201

Sibilant, whistling 's'

This is the result of too much air pressure and too large a gap through which the air is escaping. Work initially needs to be done on tongue placing and precision (page 210) so that there is sufficient closure between the body of the tongue and the roof of the mouth. This ensures that the breath only escapes down a narrow channel in the centre of the tongue. Then, it is important to work lightly and effortlessly so that the breath is released at a lesser pressure.

Lisping 's'

This occurs when the tip and sides of the tongue protrude between the teeth on the 's' producing a sound closer to 'th': i.e. 'theethide' instead of 'seaside'. Work needs to be done to train the tip and sides of the tongue to stay behind the teeth and to get the sides of the tongue to raise, to form a closure with the roof of the mouth, so the air escapes down a narrow channel in the middle of the tongue. (See page 210.)

Weak 'r'

The so-called weak 'r', where the 'r' is pronounced as a 'w' is the result of the tongue not playing its part in the formation of the sound. Instead the lips are working on their own or with only very slight and undefined tongue movement. It is necessary, therefore, to build awareness of and strengthen the movement of the tongue, firstly, by working with other more tangible front of tongue consonants, such as 't', 'd' and 'l' (see pages 222–224) and, then, moving on to the 'r' itself (see page 203).

Useful Contacts

Society of Teachers of the Alexander Technique
129, Camden Mews
London, NW1 9AH

Tel: 020 7284 3338
Fax: 020 7482 5435
Email: info@stat.org.uk
Web site: www.stat.org.uk

Body Control Pilates
14-16, Station Road West
Oxted
Surrey, RHX 9EP

Email: info@bodycontrol.co.uk
Web site: www.bodycontrol.co.uk

Feldenkrais Guild UK
PO Box 370
London, W10 3XA

Tel: 07000 785506
Email: enquiries@feldenkrais.co.uk
Web site: www.feldenkrais.co.uk

Shiatsu Society
Eastlands Court
St. Peters Road
Rugby, CV21 3QP

Tel: 01788 555 051
Fax: 01788 555 052
Email: admin@shiatsu.org
Web site: www.shiatsu.org

British Voice Association
at The Royal College of Surgeons
35-43, Lincoln's Inn Fields
London, WC2A 3PN

Tel: 020 7831 1060
Fax: 020 8288 5934
Email: bva@dircon.co.uk
Web site: www.british-voice-association.com

JoEstill
Speech therapist and singer
(see footnote 16, page 122)

Web site: www.evts.com

Index

Abdominal muscles 60-64, 73-78, 89-95, 102-116
Accents 4, 129, 164, 195, 201, 204
Acid Reflux 249
Alcohol 244
Alexander Position 24
Alignment 49-55, 132-138
Ankles 28, 35, 39, 43
Articulation 193-229
Approach 6-12, 48, 66, 119, 232, 243
Attitude xiii, 4, 7, 16, 40, 66, 87-88, 129, 253, 254
Audition preparation 38, 40, 45, 133
Awareness xiv, 17, 66, 196, 217-218, 228

Back 20, 29, 41
Body Review 17-19
Breath 59-65, 67-86
Breath Pressure 130-131, 156-157
Breath Review 66
Breathiness 129, 153
Berry, Cicely x, 189

Calling 105-107, 114
Cardiovascular Exercise 55-56
Centring 27, 36-38
Chapman, Janice ix, 90, 105, 168
Chest 54-55
Cigarettes 249
Clarity 200-201
Clavicular Breathing 64
Commitment -xiii, 9, 193, 200-201, 228, 232, 242-243, 254, 261-262
Consonants 193-194, 199-216

Diaphragm 59-63, 79, 80-83, 86-89, 99-102
Disconnection 175, 187-188, 251, 255, 258

Ease xiv, 7, 16, 19, 23, 28, 35, 45-47, 59, 69, 119, 252, 254, 267
Effort xiv, 6, 7, 9, 10-11, 46-47, 55, 67, 86, 89, 128-129, 169, 183, 199, 212, 214, 251-252, 254, 267
Energy xiv, 6, 9, 16, 19, 20, 37-38, 40, 45-51, 54-55, 57, 59, 67-68, 79, 86 -93, 99-108, 163, 165-166, 174-178, 199, 212, 216-218, 228, 252-253, 261-264, 266-267
Elision 227
Estill, Jo 11, 138, 140

Face 174 -178, 216-217
Focus 17, 79, 132, 164, 168, 177, 183, 228, 255

Glottalling/Glottal Attack 128-129, 152
Grounding 39-46

Head Position 54, 121, 137-138
Hips 35, 39, 43
How to Work 6-13

Imagery 7-8
Interest xiv

Jaw 123-125, 142-146

Knees 35, 39, 43

Larynx 120-121, 126-131, 139-140
Legs 40-42
Lips 216-217, 219-222
Lisp 210, 268
Listening 10, 119

Mumbling 200, 217, 261

Neck 28-29, 31, 124-125

Over-emphatic speech xiii, 128, 200

Index

Pelvic floor muscles 60-64, 73-78, 109-110
Periods 240
Pitch change 182
Pollutants 249
Posture 17-55, 69, 83, 132-138
Power 59, 64-65, 91, 107, 114, 125, 182, 197
Practising 3
Preparation 38, 40, 45, 235-241, 247-248

Range 182-191
Relaxation 19-30, 246 (see also Ease)
Release
  physical 19-36, 157-159
  vocal 118-159
Resonance 162 -179
Rest 245
Ribs 59-60, 62-64
Rib Reserve 64

Self-consciousness 16
Screaming 108
Shoulders 30, 135-136
Shouting 107
Sibilant 's' 210, 267
Sluggishness 16, 46, 48, 102, 163, 164-165, 175, 264, 266
Soft Palate 126-127, 150-152
Sound
  how we make it 97, 127
  initiating sound 98-108
  sustaining sound 109-112
Speech
  initiating 112-114
  sustaining 115-116
Spine 31-33, 49, 52
Standing 34-36
Stage presence 35
Steamers 245
Stretching 20-23
Support -x, 65-66, 86-95, 97-116, 182, 185

Talking over noise 246-247, 256-257
Technique 5
Tension 6, 11, 17-19, 45, 51, 62, 64, 67-69, 74, 78-79, 91, 107, 118-119, 123-124, 126-128, 135, 146-148, 153-154, 163, 165, 176-177, 216-217, 250-252, 259-266
Text Work 42-5, 68, 107, 112-116, 141, 144 -146, 148-149, 154 -159, 167, 171-172, 174, 176, 178, 188-191, 194 -195, 197-202, 227-229, 241-243
Throat 10-12, 24, 27, 61, 64, 71-74, 88-89, 91, 97-101, 105-108, 118-120, 122-124, 126-127, 138-142, 147, 153-154, 157-159, 163, 166-168, 171, 182-183, 185, 235, 244
Tongue 126-127, 146-149, 217-218, 222-226
Top Chest Breathing 64
Touch 8
Trust xii-xiii, 8-10, 12, 15, 97-98, 118-119, 128, 130, 187-188, 266-267

Upper body stability 121-122

Vocal fold closure 128-130
Vowels 193-198
Volume 254

Warming-up 235-241, 247-248
Water 244
Weak 'r' 203, 268
Worry 246

Exercise Sections

Body Work
Release and Redirection 19-36
Centring and Grounding 36-46
Toning and Alignment 46-55
Cardiovascular Exercise 55-56

Breath and Support
Breath Review 66
Freeing and Centring the Breath 67
Developing the Out-Breath 73
Developing the In-Breath 78
Bringing the Work Off the Floor 83
Building the Support Energy 86
Sustaining the Support and Breath 93

Breath and Sound
Initiating the Sound 98
Calling for Greater Energy and Greater Release 105
Sustaining the Sound 109
Taking the Support Work into Text 112

Releasing the Sound
Stabilising the Upper Body 132
Releasing the Shoulders and Neck and Balancing the Head 135

Opening the Throat and Releasing the Sound 138
Loosening the Jaw 142
Loosening the Tongue 146
Bringing the Soft Palate to Life 150
Removing Harsh and Breathy Closure 152
Getting the Breath Pressure Right 156
Whole Release Exercises 157

Filling out the Sound: Resonance
Creating More Space in the Mouth and the Throat 166
Focusing the Sound Forward 168
Building up the Resonance 171

Extending the Sound: Range
Freeing and Extending the Range 183
Connecting the Range 187

Shaping the Sound: Articulation
So to Work on the Vowels 196
So to Work on the Consonants 201
Limbering up the Lips and the Tongue 216
Strengthening the Lip and Tongue Muscles 218
Working with text 227

Troubleshooting Index

Breath
Inability to breathe deeply 250
Little or no rib movement 251
Noisy in-breath 251
Running out of breath 250

Vocal Support
Difficulty with dynamic/high-energy scenes 253
Lack of vocal support 251
Strain when screaming and shouting 253
Throat tension/strangled voice 252
Tired/strained voice 252

Being Heard
Difficulty being heard when doing intimate scenes 255
Difficulty being truthful when working in large spaces/having to project 254
Speaking over noise 256
Touring:
Working in different spaces 257
Working in acoustically dead spaces 256
Working in spaces with a lot of echo 257
Working outside 255
Voice too loud 254
Voice too quiet 254

Head, Neck, Shoulders and Jaw
Head pokes forward 258
Jaw tension 259
Neck tension 258
Shoulder tension 259

Lips, Tongue and Face
Face over-expressive 262
Face under-energised/sluggish 262
Lips lack energy and precision 260
Stiff lips 259
Tongue lacks energy and precision 261
Tongue tension 260

Resonance and Range
Lack of resonance 262
Voice lacks energy 264
Voice lacks expression/is monotonous 264
Voice shrill 264
Voice too high 263
Voice too low 263

Clarity/Articulation
Lack of clarity/mumbling and rushing 265
Over-emphatic/over-articulated speech 266
Lisping ‘s’ 266
Sibilant, whistling ‘s’ 266
Weak ‘r’ 266